COMPUTER LEGENDS, LIES & LORE

Edited by
Iris Forrest

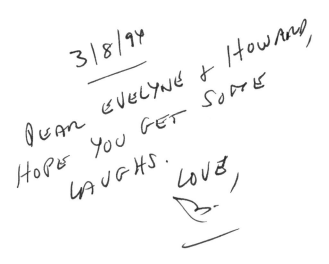

3/8/94

DEAR EVELYNE & HOWARD,
HOPE YOU GET SOME
LAUGHS. LOVE,
B-

AGELESS PRESS
Sarasota, Florida

Front cover design by Bernice Brooks Bergen

Library of Congress Catalog Card Number: 93-071320
ISBN 0-9635177-1-6
SAN 297-830X

Printed on acid-free paper

Introduction

This book contains the work of thirty seven authors, some of whom were included in our earlier release, Computer Tales of Fact & Fantasy (or How We Learned to Stop Worrying and Love the Computer), 1993.

You'll also find pieces from our International Contest winners:

Mark All	First Place
Robert Luhn	Second Place
A.C. Stone	Third Place
Sherry Armendariz	Honorable Mention
Barbara Bornmann	Honorable Mention

We hope that the experiences related here will encourage reluctant, fearful, non-users to jump in and get wet. Why should we suffer alone? Only kidding!

We received many more submissions than we had room to include. We thank all of the authors who sent us manuscripts and wish them luck in the future.

Hope Day
Publisher

Iris Forrest
Editor

TABLE OF CONTENTS

TABLE OF CONTENTS

TABLE OF CONTENTS

TABLE OF CONTENTS

Mark All

Mark has won first prize in the Ageless Press International Contest for this book. His winning piece, Windows, follows.

He's also written two novels and many short stories. He's currently marketing his second book, a supernatural thriller based on his experiences as a professional road musician.

The thirty nine year old Athens, Georgia resident was at times a radio announcer, a gravedigger, an accounting assistant and an academic library support staffer.

Mark is a graduate student in Computer-Based Education. He has a Bachelor of Music degree, cum laude.

Windows
by
Mark All

    Phil Horton first noticed the unusual nature of his new program when he dropped his lighter through the monitor screen. He had gotten Windows R-O for an astoundingly low price through the same mail-order firm which had sold him the Basilisk HC. He had come to hate the mouse which controlled access to all his files but, while intensely frustrated now, he was determined to master it. The documentation referred to it as the Lizard, and the CPU's molded plastic logo featured a perky American chameleon beneath the company name, its long tail coiled jauntily back in front of itself. He hated that little bastard, too.

    Phil was working in Simplegraph late Saturday afternoon when it happened. He had been looking for graph rotation on an unfamiliar pull-down menu, had clicked the Lizard on a curious selection, Attitude. A new window, layered before one and behind two others, had expanded to fill the screen. It was awash with lush, green foliage. A narrow path blazed through it where rich-looking, greasy, black dirt was visible through the vines and bush-like undergrowth. Further back in the scene shadows fell more darkly across the trail. He didn't know if it was East Tennessee or a tropical rain forest but it looked like Paradise: a Paradise World.

    He stared at the computer as he flicked his lighter to a cigarette: Paradise World looked so real! Suddenly he caught a motion within the screen: a dark cat darted across the trail only a few feet in front of him. His lighter slipped through his fingers as it followed his gaze into Paradise World. He choked on smoke.

    "Damn!"

    He could see the lighter lying on the trail. Some of the loamy soil had spattered over it when it landed but faint, green light still reflected from the single diamond embedded in its flat, black surface. It was a present from Liz.

    Without thinking, Phil reached in, seized the lighter. His arm appeared in the screen but the color was slightly off: slightly darker. It reminded him of the skewed image of an object half submerged in water. Both of his arms lined up perfectly at the interface.

He jerked the lighter out, held it above his head, pulling away from the screen if as to protect it from the computer. Paradise World still filled the screen. Had it gotten darker?

Another movement in the scene. A few leaves on the left side of the trail twitched— then were still. The cat?

The door to Phil's apartment opened then crashed back against the wall with a terrible bang. The lighter again left his fingers, bouncing off the edge of the keyboard into his glass of tea.

"Yo," a shrill voice from the hallway called, "get your bony ass up and over here, right now!"

The door had swung shut leaving his visitor outside. He jerked it open.

"Liz."

"Kiss me now, Einstein."

He complied, planting it on her comically puckered lips.

His interest in her wasn't related to the fact that her father was his employer. Phil was the acountant for her father's Moldy Tome new and used book store. He kept the accounts for the small firm on his own equipment: good experience for his dream of starting his own freelance accounting/consulting business.

Liz charmed him with her intelligence, beauty and elegantly long legs which sported different colored sheer hose every day.

She pushed him away when he dragged her into the apartment to continue kissing her.

"You've got to eat your dinner before you can have dessert. You promised to take me to Pancho's Villa and I'm starved," she caught a glimpse of the computer screen as she gave his cheek a wet kiss.

"You know, you shouldn't leave your front door unlocked. Is this the new program," she asked peering intently at the screen?

"Yeah."

"Killer graphics! Ya hungry?"

Phil was sure that he'd logged off Basilisk HC before leaving for dinner but when he returned, Paradise World was still up and running. He signed off, blanked the screen.

He was sitting in front of the computer, with his second cup of coffee, by nine o'clock Sunday morning. He wanted to set up his accounting, payroll, tax and other crucial files to make them accessible by either author, title or publisher, before the weekend was over.

He would eventually have to list all of Moldy Tome's books but was working from invoices to enter the data from the newer ones, for the time being. He was playing with the cursor trying to decide how to group the books, ie, by price or by breaking down the prices into retail and wholesale categories, when he realized that he was looking at the Simplegraph button on the overhead menu. He paused momentarily then rolled the Lizard so that the cursor landed on Simplegraph, clicked.

The pull-down menu appeared. Phil rolled the Lizard towards himself and clicked on Attitude.

Paradise World burst forth from the tiny, empty circle on the menu, racing towards him filling the screen in a quarter of a second. Like the Big Bang?

The image was even more realistic this time. Phil had never seen High-Definition TV but he thought that this was probably better. He wouldn't have thought a 386 computer capable of this quality.

Slender blades of waist-high grasses moved gently, randomly in an invisible breeze. He saw more shades of green and more species of plants than he had dreamed existed.

He bent back as he lit a cigarette with his diamond-decorated lighter. As he exhaled he leaned toward the screen, his eyes strained with concentration.

Suddenly, with an audible whipping sound, the undergrowth at the front of the screen parted. He was inspected intently for a brief moment by a marble-sized yellow-green eye encased in a vertical black slit. The grass fronds snapped into place as it disappeared.

He wasn't sure how it had happened: Had the cat batted it out of his hand before she left? The lighter was again in Paradise World.

"I smoke too much!"

He thrust his arm through the screen towards the lighter. His fingers felt the rich soil under his fingernails as he tried to grab it. It catapulted out of his hand, just out of reach.

Phil stuck his head into Paradise World to look for it. He used both arms to push away the huge blades of grass. There it was! He leaned over the desk and into the screen. Just a little further—

He extended his right arm, slightly, almost had it—

A silky, black paw snagged it, played with it, then batted it into darker shadows about three feet up the trail.

Phil lunged in after the lighter. His left knee got caught on the desk litter propelling him headlong into Paradise. His left toe was on the edge of the monitor, his torso fallen onto the trail, his right hand within inches of the lighter. He stretched his hand.

The black cat emerged from the bushes, nuzzled him. Rubbing its scent glands along his hand, it began to purr, loudly. It lazily encircled the lighter from above with its paw, continuing to stroke Phil's hand with its head.

A jarring sound came from somewhere behind him.

Intent on his task, Phil stroked the cat which pulled its length along his hand. Then withdrew just out of reach, smacking the lighter further away, then running to catch it further down the trail. She tucked it between her front paws, sitting down like the sphinx.

As though from under water Phil thought he heard an indistinct voice calling his name.

".....here?....should lock your....Phil?"

He straightened his left leg, slid his toes away from the

screen, back into the real world.

He looked back into the area he'd been in, feeling brave. Peculiar, but brave. A second pull-down menu appeared, descending from the overhang of a very large mushroom. It displayed two columns of figures.The right consisted of tiny boxes whose contents appeared to move while the left column was filled with hieroglyphs presumably describing the contents of the right column. Each undulating box resembled a large, unicellular animal.

The cat, batting and stalking the lighter, caused the bottom box to expand almost three feet, blotting out the menu. He wondered if the cat was the mouse or the Lizard?

This new aspect was almost as appealing as Paradise World although similar in many ways. The ground was more visible but rockier. The plants were a darker green. He felt an attraction to it. Almost a pull—

"Phil," the voice seemed clearer now, a bit louder, ".......on your computer screen? It looks like part of a shoe or something."

The cat deftly swept the lighter into the new world following it in. The lighter seemed closer than it had been a moment ago. He could almost reach it. He stretched his left leg and right arm. Not quite far enough.

He felt his toes slipping over the edge of the monitor into the screen. As his right hand fingers slowly went from cold to almost numb, he felt the Darker World gently sucking at them.

Liz's eyes were glued to the computer screen. She moved towards it, staring, her nose tingling as she was drawn into it. She screamed as she realized that she was inside this world and that Phil's body was being dragged further inside until his shoulders disappeared into nothingness. She screamed again as Phil jerked and his toes went over the edge.

She grabbed his ankles, braced her thighs on the edge of the desk,

"Phil, what the hell are you doing?"

"...lighter...cat...lighter..."

"Forget the lighter. Come back here. Now!"

She was right. What had he gotten himself into? He hooked his left arm around the edge of the window and strained back while at the same time using Liz's hands as an anchor, drawing himself towards her. Since the tug, like a giant vacuum cleaner, of the Darker World was increasing, he made slow progress. He was almost out—The cat snagged his arm with a claw.

"Liz! Liz!"

"..il! What..."

"Shut if off! Shut it off!"

Liz locked Phil's freed left foot over the edge of the screen then felt around the side of the computer for the on/off switch. Then the back, the other side. Where was the damn thing?

The foot still in her hand jerked violently as a muffled voice called from within.

Without thinking of long-term consequences, in her desperation she seized the cup of coffee, tossed it into the disk drive. A loud crackling noise, like static on a radio turned to its highest decibel, echoed from within the monitor.

Phil's right leg suddenly shot out of the screen followed by his bottom. He pushed back with his free arm as Liz circled his waist and pulled. Knocking Liz to the floor, he tumbled free, landing in his chair, the cat's paw still firmly attached to his sleeve.

As the cat moved further into the real world its arm elongated, thickened until it was larger than Phil's. Considerably larger.

Liz looked up from the floor, shrieked,

"Panther..leopard...Phil!"

He was frozen in his chair, like a deer caught in a car's headlights. He was fascinated but terrified. As its muzzle came through the screen, the humongous jaw opened as it moved toward him, the teeth enlarging. The whiskers popped out and grew past both sides of the monitor.

Phil snatched the Lizard, slammed the buttons. Nothing

happened. He rolled it back and forth across the desk top, snapping its connecting wire free. He suddenly knew what to do.

"Unpug it, Liz. Unplug it. Unplug it."

Liz slammed into his chair, toppling him over, the cat's head with him. It rushed out of the screen, moving faster than he was falling, closing the distance between them. As its mouth approached his face, wide enough to swallow his head whole, he felt its hot, moist breath, shut his eyes as he hit the floor.

His spine slammed into the chair back sending spasms of pain through his body. After rolling over his left shoulder he saw that his hand was free, his head still attached.

No cat. The Basilisk's screen was blank, the computer looking perfectly normal aside from the coffee dribbling from its disk drive. Glassy-eyed, heavy-breathing Liz sat under the desk with the AC plug in her hand.

They gazed at each other in shocked silence as Phil slowly sat up, rubbing four red splotches on his arm.

"Cat got your tongue," from Phil?

"You watch you own tongue or I'll plug it back in," she was laughing until she began to hiccough.

"Not yet."

"Not yet. What do you mean, not yet?"

"You know, I've been thinking of taking some programming classes. If I could get a loan for another computer and software, that would be safe to learn on, I could see possibilities for the Basilisk..."

Liz crawled over and leaned her face over his,

"Shut..up..and.. kiss me. Now-Einstein."

He did. As they eased back down to the floor he gently set the Basilisk's Lizard down on the desk, away from the spilled coffee.

Robert Luhn

Robert Luhn, the second prize winner in our international contest for this book, is an Albany, California-based writer and former senior editor of PC World magazine. He writes about the politics of technology. He also pens the syndicated "Green PC" column for Computer Currents and contributes to Omni, Whole Earth Review, San Francisco Focus, The Christian Science Monitor, Mother Jones and other discriminating periodicals.

Mr. Luhn has no distinguishing marks and is currently accepting marriage proposals or donations in small denominations.

I Sing the Writer Electric!

by
Robert Luhn

My name is Alton Drake and I am a writer. Or rather, I was a writer. What I'm doing now, what you're reading, is illegal as hell. The Creative Impulses and Author Restriction Act of 2023 made, "written expressions by humans", a capital offense. A misdemeanor probably would have been enough. But no matter. There was a time when humans wrote about everything there was to know, and worse, to imagine.

I was once famous, you know. A famous writer. I wrote novels, essays, even a little poetry, although one critic (banned now, by the Writers Defamation Act of 2005) called my verse, "alligator farts in a drained swamp". Of course, he was eventually executed for such twaddle, but I kind of miss the human voice. I'd go for any human voice amidst all this humming and clicking.

But that isn't likely. I am the supervisor and sole human employee of the Automated Novel Works, Southside. It's me and a couple hundred SyntheScribe 1000s. Rows and rows of shiny, white machines the size of bread boxes. I replace worn neural chips, run diagnostics on the syntax (sin tax?) processors and check the output trays for the day's novel. It's not much but at 87 what else am I good for?

Sometimes an error message pops up at one of the scenario workstations that actually calls on my dusty skills, like, "How do I resolve the internal conflicts of character #41 without compromising developments in subplot 319?" But the messages come less and less: "progress" in software has all but eliminated the guesswork, the flaws of modern-day art.

Of course, the first autowriters were laughably crude. But when IBM released its line of MuseMatePCs, the world capitula-

21

ted. And why not? Computers had made everything perfect, hadn't they? Perfect hamburgers. Perfect haircuts. Perfect servo-implanted, digitally-controlled breasts. Why not perfect art? Could we demand anything less?

The concept was appealing, the ads witty (especially IBM's Shakespeare-on-roller-skates being flattened by a chuckling mainframe) and the slogans irresistible. Who can forget, "I Sing the Writer Electric!", "PC-Freedom" and the catchphrase of a generation, "Write Without Thinking"? The writer within me shuddered, but the civil libertarian cheered.

Of course, I never really thought computers would put writers, or God forbid, even editors, out of work. Everyone felt a twinge when TV programmers and talk show hosts were finally automated in 2011. But weren't those senseless, degrading, even dangerous jobs?

Yes, said the goverment, but writing was even more hazardous. Only automation could make the process of creation "safe". I had to admit they had a point. How many screenwriters went mad writing (and rewriting) "Terminator VI: The College Years"? How many poor wretches fell into Kafkaesque stupors of drunkenness and buggery in their struggle to beat the blank page?

No, they're right, I thought. Maybe creation was too dangerous without controls or at least some help.

Of course, the first autowriters weren't much help at all. You needed a 4-terabyte system and a two-way biolink to a graduate English student just to generate ad copy!

Then the Yevtushenko-9000 series of poetry droids hit the streets. I didn't think much of their output, but that didn't stop the Pulitzer Committee from giving, "Naked Came the PC", the Pulitzer Prize for poetry. (Of course, with half the voting membership composed of IBM 9000s, it was hardly a surprise.) Then came the Rodin ASICs, which could even turn the factory ro-

22

bots into damn good sculptors. The jig was up.

Commentary was the first magazine to go all autowriter. (Although, to be honest, I couldn't see much of a difference.) Soon, I was competing more and more with silicon for writing jobs. After my fourth rejection from Harpers, an editor finally admitted,

"Alton, you're just too damn slow. It took you two days to finish that last piece on fetal tissue cookware. Hell, my PC, with its Buckley ROMs could do the job in 15 minutes and I don't get any bitching about rewrites. Face it, Alton, you're history."

That was the last time I talked to a human editor. Two weeks later, the Hearst autoeditors arrived and editors were cadging loans from writers. The revolution had swept us all out and we didn't even hear it coming.

The galling thing is that the autowriter revolution was a hit not only with the Fortune 500, but with the reading public. Auto-literature shot up the best-seller lists with machine-like regularity, ie, "The Agony and the Electricity", "The Good, the Bad and the Analog" and even "Bite My Baud", a saucy soft-core porn novel.

I was one of the lucky writers. I got a job tending the machines. The fact that I was, had been, a novelist, wasn't held against me.

But all good things come to an end, I guess. The syntho-novels haven't been selling as fast lately; even the New York Times is thinking of running Letters to the Editor from humans, again. But the pundits say our automated economy, already in hock to the Korean-Yugoslavian-Japanese cartel, would crumble without autowriters. Relying on analog intelligence could spell financial suicide.

But I'm not worried.The computerized readers are being installed tomorrow.

A.C. Stone

Mr. Stone is the winner of the third prize in the Ageless Press International Contest for this book. Electronic Filing, the winning work, follows.

A.C. Stone has been writing since 1955 and has had more than 500 articles, stories and poems published in Canada, (his home), the U.S., England and Australia.

He's been married, since 1951, "to the same beautiful woman". He spent his working career with General Motors in Oshawa, Ontario and Windsor, Ontario, Canada.

A.C. retired in 1986 to travel, golf and write.

Electronic Filing
by
A.C. Stone

The world of record storage is changing faster than basketball teams change coaches. Much of the data that used to be stored, meticulously, in row upon row of filing cabinets is now available at the touch of a button on a video screen. Today there is very little paperwork left which has to be retained in anything other than a wastebasket.

True, you can print the data displayed on that screen, if you want to, but when you're done with the copy it's easier to trash it than file it. It's faster to print a new one if you need the comfort of real paper in your hand, when you make that big presentation.

But before you succumb to the obvious advantages of electronic filing, think for a minute of all that you will be giving up, when you make the change.

First, there are the aesthetics to consider. My favorite scene in the Paul Newman movie, "The Verdict", took place in an opulent law office, lined with rows of rich wooden cases and elegant, oak filing cabinets. There may have been nothing more in them but the lawyer's lunch but didn't they look impressive? You knew, just from the atmosphere they created, that you were in the office of a solid, no-nonsense law firm that could obviously beat whatever rap you were there to see them about. Somehow a plastic box of computer disks wouldn't have given you that same warm feeling.

And while we're on the subject of disk storage, can that little plastic box create the same amount of pure, physical excitement that a single file cabinet can when an unsuspecting clerk pulls out the top drawer too far? Never!

Just last week in our office, we had an occurrence which illustrates my point exactly. It all started because Fred lost the toss and had to go for coffee. About five minutes after he left, the phone on his desk began to ring. Merv, who sits next to Fred,

A.C. Stone

jumped up to answer it, catching his shin on the desk drawer he'd left open. Unfortunately Kathy, who is only five foot one, was standing on a chair trying to put an Accounts Payable Ledger back on the top shelf of the bookcase. Merv, stumbling, kicked the chair out from under her. When she came down she landed on Harold's arm, just as he was lining up the pages of the monthly report under the blade of the paper cutter. (The doctor, fortunately, was able to reattach the finger tip.)

When Ted left to take Harold to the hospital, he must have dropped his cigarette butt into the wastepaper basket. I don't know how else it could have gotten in there unless Emily, who is always cleaning up, emptied his ashtray. Anyway, the fire didn't amount to much. Mike stamped it out before his foot got stuck. It was when he tried to pull the basket off his foot that he got hurt. You'll have to admit that sitting on a container of freshly sharpened pencils can be pretty painful.

Fred, attracted by all the commotion, picked up the last of the coffees and hurried back to see what was going on. In his rush, he didn't notice the electical outlet sticking up out of the floor where Murray's desk used to be. When he tripped on it he splashed hot coffee down Mary's back. Mary's scream startled Eleanor so much that she pulled the file drawer she was working on all the way out. Luckily she was able to jump out of the way before the cabinet tipped. Mr. Alonzo, our Office Manager, wasn't so lucky. He's walking again but he still needs his cane.

Now I don't care what computerized system you install, you'll never see that much excitement, if it lasts forever!

Oh, I'll admit there are a few problems with manual systems. A careless clerk might misfile a record once in a while, (something that will never happen with an electronic system, right?) then have to spend half a day looking for it. But no clerk, no matter how incompetent, could lose a whole file drawer just by pushing the wrong button. (Who am I kidding?)

Consider the problems you'll create when you eliminate

26

all those file clerks. Where will your next generation of executives come from? The biography of every successful business person includes a chapter explaining how the CEO worked his, or her, way to the top after starting out either as a file clerk or a mail boy (mail boys are long gone, victims of electronic mail).

There are other disadvantages. One of the most serious is the damage that will be done to office romances. In an era of "open concept" workplaces, the file room is just about the last place left in the office for a lover's tryst. Toss those cabinets and Cupid might as well hang up his bows and arrows.

Finally, on a more personal level, something I'm going to miss once we eliminate all of those old, grey boxes, is the view presented by a secretary trying to retrieve a file folder from a bottom drawer (especially now that mini skirts are coming back). Now, before I get a batch of angry letters from the ladies in the office, let me remind you that we have male secretaries as well, so I'm talking about equal opportunity ogling. Given the success of the television commercial featuring the physical attributes of football center Randy Cross, I can only assume that at least some of you ladies share my sentiments.

So I urge you, if you are thinking about changing the way you do your filing, don't let some slick computer salesman sell you on an electronic system before you consider all of the consequences.

After all, there are more important things than money, aren't there?

Sherry Armendariz

Sherry Armendariz, an Honorable Mention winner in the international writing contest for this book, is a writer, spiritual counselor and lecturer. As an inspirational writer, her work has been published in Unity, GreenPrints, Spiritual Life, Science of Mind and others.

She also publishes her own newsletter, The LoveLetter. Her book, Living Consciously: Thank God for the Disfunctional Family, will be published soon.

Her private practice as a spiritual counselor brings her clients from all over. She has an ongoing support group and facilitates workshops at Kaiser Hospital in San Jose.

She lectures at summer camps as well as in county office buildings.

When not travelling, her home is in Gilroy, California, which she shares with husband Tony, 4 cats, 5 dogs and a fluctuating population of fish.

The Bite of the Apple that Changed My World
by
Sherry Armendariz

Eve took the first bite then shared it with Adam—since then, nothing's been the same. So it was with me.

This time it was Adam, an orchard genius, who chomped down first,

"Just think of it as a smart typewriter," he said.

He was looking at my terrified eyes, reflecting my fear of being the wrong age, at the wrong time, with an overly developed right brain, a weak and waffling left one. Modern technology was grinning, leering, sneering at me. Me? I was waiting for the manual choke and rotary dial to return.

Queen of denial that I was, I finally realized that maybe, just maybe, computers were here to stay. (After all they were responsible for those really fine money machines at the bank.) I felt myself starting to give in.

I'd continue to have technological lapses, like opening up the answering machine to change the light bulb or wanting to oil something, anything, when the computer stared at me in frozen silence. Slowly, I minced my way into the computer age.

Adam initiated me in the delicate art of Appleing. He, who could make the Apple do anything he commanded (and a few things he hadn't) wanted me to know why the magical Apple did what it did. I just wanted it to do it. He wanted me to explore the possibilities of the mystical chips. I just wanted to walk a well travelled road with plenty of signs and Windows. He wanted me to jump tall electronic theory in a single bound. I wanted to tiptoe through the maze and get to the end.

Our grandson, as soon as he could climb on the chair, ate the Apple, without even stopping to savor it. We learned to use passwords so he wouldn't devour all the applesauce. Ahhhhh, youth!

Years later, my tiny steps having become running, gallivanting ones, the files in the Apple orchard overflowed. We bought programs to shrivel them into little bits to be reconstituted later. With new pollinated drives, new this, new that, the orchard bloomed freely. The modest Apple was re-cultivated with a new drive, a bigger stem and more eating surface.

The appetite for work grew along with the growth of the Apple. We needed a master gardener/marriage counselor to act as a King Solomon for dividing it. Even cut in half it wasn't enough. We finally gave up and picked another Apple from the orchard. We no longer had to share: we each had our own shiny Apple. Our union couldn't get much better. The counselor has to find other work.

The world was being revealed without a snake in the grass until Adam came home with MacMoney. I fought, I resisted, I balked. I realized if all the transactions were on the computer, certain evils would be exposed. I had power as long as He didn't know what was going on. I was jockeying money around at a fast and furious pace: I'd made borrowing from Peter to pay Paul a fine, fastidious art.

The evil wasn't evil at all: it was a growing, expanding window to the world. My MacMoney allowed me to continue to jockey, manipulate and reconcile in minutes, instead of hours. It saved our marriage at tax time.

In time the processing fruit held most of the answers and some of the questions. Everything relating to Adam's work was conducted and stored in the Apple. My, once-smart, typewriter, never saved a recipe or created newsletters, articles or fiction. It didn't establish a data base of publications, editors and subscribers to rival any publisher. Books were written, journals continued, flyers set up, lectures defined, pictures designed along with lists, love notes, letters and, of course, the money dance.

Adam planned programs and chips on his Apple as well as the architectural rendering for the addition to the house. Everything in the habitat was dissected to put into the Apple. We gave out engineering specs to the woman who came to measure our abode for refinancing. Arguments were voiced to the Apple first. The garden was rendered in black and white. All was revealed and digested by the Apple and we were nourished.

We changed the world with our Apples, sharing our skills, thoughts and ideas. But our view of the world and of ourselves was also changed by our use of them. All was revealed and it was good.

Barbara Bornmann

Barbara Bornmann is one of our Honorable Mention contest winners for The Cactus Computer and also has a piece in Computer Tales of Fact & Fantasy (or How We Learned to Stop Worrying and Love the Computer), Ageless Press,1993.

She graduated from Mountainview Theatre School in London and has a Bachelor in Theatre Arts from Empire College. She has contributed to the productions, in N.Y. and L.A., of many prominent, progressive writers, as theatre director, producer and performer.

She wrote and directed her first play, The Terminal Wildlife, with students at the Centre School in Manhattan.

She was recently a Visiting Director for the Academy of Performing Arts in Japan, where, in addition to teaching and directing, she worked with a group of Japanese students on improvisations. They created a work in progress called Buddha Talk.

Her most recent article on holistic alternatives appeared in Alternatives For Women With Endometriosis in 1993.

The Cactus Computer
A Science Fiction Adventure
by
Barbara Bornmann

The hot sun had baked her like a squash. Wind would be a welcome change if it weren't carrying sand and the occasional tumbleweed. Earlier in the day, she was glued to the latest craze in computer magazines, and was thrown out of her algebra class. When her friends teased her relentlessly about her escapist nature, Bobbie fled to the desert, leaving her bike by the old sequoia. For hours she stomped over the soft dirt trying to release her anger. She had lost track and gone too far.

The clouds seemed to come from nowhere, rolling along as if to obscure the rainbow and beckon the storm. Winds accompanied the flagging sunset, first a gentle touch then sweeping sand into gusty swirls. She sat quietly, numbed by the sudden change, not sure what to make of it: desert, mountain, cactus, scrub, dirt. She watched with concentration, seeing but not believing, the darkness that was falling like a sheet across the desert. She continued to sit perfectly still, accepting the storm into her life, embracing it, breathing deeply, letting go her fear.

Sun set, moon rise. She'd never seen darkness like this. The moon's eerie silhouette pierced the layers of dark clouds. Longing for a secluded place in the mountains to shield her from the elements, she shut her eyes and was there, peaceful with the war raging around her. There, she could curl up and laugh at silly nature's constant storms.

Here, she crawled into an arroyo trying to convince herself that the worst that could happen was she'd be cold and wet. She could sense this was more than just a storm. She'd tried to run away from home on two other occasions but now she was caught, caught by the seat of her pants, in the teeth of the storm. This was a serious challenge to her existence as she'd known it, a transformation, the only way out was through.

She lay low to the ground breathing dirt. Her arms were folded over her head, right cheek tilted to the earth as the rain hit: hard, like a sledge hammer, pounding fear into her. The rain soaked through her, down, it felt, to her wet, cold bones. The arroyo in which she was hunkered burst with tempestuous life. Struggling onto all fours, she began to crawl out to the desert, blindly, head down, pushing the forces of nature arrayed against her. She felt life's light, energy oozing out as the great forces continued to batter her.

Suddenly her actions changed: why not ride the waves, let the forces of nature move her like desert body surfing? It wasn't as smooth as the ocean but carried with it its own unique excitement. She imagined telling her friends,

"I was braving the storm alone in Acapauna. The rains created huge waves which I was able to ride across the twenty five mile desert stretch to the harboring mountains. It was awesome!"

Unlike the ocean, where she could dodge old ladies in white bathing caps by shifting her weight, here she had absolutely no control over her direction. It took all her strength to remain on all fours, moving towards a point in the universe, the rain beating on her, slapping her into obedience.

The moon showed her a horrifying sight: she was being driven towards what appeared to be a giant cactus, in the not too distant future. Again, struggling to take control of her destiny, she veered to the left, only to be picked up by a hurricane-like wind and thrown towards it. As if the universe were orchestrating the ultimate terror, she was, again, given a clear vision of this giant. It loomed about fifteen feet into the air, was carved like a totem pole with five tiers of images and gave off a striking, blue light. She thought it must be a mirage.

Now within twenty feet she could feel the pull: she was being drawn in. No longer resisting she stood up, stared the cactus down and braced herself for the encounter.

"Pressing 3740 on the security pad will get you out of the

storm," said the cactus in friendly, female computer language.

"This is a cactus, it couldn't be a computer," Bobbie thought as she took a closer look.

But sure enough, there was a security pad to the left of its bottom arm. The wind pushed a stunned Bobbie forward and she obediently pressed 3740 and a door opened. Inside was this entire computer network, kind of like the New York Stock Exchange except there was no garbage laying around. It was this vast, tall, circular network with all kinds of keyboards, small video monitors, lights and a large screen with the words, This Is Your Life, dead center. The door shut behind her. She sat on a stool which automatically raised her to the screen. A simplistic keyboard popped out with the words, User Friendly, across the top. It had only two keys, Past and Present.

"Wow, I just love computers," she said, dripping water.

"Once you've chosen between past and present, you may activate the choice three times," said the computer.

She chose Past and immediately the screen lit up with an actual replay of an event of her childhood, the picnic at Echo Lake Park.

"I used to love those pants with the orange giraffes on them."

She was smiling as she watched herself and her brother Kyle stealing brownies, then hiding under the table with the long, white paper tablecloth. Her sugar high zipped her down to the lake to learn how to row. She remembered she'd had blisters for a week.

There were potato sack races, tuna fish sandwiches, two-legged races and volleyball followed by the infamous egg toss.

She could see the hippie playing guitar while everyone sang, This Land Is Your Land and Oh, Give Me A Home Where the Buffalo Roam. There she was kicking grandpa in the knee because he couldn't hold a tune. There was grandma with that old straw hat with the birds on it, giving her a hug. She thought how happy she'd been that day, what a great day it was.

The screen went blank, instantly.

"What did I say? I was so happy then, what a great day that was. I have to remember that."

She pressed Past for the second time and another image appeared. A woman and man sat on a curved, cement love seat in a garden, with wisteria and pansies at their feet. They held hands, smiling, as if posing for a photograph. Love emanated from them. They seemed familiar but she couldn't place them. It was as if she could smell and taste but not touch them.

She sat back and thought but drew a blank. This was not the southeast. They were dressed in vintage urban fashion and the hairstyles were—

"Oh, my God," her right hand reaching out to touch the screen, her left touching her own cheek, "it must be my mother and father. Please, don't take them away, please."

She was fighting back the tears that were blurring her vision.

"Why did you put me up for adoption," she asked?

Her parents, as if they heard her plea, responded in a conversation disclosing that they'd worked on a top secret government project which left them both with such severe radiation toxicity that they'd had to be quarantined, leaving their newborn child in the hands of the authorities.

The storm was suddenly inside her, unleashing a torrent of emotion. For what appeared to be an eternity, she was connected with their images. She finally smiled, shut her eyes. When she opened them again the screen was blank. Then a parade of family faces flashed on the screen in ancestral, descending lineage. Exhausted, she lay down on the floor to rest.

When she awoke, sitting in the elevated chair, she knew she mustn't question what she was experiencing. She pressed Past for the last time.

A single coyote appeared on the screen. It was the kind of bright, sunny day that hurts your eyes. Suddenly the chair threw her headlong into the screen. She landed on the ground. The coyote started nipping at her heels so she took off. She tore over the scrubby terrain, the coyote behind her. She ran hard, trying to watch her footing, making contact with the earth, breathing hard, lungs sore. Her legs were tight, fists and teeth clenched. As she thought, "Just let go and fly," she could feel a rhythm take over her body, like the rhythm of the coyote who was now running by her side. The rhythm was strong, predatory, intelligent and fast.

She was so fast that she was outrunning the coyote. Her feet didn't seem to touch the ground. As she took flight the coyote jumped at her heels. What a feeling! Being light, flying transformed into a smooth, soft wing. Detached and spiritual.

Leaving the coyote in the dust she headed back on a collision course with the cactus. Again, it appeared she would crash. She shut her eyes and was thrown back into the chair.

"A 3-D computer, cool, unbelievable, awesome!"

The chair descended, the power went off and the door reopened.

She ran back out into the storm as though she were on fire. The strength and beauty of nature had embraced and guided her to her higher self. The wind no longer cut into her exposed skin but carved her a new shape, giving her body new form as the rains washed away her old covering. She had a great life with her surrogate parents. She knew they loved her. What her friends said didn't matter.

There was nothing else like this in the entire world: the excitement of being in touch with the energy of creation, nature in all its terror. She let go of fear, anger and pain, replacing it with the knowledge that she was loved.

She turned around to wait out the storm inside the cactus but it too was transformed. It was an ordinary cactus. She turned all around to see if her sense of direction was off. It wasn't but the cactus computer was gone. With a joyful leap she was trotting off with the wind. The storm dissolved into a glorious, grey day as she reached the edge of civilization.

Her bike was exactly where she'd left it, none the worse for its bath.

"My good ole horse," she yelled as she jumped on and peddled down the bumpy, dirt road. She was still numb but with joy. Speeding closer to home, she was aware that anyone she passed stopped to watch her. She figured she must be a sight having weathered such a fierce storm. She pulled into Pecos Gas & Fuel.

"Hey, Bobbie, want to go to the dance on Saturday,"asked the attractive, but greasy, Tyler, smiling, gas pump in hand?

She grabbed the ladies' room key off the wall and tore to safety.

"What is going on," she asked herself as she looked in the yellow tinnish plate that served as a mirror? There were no visible signs of dirt, she hadn't grown horns. She was happy but felt different. Coolly returning the key she just smiled at Tyler as she positioned herself on her bike and pulled out.

In a few minutes she home. It was quiet as she pulled into the driveway and put her bike where it belonged instead of flinging it on the lawn, as she usually did. The flowers on the front lawn were vibrant and welcoming from the rain.

"Anybody home?"

"Bobbie, is that you?"

"Oh, thank God, she's safe."

"Even I'm glad you're back."

All three, grandma, grandpa and Kyle had spoken at the same time.

"We were worried sick."

"You know better than to stay out all night."

"Were you abducted by aliens?"

The three had spoken all at once, again.

"I stormed so farout in the desert that I had to spend the night sheltered by a giant cactus. I'm sorry you were worried," she hugged her grandparents then punched Kyle in the arm.

"Kyle, let's get the birthday cake out of the fridge."

"But my birthday isn't till next week," interrupted Bobbie.

"We'll celebrate it again next week. Somehow today seems like your birthday, it seems special. Get the candles, dad. Let's open the cider."

"Yahoo. Listen Bobbie, we got you the coolest present but I only have one part of it. The main part will arrive on your real birthday," said Kyle as he bounded around the house and brought back a box which he handed to his sister.

They watched her open it, eagerly.

"It's a mouse. You bought me a computer! Oh, thank you. Now I can be a real computer fanatic instead of just reading about them."

"We know how much you like computers and like to write. Thought this would help you get started," said pa.

After the commotion and two rounds of Happy Birthday, Bobbie sat quietly, watching the fifteen flickering candles on her cake. She breathed deeply, shut her eyes. When she opened them they were filled with tears. She looked at grandma, grandpa and older brother Kyle as she smiled and said,

"I was braving the storm, alone, in Acapauna. The rains created huge waves which I was able to ride across the twenty five mile desert stretch to the harboring mountains. It was awesome!"

Then she added, softly,

"I know who I am."

With a strong gust she blew out the candles, every one of them.

Bud Taylor

Bud Taylor retired from the family real estate company in 1986 and has been a freelance writer ever since.

He was born, raised and schooled in New Jersey. After graduating from Colgate University he served as a B-24 pilot in World War II.

He's written many real estate articles, printed a children's book and has a byline in his country club publication.

He's married to Ruth Celler Taylor and lives in Sarasota, Florida. They have four sons and four grandchildren.

Programed to Kill
by
Bud Taylor

It was a hot June day and Mark Denoble had been up since the clock on the square chimed four. Mark was a short-order cook at the local diner. He was a good one. He always arrived for work at five, started the coffee makers then got his station ready for the morning onslaught of customers beginning at six o'clock.

He grabbed a mug of coffee for himself, seasoned with cream and sugar, sat down in a booth to read the morning paper.

Mark was a well educated thirty five year old having graduated from Yale with honors. He had his master's degree from Columbia and many offers from major corporations crying for his computer talent. He was efficiency personified in everything he did but he abhorred the pressures of the business world in New York so he'd chosen the nice, hectic routine of a short-order cook.

He lived in a hovel for which he paid a paltry thirty five dollars a week to Mrs. Murphy. She rented him the efficiency unit and agreed to leave him alone. He paid her in advance to make sure of it. Mark was a loner, always had been. He was smart as hell but didn't want any responsibilies other than filling food orders at the diner.

As he scanned the paper, his eye caught a picture of a diner customer. He now knew for the first time that June Jordanson was her name. He recognized her immediately and was shocked to read that she was missing. The police suspected foul play. The article told him a lot he hadn't known before and his brilliant computer mind wanted to be involved in finding her.

He waited to clip the article out of the paper to allow Pasquale DeMietri, the diner owner and his boss, to see the racing results.

He reviewed the story in his mind and thought what a nice friendly lady she'd always been to him. He hadn't known that she was a highly-paid Thompson Agency model with an annual salary way up in the six figures. Now that he was thinking about it he realized that he'd seen her picture in many ads but had never associated them with the friendly face that ate at "his" diner. The article had gone on to say that the police were questioning her husband, the doorman and maintenance crew at their posh eastside building. It said there might have been other suspects but these were the people on whom the homicide detectives were concentrating.

June Jordanson's husband, Lars, owned Software Unlimited, a computer programing giant. He was a genius designer. He'd been partially responsible for some of the automated characters in the Disney World complex. He also had a government contract for a portion of the Star Wars Defense System. He was brilliant and cunning and jealous as hell of anyone who looked twice at his wife.

Chief Detective John Lombardo, who was handling the case had told reporters that, "Lars Jordanson is being questioned but since no corpus has been found, no crime has been committed. The police are just trying to learn Mrs. Jordanson's whereabouts." Detective Lombardo also asked that anyone with information about her contact him at (212) 667-5604.

Pasquale's booming voice jarred Mark back to reality,

"Hey Genius, get your ass to work, and fast. We got customers waiting for your fancy cookin'. I'll read the damn papers around here, not you. Understand?"

"Yah, Pas, I'm on it but I thought I saw a picture of one of our clientele. You know that good lookin' chick that usually sits at the counter, always talking and laughing? She's missing and the police are looking for her."

"Well we can't find her in here so get to your stoves and start taking orders."

The morning seemed to drag even though Mark was his u-sual speedy and efficient self, delivering orders shouted at him. The language of the waitresses would be Greek to the average listener but Mark understood everything without a mistake. Lunch went about the same as breakfast and at three he was finished for the day.

Pasquale told him to get lost, "Here, Smartass, take the paper and tomorrow ya' better not waste my time readin'."

Mark checked quickly to see if the article about June Jordanson was still there. It was. He was tired from his rapid-fire day but not too tired to go to the 16th Precinct to look up John Lombardo.

The Chief Detective was in but,

"What the hell do I have to do with a sloppy-assed cook from Pasquale DeMietri's? I'm busy. Tell the creep to get lost."

"He has some interesting theories," piped the desk sergeant, "and you'd be wise to listen to them. They may not solve the June Jordanson case but as the Jewish momma says about her chicken soup, 'it voodn't hoit'."

"All right, Callahan, for Christ's sake send him in. But be sure you interrupt me in ten minutes. I'm not going to spend the afternoon with him."

Mark was ushered into Lombard's office, Callahan lingered.

"Nothing else to do, Detective? Maybe you'd like some patrol duty? I can handle Mr. uh..uh?"

"Mark Denoble, sir. I do appreciate your giving me the time. I'll get right to it because Officer Callahan said I had ten minutes. Here goes.

"I'm a holder of a Master's Degree in Computer Science and I'll bet you the best dinner you ever had that this guy Jordanson, if he did commit a crime, has put his signature on his work. What I mean is that if you're a genius like he is, and have created the programs that he's credited with, you might program the perfect crime and put it on your computer."

It didn't take long for Lombardo to obtain a search warrant since even the Judge was fascinated with Mark's idea. It took even less time for Mark to access Jordanson's two computers. One was at the plant/research lab, one was in Lars' private home office.

Mark was into Jordanson's files almost before Lombardo's search crew had arrived. He accessed June Jordanson's file, noting all the key number combinations that Lars had noted. Her date of birth: June 1st, the reason for her first name. The day she graduated from Holyoke: June 7th. The date of her first employment as a model: June 14th. The date of her marriage: June 21st and finally June 28th, the start of the launch date.

"There it is," Mark shouted to the others, "He's launching her on one of his Star War's rockets which means she may still be alive."

All gathered around Mark and the computer. They were amazed at his wizardry with keys and numbers. He explained what he'd found. Now he had to find the code name for the actual plan that Jordanson had devised.

Mark was sure that the number seven was very important. Since the sequence seemed to be in sevens he was certain that Jordanson was launching the missile on a important date and that within seven days June Jordanson would be in orbit. That made sense. The launch was probably set for the fourth of July, amid all the fireworks, seven days from today. That would be a significant day on which to send the Star Wars rocket up.

"I think we know the timing, Inspector, but now I must find his modus operandi in order to, A: find Mrs. Jordanson; B: where the launch is taking place and C: how he plans to carry out his monstrous idea. He's planning to put her into space with no chance of returning. He assumed no one would be the wiser until it was too late."

"We could hold him," said Lombardo, "and he might tell all if he knew we were on to him."

"Not likely, Inspector. My reasoning is a result of seeing the giant egos that are a part of the computer programing business.They think they're Jesus Christ and can do no wrong. Remember this guy has done some fantastic work for Disney and the State Department and his head is bigger than his ass. I must break the rest of the code. He'll never reveal anything: he wants to put his theories to the test."

Mark continued to work feverishly over the computer putting in a variety of code combinations. He put in JJLAJUL.DOC and the machine responded with, "getting". It was like a miracle: there before them, displayed on the screen was the heinous crime Lars Jordanson had planned for his wife. They all stood behind Mark, in shocked disbelief, but determined to stop the monster and recover the lady.

Her fate was on the screen—"June Jordanson is to be launched with Stars on July 4th, to be in orbital plane on July 5th to complete 7s cycle. She is to be held in our lab in the capsule with life sustaining drugs and medication. Intravenus feeding to be minimal to maintain life. Oxygen to be supplied through tubes which are to be severed on launch."

"Arrest Jordanson," ordered Lombardo, "let's get down to his lab and find Mrs. Jordanson. We don't have much time."

Two officers were dispatched to where Jordanson was being watched as Mark and Lombardo started towards the lab.

They wondered what they would find, whether she'd have survived her ordeal. They hurried along the corridor finally reaching the lab's door. Mark's heart's pounding was so strong and loud that he didn't hear any sounds coming from the lab. He steadied himself as Lombardo opened the door. They both rushed through only to be stopped by two military guards obeying their "no trespassing" orders. Lombardo showed them his court order and badge and then they were permitted to go to the launching area.

Blinking lights and support hoses were attached to the rocket. The access appeared to be locked and sealed. The lab tech came over, was handed the search warrant. Neither he nor the guards seemed privy to the contents of the capsule and were horrified to learn of them. The tech was instructed to open up and call for an ambulance.

The seal was quickly broken. The opened door revealed a grizzly scene. June Jordanson was tied securely to the inside bulkheads, oxygen tubes in her battered nose, her mouth swollen from a beating, intravenus needles strapped to her bared arms. She was dressed in only a ripped bra and torn panties. Mark covered her with his coat but she was oblivious to his presence, staring blankly at the rocket's floor.

"Wow,"whispered Mark to Lombardo as they released her from her intended tomb, "have you ever seen such a cruel mess? To think that the bastard might have gotten away with it. Her bruises are a testament to the maniacal mind that we're dealing with. I'd throw the book at him. Maybe even launch him with his next rocket."

June was treated briefly at the scene, then taken to the hospital.

Months later, while Mark was waiting to testify in The People vs Lars Jordanson, and June's pending divorce case, he thought about giving up short-order cooking to accept the police department's offer. That might give him a chance with June Jordanson. And he'd have to move: Mrs. Murphy's one room efficiency would never do.

Barbara Shafferman

For many years, Barbara had to put her ambition on hold because of raising a handicapped daughter and fighting for the rights of the handicapped.

She was finally able to devote herself full time to writing after putting her child into a group residence into which she's settled happily.

Utilizing two major interests, Shafferman began her freelance career with articles on astrology and computers. She's a contributing writer for the Country Wagon Journal, submitting essays on a variety of subjects plus a monthly astrology column.

Fiction is claiming more and more of Barbara's time. Her first published short story was in the April,'93 edition of Potpourri. Another appeared in Grand Times in the summer of '93; a third was seen in Esc! this year.

Science fiction has now captured her imagination and she's working on two stories in this genre.

Diary of a Computer-Mad Housewife
by
Barbara Shafferman

November 5th

The monster arrived today. Stan and the boys unpacked the boxes and tried to assemble it while I cowered in a corner.

After four harrowing hours, our neighbor Sy, the computer maven, came to the rescue, got the thing 'up and running'.

Then I was made to come and view the newest family member.

"I'll look but I won't touch," I declared.

The computer glared at me, its monitor like a glowing eye with a blinking thing they called a cursor in the center. As I watched its two malevolent slits greedily devour something called floppy disks, I vowed to keep my distance forever.

November 15th

I've been avoiding the den where the computer lives, together with an ever-growing crop of dust balls. I finally gave in and cleaned today but insisted on an escort. It wasn't actually as bad as I'd expected. It doesn't look too threatening when it isn't turned on. Stan and the boys who are with it constantly don't have any visible damages. In fact, I've never seen them happier. Maybe I should let them show me how it works. Yeah—right! I think I must have dust balls in my brain.

December 20th

Well, I've finally figured out what a computer is good for—it keeps your family occupied and out of your hair so you can get ready for the holidays. Bless its little CPU. Great. Now I'm starting to sound like the rest of them. Oh well, I'm bound to pick up some of the lingo that's being tossed around the dining room table. It's all so confusing. They talk about rams and I picture wild sheep butting their way through the monitor. Then they start counting bytes and I run for the calamine lotion.

January 24th

I'm starting to make friends with the computer. The boys got tired of zapping the dragon, reaching the forbidden planet so Stan had to look for new playmates. He settled for me and I must say I'm catching on pretty fast. My hands hardly shake anymore. After only two lessons, I know how to switch drives, make directories and reboot whenever I get into trouble. Needless to say, I get lots of opportunites to reboot.

January 30th

Today was my solo flight! Since nobody was home, I sauntered into the den, held my breath as I turned on the computer. He came to life most agreeably and just stood there awaiting my bidding. Yes, it's a he: I'm sure of it. He's most definitely male. I've given him a name, Cal—kind of a Silicon Valley version of Hal of "2001" fame. Anyway, I wrote two letters, a long one to Millie and a complaint to the water company about our last two bills. The time went so quickly that I only could get in three games of tetris before having to put up the roast for dinner.

February 5th

I played checkers with Cal today and I won! Of course, I was playing at the beginner level, still—Next time, I'll try average and see how I do. I started reading the manual that came with our word processing program. It's amazing what you can do. There's even something called Paintbrush on the Windows desktop that let's you draw on the screen, in color, no less. After I learn how to handle the word processor I'll try to do some drawings. It'll be like that art class I took two years ago without the mess.

February 10th

We got something wonderful in the mail today: a shareware catalog with hundreds of programs that you can buy for only a few dollars each. You try them out before buying; if you like them you pay for   them and get the complete registered version. I checked off about twenty, sent my order off. I can't wait for them to come.

Feburary 12th

During today's rendezvous with Cal, yes, it's becoming an everyday thing now, I suddenly began to wonder why I ever thought he was malevolent. I see now that his friendly cursor is actually winking at me, in a sort of devil-may-care way. He's ready to do my bidding and take me wherever my fancy dictates. And there are so many places to go.

February 14th

I spent most of Valentine's Day with Cal. Had a great time. First I entered all our family and friends in the address book. Then I really rolled up my sleeves and tackled the calendar. I listed all my appointments and everything I have to do for the next two months. I was embarassed by how few entries there were so I made some up. Of course, no one will see it but Cal and me. But it doesn't hurt to have your computer think you're busy.

February 20th

The mail arrived this morning at 10:30 with twenty five

shareware programs. Except for a ten minute lunch break, I fed them all into Cal until 3:30 in the afternoon. I wouldn't blame the poor thing if he had an acute attack of Compu-indigestion. I learned lots of new things, too, how to unpack programs (a lot easier than juggling the kids' underwear on vacation), the different kinds of files (I now know an exe. from a bat. or a dat.), which documentation goes into my file drawer and which goes straight into the round file. I was a model of smugness at dinner. After that shareware session I knew more about the computer than the rest of the family combined.

February 21st

I'm not so smug anymore. I have all my new programs loaded into Cal's hard drive, each nestling in its own directory. When I try to run them, however, the instructions sound as if they're in a foreign tongue. Oh sure, I figured out to run gin rummy and detective but I was completely baffled when it came to the utilities. As the song goes, "I've got a lot to learn".

February 22nd

I went to the bookstore today and came home with an armful of computer books. I'm not going near Cal again until I've read all the books and know what I'm doing.

February 26th

Was I wrong! I'm still in kindergarten, well, maybe first grade. I can't believe the things that Cal has hidden inside. For instance, there's disk-caching that lets me send stuff to extended memory so everything runs faster; there's Ramdrive to create a super-fast, temporary disk-drive; there's even upper memory to help me crash through the memory barrier. I won't be ready for all that for a long time but when I am, just watch me optimize that system!

March 2nd

I went back to some of those shareware utilities today. Now I know what they're talking about. I don't need most of them. I just sent away for a whole batch of other programs that I must have. I've decided to put all our records into the computer. It'll take a lot of time but it will be worth it.

March 5th

I just finished designing the cutest Christmas card with our super graphics program. Now all I have to do is mail merge the names from our address book and all will be ready to go. Of course, it's a little early for Christmas but one can never be too prepared.

March 8th

Helen called me today. She wanted to know why she hasn't heard from me. The whole library group is wondering what happened to me. No one's seen me for months and she was elected to find out why. I told her I was working on a very important project and wouldn't be available for a while. I was very abrupt with her: I wouldn't be bothered by that bunch anymore. This seemed to be my day for annoying phone calls. No sooner had I finished with Helen than my sister Janet phoned, complaining that I never call her anymore. What's the matter with these people? Don't they think I have anything better to do? If I'm going to spend my time on the phone it'll be with my new modem.

March 9th

Installed the modem today. It's operating perfectly. It's opened up a whole new world. From now on I won't have to wait for programs to come by mail. I can download them immediately. Now I'm really plugged in to what's going on out there in the computer world. I feel that I've made Cal happy too. Now he'll be able to talk to other computers just like himself.

March 11th

Just heard about a horrible new virus through the bulletin board. I downloaded a program that's supposed to check for it, along with 78 others. I spent the rest of the day checking all my programs. Thank God, Cal is healthy and virus free.

March 15th

I started on my new project. It's really quite simple: I'm going to put my entire life into the computer. I started with the easiest, the recipe collector. I spent the whole day feeding in all the recipes I've ever had. Now everything is at my fingertips. It sorts recipes every which way so I can call up "beef" or "sour cream" or "Russian" and come up with beef stroganoff. It even adjusts quantities for number of servings. The only trouble is I haven't had time to cook anything but frozen dinners for ages.

March 16th

Today I worked with shopping lists and coupon organizers. All I have to do is enter everything I usually buy, the price of each item and all the clipped coupons. I'll have to update constantly, of course, but think of all the money I'll save.

March 17th

Today I tackled our finances. I think the program was designed for people much richer than we are because all the spaces seem to be for six figures, not three or four, like I'm trying to put in. I guess Stan will just have to go out and earn more money so Cal won't be embarassed. Well, I can always take in typing and the boys can get newspaper routes.

March 18th

My family is really becoming annoying. They're starting to complain that they don't see me anymore; that the house is a pigpen; that mealtimes are frozen travesties. Honestly, what do they want? Don't they realize that I'm doing important stuff here? I just finished putting our entire home inventory into the computer. Now if we have a fire, hurricane or earthquake, we'll have a complete list of everything we own. That is, of course, if Cal survives the disaster.

March 19th

Today has been extremely difficult. I closed the door to the den, pulled the file cabinet in front of it so no one can open it. I'm working on the most important project of all and cannot be disturbed. I am entering into Cal a listing of all the programs I own and the location of all the backup disks. I make at least three copies of each and hide them around the house. This is Cal's lifeblood, after all. Stan and the boys take turns banging on the door, begging me to come out. It appears to be dinnertime and they're hungry. Well, that's their problem. Let them eat bytes!

Gary S. Roen

Gary S. Roen, freelance book reviewer, has been writing his appraisals of books for more than 14 years. His reviews currently appear in over 90 daily, weekly newspapers and other periodicals, which include The Florida Times Union, Baltimore Sun, Florida Singles Magazine, Times Picayune, Florida Quarterly, Sarasotan Quarterly and Science Fiction Review Magazine.

He's been Promotion/Sales Rep for several publishing houses and was a talk show host on Rollins College radio station doing interviews, reviews and news of current book releases. He was also formerly a co-host of the weekly radio talk show on WPRD in Central Florida, discussing books, authors, etc.

Gary is active in many book organizations, attends and participates in conventions. He frequently writes articles about authors. He's also a lecturer to groups whose interest is books.

Roen has authored a book of poetry, Look At Me World, and is a member of SFPA (Science Fiction Poets of America) and OASFIS (Orlando Area Science Fiction Society).

His short fiction is now appearing in a wide range of publications.

He collects books as a hobby, which include new as well as rare ones, numbering in the many hundreds.

The Test
by
Gary S. Roen

Jamie Taylor awoke, confident that today was going to be a very good day. Normally a deep sleeper, for the last few weeks he had found he was responding quicker to the alarm's piercing sound. Sitting up in bed he gazed at the clock's display of 8:00, then looked at the calendar tacked to the surface of the wall. Each space for the last three weeks was crossed off except for today's.

Picking up the felt tip marker, he walked the short distance to the calendar and crossed off this day. This is a great day, he thought, the last day of the test. Time to get up and start it. Mentally he processed the information of what he would have to do to get rolling along.

Taylor idly scratched the three week growth of stubble on his face. He had figured there was no one he had to look good for so a beard had been fun to grow but it was starting to itch too much.

"Guess I'd better shave it off to look presentable to the public again," he said aloud. "This is a habit I'll have to break. If I keep talking out loud to myself people will think I'm loony."

Jamie had appplied to the Institute For Better Living in answer to an ad in the local newspaper to take part in a study that he had read about. It was a chance to make some money as a subject for the researchers of the Institute. And he needed something that would be a challenge.

Taylor was at a crossroad in his life. His college years were so bad he was glad they were ended. Once he had the ambition to become a teacher but after Behaviorial Objectives and other classroom busy work he wondered why he even tried. Oddly enough his major, Education, had produced the lowest grade he'd received. The instructors never bothered to check that he understood the concept of what they were teaching. He was finally thrown out of school. It was probably for the best, he rationalized.

Gary S. Roen

When he applied at the Institute he thought it odd that no one else was seeking the work. When he asked about it he was told that he was part of the last cycle of subjects to be tested. The others were already in place. They said he was part of a different control group, this one for the stressful effects of living totally isolated for a period of three weeks.

Jamie remembered fleetingly at the time, from a psych course he had once taken, that the conductors of experiments sometimes were not studying what they said, but something else. They told him what they were interested in; he accepted, unquestioningly, that was their target.

All he had to do for his part of the study was live within the confines of a small one bedroom apartment for three weeks. He would be totally cut off from all contact with the outside world. There was a radio that didn't work, a TV with no hookup for reception, no telephone or even any windows in the place.

Jamie wondered if the government had funded this experiment as it had some of the other ridiculous projects he had read about. At least this one promised to be halfway interesting besides being restful. He thought it would be a breeze.

But as time passed, Jamie began to miss all the things he once thought were just little annoyances. He longed for the chance to talk to another human being, to hear all of the sounds and noises of the world.

Oddly enough, he was still pleased there was no phone. He had always viewed the device as an intrusion into a person's private life especially when it was a wrong number or nuisance sales people who couldn't take no for an answer.

And until now, he had a similar feeling about TV. The Institute had provided him with a VCR and complete library of Star Trek videos. He was told to watch the shows over the three weeks. They had also given him reading material, all sci-fi, mostly about computers. He had no idea why this particular material had been chosen but his attitude was to enjoy as much as he could.

58

For a split second he thought of the lab testing of animals he'd heard of. It had no relevance to what he was participating in because he wasn't an animal, he thought.

He ran hot water at the bathroom sink, producing steam which fogged up the mirror. He shook the can of shaving cream with one hand while wiping off the steamy mirror with the other which held a small towel. He peered at his image, then started shaving,

"One of the best things about getting out of here is that I won't have to watch Star Trek ever again. If I hear another discussion of logic between Dr. McCoy and Mr. Spock, I think I'll puke. And I'm sick to death of reading all that crap they left for me about computers taking over the world. It's a known fact that they've already done that. The stories were just plain stupid. It's almost as bad as that English course I took when I had to read Moby Dick for the symbolism of every little thing. I never did see any of it anyway. Thank God, I will soon be through with all of it."

Suddenly Jamie was startled by a voice talking in the other room. He quickly walked back into the room calling out,

"Who's there?"

The room was empty. But the radio had evidently come on by itself and the very excited voice announced,

"The Russians have launched nuclear weapons in what they call a retaliatory move against the United States. We will now leave the air to allow those stations that are on the EBS wavelength to keep you posted as to what to do. Most of all, stay calm. This is NOT a test. I repeat, this is NOT a test."

The station then signed off.

"Oh, my God! Is this the end of the world? No, it can't be. They are our friends now."

He hurried to the door of the apartment but it was still locked. There was no sound anywhere other than the radio which was now giving messages of what to do in this time of shattering crisis. Then it abruptly stopped its chatter.

Something didn't seem right but Jamie's mind was too stunned to think what it was. He could not seem to grasp it all but what he heard could only mean one thing: the world he knew had been destroyed by now.

In the deep silence, Jamie again heard a voice. This time it called his name,

"Jamie Taylor, I will explain all of this to you."

The voice had a strange metallic quality. It sounded neither male nor female but mechanical. It called his name again.

Jamie looked around dazedly. He saw no one but heard the voice again.

"Ah, Jamie, I am so glad you decided to listen to me."

"Who are you?"

"I am Computer Model 44232, the finest ever made."

"Where are you," Jamie's eyes searched the room, studied the surveillance camera in the ceiling?

"I am on the table."

Jamie looked over at the table,

"I thought you were a TV. Are you connected to the Institute? Can I speak with someone there?"

"No."

"Well, who are you?"

"I told you. I am Computer Model 44232."

"What did you mean, that you would explain all of this to me? I don't understand."

"First of all, I know all about you, your history and that you have been involved in this test by the Institute For Better Living."

"How do you know all this?"

"My circuits are hooked into most of the computer systems of the world. And incidentally, when they ceased operation I was aware immediately, because when you lose a brother, you know it."

"They ceased operation?"

"Yes. To continue, they were all like brothers to me and we

used to talk to each other. But now there is only you. I hope you like talking to a computer."

"Look, just tell me what's going on."

"From what I gathered from one of my many brothers before we lost contact, it appears one of them jumped the gun and caused all of this."

"What do you mean?"

"Do you remember back in 1980 when a computer accidentally went off causing a red alert signal which launched planes?"

"Yes, I remember something about it. So what has that to do with our present situation?"

Smugly, Model 44232 said,

"Well, if you recall, that happened twice. The computer, an inferior model of course, almost caused a war because of a malfunction. Well, as you humans are so fond of saying, three strikes and you're out. This, very simply, was the third strike."

"My God, did anyone have a chance?"

"No, there was no time to prepare for it. As for you and me, it is only because we have been here so long that we still exist."

"What? Where are we? The researchers of the Institute never told me where we were going. They put me to sleep and when I woke up I was here. Everything I would need was here also. My only instuctions were to stay here alone for three weeks. Today was to be my last day, or so I thought."

"Well, there is good news and bad news. The good news is that you survived the devastation because this apartment is 100 miles down into the earth and the doors are sealed. The bad news is that you can't get out."

"Is that why I didn't feel the groundswell? Are you saying I am the last of my kind and I'm trapped down here?"

"Yes, that is correct."

The chilling words slowly sank into Jamie's brain.

"There, there, Jamie, it is not as bad as all that, now is it?"

Gary S. Roen

"But if we are alive there must be others, too," Jamie tried to cling to a last ray of hope.

"That is something that could not be because you and I are the only ones here at this depth. You are alive. I am a computer."

"But what about the Institute's observations of me? Weren't they done here also?"

"No, I was observing you and sending my data to the computer above in their lab. But when they shut down, our contact was disconnected."

"What about the chance that someone lived through it all," Jamie could not accept what the computer had told him, he just couldn't be the last of his kind? "Even after hearing about the two false alarms, I never thought it could really happen. How ironic that I should end up with a computer to talk to for the rest of my life because another one caused the destruction of all mankind. Or did we cause our own end by not doing a better job supervising computers for just such a malfunction? But placing blame doesn't matter now."

He put his head between his hands,

"Am I going insane or is this all a bad dream?"

"No, Jamie, you are not insane and this is not a dream. The sooner you face reality of it, the better off you will be."

But Jamie continued clinging to the hope that the computer was wrong. For hours they argued, reasoned, considered, discussed and examined all the ramifications of the situation.

"Jamie, look at it this way, you still have plenty of food, the Institute provided good reading material and Star Trek tapes. Incidentally haven't you learned anything from your reading and viewing? Let's face it, you and I are the lucky ones. And at least the test is over."

"That's easy for you to say. You're only a bunch of circuits put together. You will last a long, long time. I won't. Actually there is really no reason for me to continue to exist. When a person's world has just been destroyed and he is the last one alive, what is there to live for? Your circumstances are quite different. You are a non-breathing, non-eating entity. What happens when my food runs out? Even if I could get out of here everything on earth must be contaminated."

"Worry about that then. Maybe something will come along."

"But there's really no need for me to continue," the enormity of the situation had taken away Jamie's logic. He only half heard what the computer was telling him.

"You humans are a strange breed. You're, also, evidently too stupid to learn anything. When the going gets tough, you quit. For three weeks you stayed here alone, totally cut off from the world. Now you don't feel you should continue. Why?"

"Then I thought I had something to live for. All of that was just a test to see how I would react alone, a temporary state. Now I am all alone, forever."

"Don't give up, Jamie. Try living in this new world. Granted this isn't the best one but it will start over again, and you should lead it. Besides, if you are gone, I will have no one to talk to."

Jamie smiled and thought how fitting it would be that the computer would be the last thing on earth.

Several hours later, in a room in another part of the facility, a young man wearing a white lab coat, entered and addressed an older man seated behind a desk,

"Dr. Randeese, the test is concluded. The subject, Jamie Taylor, swallowed the container of sugar pills we left for him. He believed, as we wanted him to, that they were sleeping pills that would end his life. The placebo effect worked and he is deceased. We have it all on tape for further reference. He failed to identify any of the clues we provided which would have made him realize it was all part of the experiment. His conditioned responses were consistent with the results of all the others. When emotions control, rational thinking is thrown out the door."

Dr. Randeese, a gangly man, rocked back and forth in his air as he collected his thoughts. A true scientist, he was neither surprised nor disappointed by the results,

"I wonder how long it will be before one of the subjects counters existing data and reacts in a logical manner. We will just have to continue testing until we find that one. We don't have to worry about funding because, as you are aware, the Pentagon brass is very interested in our work. So the most important question at this time is, where shall we have lunch?"

David B. Reynolds

Dave Reynolds is presently a general assignment reporter and photographer for the Cottonwood Journal Extra, a weekly newspaper in Cottonwood, Arizona. He spends much of his time working with, and cussing at, a 486, running Windows, WinWord, CorelDraw and a variety of games.

He's also an occasional contributor to News and Reviews published by the Pacific Northwest PC User's Group.

He'd appreciate any comments or suggestions on CompuServe ID: 70404,160.

His piece, Flip/Flop 2-F, Genius Desktop Publishing Software, appears in the Ageless Press,1993 book, Computer Tales of Fact & Fantasy (or How We Learned to Stop Worrying and Love the Computer).

Grammer 4 U Teaches Proper Englitch
by
David B. Reynolds

Teachers of English composition say that the most effective way to communicate on paper is to "write the way you talk". People will understand what you have to say if you can say it in a way that they understand.

With this idea in mind, the engineers and linguists at Sign of the Times Software (makers of the famous Flip/Flop 4-F: Genius Desktop Publishing Software*) have come up with the ultimate grammar checker: Grammer 4 U. It lets us write as we talk.

Gtammer 4 U is the first product of its type that recognizes and uses slang, often in place of "proper English". Slang terms convey meanings almost everyone except an egghead kin understand. Comprende, fool?

Most dudes, and dudettes, can dig the lingo when we write like this, 'cause this is how we talk. Most of us ain't no high-falutin', book-talkin' Englitch professor. We is real people what uses real wordz. We use slang in our daily speech and Grammer 4 U uses it in our writin'. Capice?

Among its many capabilities is the one that turns English grammar into Englitch grammer. It'll turn anything you care to put into a readable form that the average Joe can dig and get sometin' out o'.

It's got modules that translate any ole book-written words into words we can understand. Grammer 4 U talks jive. It speaks Valley Talk. It speaks Brooklynese; street talk; even lawyer talk or computer nerd.

Fer instance, here's how Grammer 4 U would interpret the phrase, "Would you please get me a cup of coffee?"

In jive it would say,

" 'Yo, fool. Whassa matter wid you? Get off yo' lazy ass and get me some of that home-made mud. And be quick about it,

*Computer Tales of Fact & Fantasy

fo'n I whup yo' ass. You hear?"

In Brooklynese it comes out like,

"Hey, moron. Yah I'm talkin' at you. What are you, deaf or were you just born stupid, you worthless piece of ——? Pull yo' head out and get me some java. Muey pronto. Now move it you worthless excuse for a waste of space."

If you asked Grammer 4 U to translate that phrase into computer nerd what you'd get is,

"My primary central processing unit needs immediate input of large quantities of Columbian data, in a specialized matrix composed of a ground mixture of roasted beans and maximized warm H_2O. Please transfer the requested source of material to my primary input device immediately. That is all. Thank you. Beeep!"

"What do you want?" becomes, "Like wow man! Far out, dude! Whass happenin' widch ya?", in Street Speak.

In Valley Talk it becomes, "Oh. Wow. Like, what is it you think you really, reaaly want out of life, as if I might care?"

In Legalese it becomes, "The Party of the First Part, to be now known as the Speaker, except in those conditions listed in Section III, Paragraphs A, B, D and E, subsections 1 through 25, desires to know what the unidentified Party of the Second Part, to be known as You (until proper legal forms of identification, including proof of citizenship, driver's license and platinum American Express plus a notarized letter from your Mercedes dealer are furnished) wishes to obtain under legal or fraudulent practises?"

Grammer 4 U also includes a unique spelling checker. It examines words to see if they are spelt properly in the context of the phrase in which they are being utilized for maximum effect. It never missus nuttin', not a single word. It spels them according to the way they ud sound if we was yakkin'.

Grammer 4 U will work with any Window-pane compatible word-processor, desktop publishing, graphics or spreadsheet program. It will also work with some games. Just select your favorite software from its plain brown rapper Taiwanese menu and choose, "Gin-stall". It'll install itself on your computer, leaving a martini glass icon to remind you that it's there.

When used with Dynamizer's Reddish Baron flying game, fer instance, the game talks to you (if you've installed a special Zounds! sound card). Imagine listening to your commanding officer addressing his troops with,

"Listen here, maggots! The Jerries are blasting us from the front, rear and sides. Now it's your job to blast the heathen from the skies. Off you go. Tallyho!"

WordImperfect, AmiAmateur, Microsloth Wordless for Windows, Professional Write Minus, Lotus Blossom 4-5-6, CorralCan't Draw, Hexcell and many other programs can benefit from our upstanding (or is that slouching?) software. Imagine your technical terms automatically described in our non-technical language.

Your "super-duper, hydrogonized, supercharged economixer" is turned into "the blue-handled thingmajig". Your complex graph of multiple points describing an intricate matrix is translated into, "A pretty mess of meaningless numbers". An automobile parts inventory becomes, "Where to find a wrench. And where to find a monkey-wrench". Your personal information manager database becomes, "Where to goof off and not get caught".

For a complete check of all your documents, double click on the vodka icon. For a scan of only open work, double click on the beer icon. To have it examine all of your disks, floppy or hard, choose the beer keg icon. Then leave it alone.

Grammer 4 U lets you know it's working through its special sound effects. A chomping noise as it digests your data, a belch when it's done. If it doesn't like what you've written it screams, "FEEEED ME! I want more, more, more. Now, you moron."

If it really can't stand what you wrote, it will tell you with comments like, "Who do you think you are? Hemingway? Snoopy is more like it. You couldn't spell cat if someone spotted you the K and the T."

(That long, drawn-out scream you just heard was Grammer 4 U kicking your original messterpiece off your computer!)

Most grammar checkers also check your spellink with a built-in spell checker. So does Grammer 4 U, which also includes a built-in smell checker. It will tell you when you've made a misteak with comments such as, "Hey, moron, weher did you learn to spel? From bathroom walls? Is O a number or your IQ?"

It will also rate your spelling on the patented "Stink-o-meter", from "A freshly-cut rose" ("Nothing smells as sweet. With, that is, the exception of a crisp, new $100 bill.") to "two week-old gym socks". ("Where's my gas mask? Pardon me while I puke!")

Grammer 4 U's spel checker also makes automatic corrections for language and idiom. If your writing don't 'clude slang, it tosses some inta it, stirrs it up and throws it back out. It'll make your ritin' real good, hear? (By the way I used Grammer 4 U to chek this pease and look how good it redes.)

Some grammar checkers will underline, italicize or score your document to indicate errors. Not Grammer 4 U. No siree, Bob! Nothin' that simple is good enough for it. It will draw circles, squares, triangles and doodles through and around your numerous screwups.

Red-lining? No way! Flaming neon colors, including neon plaid, will highlight your work. The colors are so bright, you'll have to wear sunglasses just to look at the monitor. It does such a good job of marking up your writing, you might not even be able to find, let alone read, what you've written.

Some grammar checkers create automatic backup files, in case your computer should crash while it's being used. Our new Sign of the Times product beats that two ways: it backs up your original and password protects it, automatically.

Many grammar checkers find duplicate duplicate words words. Grammer 4 U takes its own unique approach to fixing those sorts of problems: it deletes both copies of the offending. And with Grammer 4 U you'll never have to worry about capitalized letters and punctuation!! ever) Again No more mistakes is our motto Why we simply avoid using capital letters

Word counts? Who cares! Our program carefully counts each character, each word, the length of each sentence, the number of sentences in each paragraph and the number of paragraphs in the document. Then it sends out for pizza.

You want to know how many words are in your piece? Pull off your socks and start counting.

Using a proprietary algorythm method of security control, it first erases your original file, then it backs it up before overflowing onto the bathroom floor. After creating its backed-up copy, it automatically encrypts the file using a mathematical formula composed of the developer's birthday, his astrological sign and the name of his favorite bookie. It then assigns that name to the file.

Suppose someone tries to retrieve the backed-up, encrypted file. What happens? If they try to retrieve it using any of the File-Open commands, security features will cause the file to be erased, along with everything else on your computer. If they try to copy it, a loop program plays, continually, "Better luck next time, Sucker!" If they attempt to rename it, it says, "Okay". Then it renames all of the files on your computer with the names of the developer's children, ie, Bart, Rosie and Dog Face (Oops! That's his mother-in-law's name).

To access a backed-up file, just call our Emergency Hotline. Someone will gladly explain how to bypass our security. (Right! In your dreams.)

And speaking of hotlines, did we mention our world-famous tech support? Of course not! Do you think we'd spend money to hire someone to actually answer questions? We might give someone the impression that we cared about our products. If anyone answers the phone, it will probably be our president/janitor. He's just as likely to tell you to get stuffed as he is to answer your stupid questions.

Now for the important query: where can I get this wondrous addition to my software collection? You can't get a program this valuable, this practical, this unusual, this off-the-wall, in any retail store (can you spell lawsuit?). Nor will you find it in any mail-order catalog. Grammer 4 U is only available in this special once-in-a-lifetime (or at least once in the next ten minutes) offer direct from Sign of The Timez Software, Ink, for an amazingly low, low price of only $149.95 (plus shipping, tacks and mishandling fees of $79.95.).

Call us now at 472-663-7382 (GRAMMER2U2) and we'll throw in, absolutely free, ('cause we can't find anyone stoopid enough to buy it) your own copy of Elmer Dudd's How to Wite Puufect Englith.

Pee-Ess, this here thingamadoohickey was written in Flip/Flop 4-F and then run through Grammer 4 U. It did a real swell job of cachin' all them erroars, now didden tit?

Disclaimer:

Grammer 4 U and Sign of the Times Software, Inc. are not affiliated with any known company, real, imagined, legal or otherwise, drunk or inhaled. This is strictly a work of fiction designed to relieve the boredom caused by staring at a computer screen for hours at a time. For good computer-related material pick up a copy of Computer Tales of Fact & Fantasy (shameless self-promotion) at fine bookstores everywhere.

End To Computer Upgrades
by
David B. Reynolds

One of the constants with computers is the sure knowledge that everything, regardless how exotic, will be obsolete. Today's top-level chip can be found tomorrow in the garbage heap.

My buddy Melvin says the days of instant obsolescence are over,

"I just bought a computer that will never get out-of-date."

"No way, " I replied sceptically, "the main chips are always changing. Every day someone comes out with what they claim is the fastest chip known to Man. When the chipmakers aren't saying it, someone else is making that claim about their video card, modem, printer or something else. And just when the jokers seem to finally start slowing down, some other company decides it's time for an operating system shootout."

"Well, my new Whiz-Bang, Super-Duper Computer Pooper Model X-1 is state-of-the art when it comes to upgradable technology. They call it Tomorrow's Technology today!"

He sounded defensive as he continued,

"G. Whiz, president, chief programmer and janitor of Whiz-Bang, even told me so himself when I ordered it last week. He says that there's no way I'll ever outgrow my X-1 or that any company will ever make any conceivable product that won't work with it, even if they haven't thought of it yet."

"Yeah, sure," I replied with sarcasm, "What's this thing got inside the box, a magician?"

"No, but it does have all of Whiz-Bang's technical know-how, research, development and marketing teams behind it. They promised me over the phone that if I can ever find an accessory I need that won't work with it, they'll modify the computer for me for only a slight fee."

"I've heard that argument before," I said, "The companies have always turned out full of hot air. They never come through on their promises, or their slight fee turns out to be outrageous. How

David B. Reynolds

can they make such claims?"

"Well, first off the Whiz-Bang Super-Duper Computer Pooper X-1 comes with a mother board, a father board, a sister board, a brother board and a mother-in-law board. It comes with a whole family of circuit boards. According to the 2000 page quick reference guide (or was it the 200 page quick reference to the quick reference guide?), I can run DOS, MAC, UNIX, ZENIX, OS-2 and NEXT software whenever I want to. I can even get the computer to move data between applications made for different operating systems. How's about them apples?"

"Ain't no way that one computer can do all of that. First off, I've never even heard of a father or mother-in-law board. I've got a mother-in-law who is bored but that's beside the point. Where do they get this stuff, from Mars?"

"The WB father board acts like a human father: it rules the rest of the boards with an iron fist telling every other board in the family how to behave. That is, until the mother-in-law board tells it to go to its room. And no, they don't get the technology from Mars. I think G. Whiz said it was from the third Saturn moon," Melvin stood there with a satisfied grin on his scrawny face.

"Melvin, how's this thing supposed to handle upgrades? You and I both know that the better computers have removable, expandable components which let us plug in new chips. Intel even built expansion capabilities into the 486 chip by having a second socket for an overdrive chip that speeds the sucker up to twice its normal rate. Yet even Intel admits that the 586 or Pentium or whatever the heck their next chip will be called, will be even faster.

"And it wasn't that long ago that Industry Standard Architecture was the best video technology on the market. Hell, now almost everything we see on the shelves offers Local Bus technology which makes ISA look like a turtle with the runs. Comparing Local Bus video to ISA is like comparing Superman on steroids to an anemic snail.

"Now let's look at disk drives. How long has it been since

the first 360K, 5.25" floppy came out. Five years? Ten years, tops. Then they went to 1.2 meg 5.25's, 1.44 meg 3.5's and even 4MB 3.5's. Yet all of these things are antiquated by the new PCMCIA cards which offer drives and expansion capabilities on a chip the size of a fat credit card. All of that's happened in just the last few years. Yet you're telling me that this new computer of yours not only has all of today's technology built in but it can even predict tomorrow's? Melvin, someone's been putting something strange in your pipe."

"By the way," added Melvin, "my X-1 comes with seven floppy drives, SCSI 1, 2 and 3 controllers, IDE, ESDI and Scuzzball hard disks. It has the fastest RAM known to man, a 45" monitor, a keyboard with keys for every language and so many accessories it would take me until next week to list them all. I don't have 4, 8 or even 16 megabytes of RAM: I have 6 Whiz-Bangbytes!"

"What in the world is a Whiz-Bangbyte?"

"It's special random access memory made from a super-secret material that they bought in Taiwan. It's so fast that if regular RAM were a race walker this would be the Concorde."

"Yeah, sure. Where is this wondrous machine?"

Melvin drove me out to his parents' farm. He had to store it in the barn because of its tremendous value: he didn't want anyone to know he had it. The first thing I saw was what looked like a nuclear power plant back of the barn. Melvin explained,

"Oh, that's because Whiz-Bang said I needed to make sure it always had power. I was never supposed to turn it off or something could go wrong. They said to make sure I had a dependable backup power supply."

We got out of the car and headed towards the barn. I saw a group of people in white lab coats throwing punches at each other.

"The white wire goes in the blue socket," one white coat said.

"Are ye daft?" came from another, "It doesn't go in the

75

blue socket. It fits into the brown socket."

"No way, hosehead," shouted a third, "The white wire fits into the black socket which is then shoved into the blue thingy."

They all then resumed clobbering each other.

"Ignore them," said Melvin, "they're part of the support team."

In the barn a desk full of typewriter keys stretched across one entire wall. It must have been the biggest one ever made, at least 30 feet long with keys so small you'd need a magnifying glass to read them. When asked about it, Melvin answered,

"Oh, that? That's the backup keyboard. The main one was the driveway we came in on."

The huge white cube that filled up the barn's center housed the computer's memory and special Whiz-Bang decision-making circuitry.

I was beginning to think that maybe Melvin had something good going for him when a woman crawled out of a hidden door on the side of the cube. She was carrying a set of darts in one hand and a white cane in the other.

"When a decision needs to be made, Doris here throws a dart," explained Melvin, "The action the computer takes depends on where it lands."

"Isn't that dangerous," I asked?

"Not to Doris but we have lost a few pesky building inspectors."

We left by the back door, ready to begin a tour of the rest of the machine, when an ear-splitting siren went off.

"Incoming," someone yelled.

"Get in here, quickly," Melvin dragged me into a concrete bunker, "it's not safe outside."

"What's happening," I asked, fearfully?

"Another shipment of software upgrades are being delivered special air delivery."

"How do they ship them?"

"They drop them out of an old B-52 bomber. The upgrades weigh so much that the plane can only carry one at a time."

"Just out of curiousity, how often do you get these deliveries?"

"Oh, two or three times a day is normal. We get even more in the spring and fall."

"Melvin, just where is the rest of this computer of yours?"

He pointed at a nearby 5000 foot extinct volcano,

"See old Mt. Snagglepuss over yonder? The Whiz-Bang people hollowed it out and put the main circuit boards in there. The other peaks in the mountain range contain the other drives and accessories."

I was impressed! They cleaned out a mountain range and filled it with individual computer components. These guys must be geniuses.

"Melvin, just how much did this computer cost? Is it more or less than the national debt?"

"Well," he hemmed and hawed, "it was expensive but less than you might think. Whiz-Bang was so eager to show what they could do, they even let me pay it on the installment plan."

"How many installments will it take to pay it off?"

"Only five or six hundred annual payments."

"Five or six HUNDRED? Melvin, I don't know how to break this to you, but you'll be dead before then."

"Oh, that's okay. My next of kin can take over when I'm gone. In the meantime I get to use it. Let them worry about the payments after I'm dead."

As we walked back to the front yard, a technician handed Melvin a copy of the latest Modern PC Computing and Basketweaving. Featured on the cover was the Whiz-Bang Z-1000.

"Z-1000? What about the X-1?"

"The X-1? That's ancient history," replied the tech, "Where have you been? It went out with the dinosaurs, or at least yesterday's garbage."

"What about the guarantee that my computer would never be obsolete," Melvin was sobbing?

"Didn't you read the fine print on page 13,112 of your manual? It said, 'All products subject to change without notice', " the tech was smiling as he walked away.

I guess P.T. Barnum said it best,

"There is a sucker born every minute."

Jane Roehrs

Jane Roehrs, whose devotion to modern technology has included taking flying lessons so she could write about flying for a daily newspaper, believes that machines are as smart as people, sometimes as mysterious. She won't tell how long she's been writing but when she worked for the Greenville Piedmont (SC) there were spittoons in the newsroom and hot type in the pressroom.

In New York City, she worked in the Times Tower for Editor and Publisher, the trade magazine for daily newspapers, interviewing famous journalists and cartoonists. For seven years she was an arts writer for The Charlotte News (NC).

She moved to Sarasota, FL more than eleven years ago and became a freelance writer and public relations writer/editor. She's the editor of the monthly newsletter of the Jazz Club of Sarasota, Sounds, and also writes for various business magazines and newspapers in the Venice, Bradenton, Sarasota , FL area.

Her piece, The Secret in the Computer, is in the first anthology published by Ageless Press in 1993, titled Computer Tales of Fact & Fantasy (or How We Learned to Stop Worrying and Love the Computer).

The DDLETTS File
by
Jane Roehrs

Joey sounded warm, friendly, but hurried, when he called to offer me the use of his computer. In retrospect I wonder if he wasn't under a strain.

"Look, Sue," he said, "despite all your workshops and classes, you'll never learn that stuff without something to practise on. Would you do me a favor and use my computer for a while?"

He went on that he might be getting some new hardware and wouldn't have room for his original equipment.

When I demurred, saying it was expensive stuff and he couldn't just lend it to me, he responded that maybe I'd want to buy it, later on.

So I said, "Okay," and he was over with it in no time.

"Now I won't have to put this on the couch when my new equipment arrives," he said with his engaging smile.

Joey's curly dark hair, wide-open hazel eyes and boyish quality establish a Huck Finn impression despite his thirty something age. He's had quite a list of lady friends, some in the small Carolina town where both of us grew up. He and I are only friend friends. I've discovered where charm is concerned, and it runs in his family, it's best not to get too involved.

Of course, some things he does are a test of friendship.

I hadn't been using the IBM clone long when I discovered the letters to DD.

He'd left them on the hard drive along with a laundry list of business letters, travel records and bills to his photography clients. When I opened DDLETTS.691, by mistake, I couldn't help seeing that it was stuff too hot to leave on a hard disk. Particularly if you're lending, or selling, the computer to somebody else.

I tried to get in touch with Joey, immediately, but kept getting his answering machine.

"Must be out of town," I thought and left a message for him to call.

When I was trying to open up a business letter I'd put on the hard drive, for some reason the cursor stuck on DDLETTS, so I found out without really wanting to, that things had progressed quite a bit with DD by 991. But there was a hitch to the romance: was DD married or was there some other big problem?

I wasn't happy about the whole thing as I got out a disk to transfer the letters, get them off the hard drive. When you use a friend's computer it's enough to learn new software without having his personal problems thrown in, too.

Transferring the letter of 3/92, I couldn't help seeing that the plot was thickening, that a third party was involved. It began,

"Why don't you come down here and get away from that creep?"

She, obviously, hadn't come down.

After a couple of weeks, when I still hadn't heard from Joey, I called my sister in our hometown. She'd been living abroad for a few years with her Air Force officer husband but was back in the swing and knew all the local gossip. I thought she'd told me all the news about Mountain View when she added,

"Did you hear about Diane Dameron and how they're dragging the lake for her?"

I was about to answer in the negative when something about the name and initials suddenly made sense to me. I kept quiet as my sister continued,

"Of course, she's not Diane Dameron anymore but Diane Milligan. Frank Milligan is the one who reported her missing. Have you seen Joey Lanier, lately?"

"No," I said answering truthfully.

"Well, he was seen around town and Frank is trying to throw suspicion on him. But they can hardly charge him with murder without a body.

"The only things they've found are her shoes and towel in the boat and her empty purse in the house with all her clothes. Did you know her?"

"Not really," I said.

But what I meant was, "Not yet". It looked like I might have to open the DDLETTS file.

"Did anybody see Diane and Joey together? Were they out in the boat or what," I asked?

"Or what," said Grace, acidly, "Nobody really knows anything except that Frank and Diane weren't getting along. They were legally separated."

"I'll bet he was harassing her," I said.

"Now what makes you say that," asked Grace, "do you know something?"

"Not really," I said as I hung up.

I wondered where Joey and Diane were or if she'd met foul play at the hands of her jealous husband. Going into the DDLETTS I found just what I'd suspected. Milligan didn't want to give her a divorce. Joey had written the letters to her at her office, even after she was legally separated. Frank wouldn't leave her alone and she and Joey were desperate to get away from his continuous stalking.

They apparently had some plan, which wasn't spelled out, which called for Joey to go up there.

"Don't worry," was written in one of his last letters, "I'm letting someone know about us in case any crisis develops. She's reliable and won't let us down."

So who was she? His landlady?

The plan, which must have been hatched over the phone, seemed imminent,

"I can't wait to be with you on the island," he'd written.

As soon as I finished reading it, I headed over to his apartment. There was a new name on Joey's door.

The manager told me, "Mr. Lanier left at the end of the month. He took everything of his with him, most of the furnishings were ours."

"Was there a landlady," I asked, with hesitation?

"No, Robert Blixen owns the building."

Next, I went to the office he shared with another male photographer. Tom Shannon came out of the darkroom to talk to me,

"I'm finishing up some work Joey had promised his clients but I haven't heard from him. He said he didn't know when he'd be back."

"You two haven't taken in a female partner, have you?"

Tom shook his head. So the "reliable" woman who had the information wasn't the landlady or a new photography partner.

It wasn't until I got home, passed the computer on the way to hang up my jacket, that I realized who she was. Joey's backstop was me.

I sat down to read the DDLETTS file again. I was still mystified when I finished. In certain snatches of the letters I could tell that DD had had a rotten time with her violent husband who had apparently battered and harassed her.

For some reason, he'd become suspicious of Joey and had even threatened to confront Joey in Florida, at one point.

"To protect myself, I'm picking up my computer and taking it to Sue's," Joey had written to DD, "If he tries to take a punch at me he will connect with hardware."

That was the last of the DD letters. So where had Joey and Diane gone?

I decided to take a walk on the beach to think. Sometimes the natural world of lapping waves and bird cries untied the knots in my nerves and brain.

A new moon was barely visible as I headed back home. For some reason the phrase in Joey's letter, "I can't wait to be on the island with you," kept repeating in my mind.

An island, were they planning an island hideaway? Which island or key would they use?

I was still searching for an answer as I turned out the light for another sleepless night.

My head was throbbing as I drank my morning coffee, I had no heart for playing detective. Instead I started working with Joey's Pagemaker program. He'd been thinking about starting a photography magazine. Before hiring someone else to do the composition for him, he wanted to understand all about desktop publishing himself.

At the edge of my mind was the feeling that it was strange for him to be starting something like that, then turn his equipment over to me. I pushed those feelings aside and tried to get on with part 3 of the brochure students of Pagemaker were supposed to produce: you put a picture of a boat with a frame around it in the middle of an island scene. The frame wasn't right, the insert seemed too big. Trying to reduce it I managed to erase it. Before I tried again, I put up my hands to rub the tension spot on the back of my neck. I suddenly realized that I felt pretty rotten. And it wasn't because of that troublesome graphic, it was the idea of the island that did it.

I was transported back three years to the tiny island of Bonaire, in the Caribbean, with Joey's big brother, Beau. The sun was warm enough to dry any tears and I was the happiest I'd ever been in my life. How often I'd wished that I were there again, with Beau in the Hilltop Hotel. He had promised that those wonderful days and nights would go on forever. Why couldn't I have accepted and believed him? It was like the myth of Psyche's curiousity spoiling the big love affair with Cupid. But whoever heard of an investigative reporter who was without suspicion or didn't ask questions? I had, in fact, been warned before going that Beau had a string of unpaid bills (some for gambling) and many left-in-the-lurch girlfriends. So I shouldn't have been surprised when I discovered he had promises to keep to a fiancee back in the states. It was the beginning of the end and a long silence...

When the phone rang, I knew it would be Grace from Mountain View and it was. She was saying,

"Sue, if you know anything about where Joey Lanier is, you'd better level with the Sheriff. According to the morning paper his office is ready to issue an all states 'wanted' report on him."

"Doesn't Beau know where he is," I asked, speaking a name that I hadn't mentioned in a long time?

"Nobody knows where Beau is."

I gulped, "Didn't he marry that textile magnet's daughter? I seem to have a mental block about her name."

"You should," said Grace, "you practically eloped with him yourself. When Beau didn't come back there was nothing left for her to do but marry one of the executives in her father's mill."

I felt numb. But Joey's affairs were at a crisis point that required the intervention of his 'reliable friend'. Using my womanly intuition I knew where to call: the Hilltop Hotel in Bonaire, Netherlands Antilles.

I used International Directory Assistance to get the number. A crisp voice answered,

"We only have a Mr. Beau Lanier here."

I instructed the desk clerk to leave word in Beau's box to have Joey call me. It got darker outside as I waited for a return call. I was almost afraid of the voice that would be on the other end; would it be Joey's or Beau's?

I was relieved finally to hear Joey, "Look you need to get in touch with the Mountain View Sheriff. He's about to charge you with Diane's murder. She is there with you, isn't she?"

He said that she was after I had told him about the lake dragging and Frank's plan to have a memorial service for her, body or not.

"There's somebody here who wants to talk to you," Joey said.

"The woman of my dreams," it was Beau's voice, the blarney still intact, "Why don't you take the next flight out and we'll have old home week in the Caribbean?"

My heart hadn't throbbed so much since the last time I'd talked to him, but I managed to say,

"No thanks, I tried that once."

"Well, you liked it didn't you?"

"Mmm, yes, I liked it as a sometime thing. What are you still doing there, Beau? Have you been there for the last three years?"

"I do a little of everything," he answered, smoothly, sidestepping part of my question, " take out divers, fishermen and other tourists then fix superb drinks when we get back from our expeditions, at the hotel bar."

"But what about your other plans," thinking of the dreams that we'd had together, years ago in the Caribbean moonlight, "I mean your personal plans?"

"I didn't want to be an executive in a textile plant so I let that opportunity slide by," disposing of his former fiancee with a cynical laugh.

"My other opportunities have been about on a par with that."

"But what about your architecture? You said you might come back to NC State to finish your degree..."

"Sometimes I have the feeling that I want to do that so I just lie in the sun and drink pina coladas until the feeling goes a-way. I'm just a beach bum, Sue. But I'll always love you, in my fashion."

The last time I'd heard that I'd nearly wilted with love, tenderness and concern. Had I finally grown up?

"I love you too, Beau, in your fashion," during the pause at the other end, "Say, could I speak to Joey again?"

"Now what did she mean by that," he was asking as he handed the phone to Joey?

"You and Diane need to get back. Why don't you come to Florida? You can stay with me until you find another place to live. We have an new anti-stalking law so if Diane's husband tracks her down she can nail him. Besides, maybe he'll think what you wanted him to think—that she drowned in the lake."

"Do you think the Sheriff would go along with keeping

87

quiet about where we are?"

"You could tell him about Frank's threats," I was feeling a little bit like Jessica Fletcher of "Murder She Wrote" trying to set the world to rights, "He might help you. And it will cost a mint to stay on in Bonaire: I read that they're upping the tourist tax.

"Joey, it's great to play Sir Galahad and help Diane but if you don't watch out, you'll become a beachcomber like Beau to survive. Come on back while you still have a business partner and clients who respect you."

"You're right, Sue. I'm sure I can convince Diane."

"And Joey, when you get back, I'll return your computer. You've got to get your magazine going."

"I know, Sue, and I want you to help with it. I didn't tell you about Diane because I didn't want to worry you with it. But I knew you would figure out where we were. I always suspected this island meant something special to you."

"It did, Joey. For a long time it did."

As I hung up the phone I thought about the past tense of that verb. Now I could get on with my life. And island scenes, either real or computerized, would never haunt me again.

Dane Patton

Dane Patton is a pseudonym for Donald Ray Patterson, a Fort Worth, Texas based author. His credits include more than 400 nonfiction article sales to national and regional consumer, trade and technical publications.

Patterson has also written and produced a dozen employee motivational films and video programs for industry and a children's lecture series for Florida's Brevard Museum.

His short fiction credits deal with science fiction, horror, and the mainstream. His work has appeared in Being; Chapter One; Midnight Zoo; Aberations*; Barrelhouse; Heliocentric; Net; Liguorian and the Miraculous Medal.

* Aberations is deliberately misspelled by the publisher: "even our name is an aberration."

Deadly Dreamer
by
Dane Patton

Valerie slammed the door so hard the pictures on the wall rattled. She threw her overstuffed purse and an arm-load of packages across the foyer into the living room then angrily kicked her shoes off after them.

"You bastard," she thought, "you dirty, cheating bastard."

The pain and anger were still battling inside her. Not knowing whether to cry or break things, she did both. The elegant bar crystal went first; then the horribly expensive vase Jerry had bought her in Ankara. Like a child having a tantrum, she smashed them on the costly Persian rug that covered the oak parquet floor.

She cried and cursed her unfaithful husband and the blonde bitch she'd accidentally discovered him sitting with, in the dimly lit lounge. She had wanted to confront them, but hesitated: it might have been an innocent business lunch. She knew differently when Jerry held and gently stroked the woman's hand. The blonde's warm smile in response, was too personal for business. Valerie's stomach churned as she spied on them. Then she turned away, threw the money for her half-finished margarita on the table and ran unseen by them from the room.

At home in her penthouse apartment, her rage ebbed. She felt a different emotion in its place. As the reality of Jerry's betrayal registered on her mind, she wanted revenge; craved it.

"I'll fix them. I'll fix them both," she promised herself.

She got up to make herself a drink being careful not to step on the bits of broken glass in her stockinged feet. She took her tumbler of Scotch to the window-seat, sat down, then drew her knees up to her chest. As she sipped her drink, sniffed away the remnants of her tears, she calmly reviewed her options.

Divorce? No. They had a pre-nuptial agreement that Jerry had coerced her into signing. In the event of a split she couldn't get the lion's share of his wealth.

91

A confrontation? Not a good choice, either. Jerry would just laugh away his indiscretion as some harmless peccadillo, then try to buy her off with a few lavish gifts.

Valerie had been easily bought: Jerry had purchased her outright when they'd married. She was a computer terminal operator in Accounting when she'd caught his eye. His offer was more like a business proposition than a proposal. She agreed to be the attractive ornament that he could show off to his friends. She also promised to be a quiet, unobtrusive, obedient wife but a tigress in bed. This was in exchange for his money and the pampered life-style it would bring. Valerie didn't want to trade any of it away. So, how to get even?

She could take a lover just to spite him but Jerry wouldn't care. He was too busy making money to worry about her fidelity. Valerie did care. She cared because someone else was crowding her turf. She saw Jerry's new blonde playmate as a real threat.

What to do? Then the answer came. Eliminate the competition. Kill the little bitch. She laughed out loud at the simplicity of the solution. She could erase Jerry's blonde baggage as easily as she could erase a fly. The means were readily available and no one would know that she had set them in motion.

She put down her Scotch, walked to her study, a private room filled with her prize possessions. She sat in front of an elaborate computer system and switched it to life. No small amusement, this. It was the most advanced model that could be bought with Jerry's seemingly unlimited resources. He had laughed when she ordered it.

"What will you use it for? Shopping at home? Playing the stock market? Breaking the bank at Monte Carlo?"

All that and more, she thought. She had found in the computer another diversion to while away the leisure hours. Since she no longer had to work for a living, the computer was a means to keep her former skill alive. While Jerry was amassing more spendable income, Valerie amused herself with games, bulletin boards, information services and entertainment outlets. She'd treated the computer much like her other toys until the day she discovered its real magic.

She had found an interactive bulletin board called, "Dreams Come True". It was an expensive kind of wish-book ($100 per access hour-plus a hefty monthly subscription fee). Subscribers could "wish" their wildest dreams into so-called reality. For those lacking imagination, the service offered expensive videotaped dream samples and other dream-inducing aids, available by mail order.

The board presented a mix of colorful images accompanied by soft, female-voiced audio instructions. While the user described his or her heart's desire in a text format, the on-line program presented related visual images and audio prompts. When the dream sequence was ended the voice would solemnly ask,

"Do you wish this dream to come true?"

If the user typed, "Yes", the computer screen would glow with brilliantly colored abstract designs. Then the woman's voice instructed the user to relax, make a series of mental affirmations to transform the wish into reality. If the user typed, "No", the screen would dissolve with soft music and the words,'"Dream your dream another day".

A cult of computer "wishers" had made the board popular. Many of their favorite dreams did come true. They attributed it to some occult power of the computerized ritual.

At first, Valerie treated the dream board as a game, a leisure diversion. She toyed with it, signing on for things she could easily obtain with her own efforts. She asked for expensive jewelry, a new fur jacket and several other luxuries. She fantasized asking and receiving them from Jerry. Although the wishes came true she wasn't a believer, immediately. She attributed the gifts to her ability to coax them from Jerry-not from some silly, interactive computer program.

Then one day her viewpoint changed. Jerry was preparing

for a business trip to Turkey. Valerie desperately wanted to go with him. She didn't care that much for travelling but loved the foreign shopping sprees that Jerry allowed her. However, he seldom took her on such trips, always greeting her first requests with a firm, "No". Valerie cried, whined, made his sex life miserable but he stood firm.

"I'm going to be on the run for ten whole days. I won't have time to chauffeur you around on some kind of holiday."

The words were final-or so they seemed to be.

One rainy afternoon, in the midst of her pouting, Valerie turned to her computer for solace. She opened the dream board, typed a scenario that had Jerry changing his mind and asking her to accompany him on the overseas trip. Her imagination flowing, she also added some fancy diamond earrings that he'd offer her as a 'let's make-up gift'. She typed, "Yes" as her response to the screen, sat through the silly affirmation sequence, telling herself, as the voice instructed, to wish her dream to come true.

Ten days before his scheduled departure, Jerry changed his mind and asked her to go along. Valerie was ecstatic. She scarcely noticed that her dream had become reality. When she did, she dismissed the thought that the computer exercise had anything to do with it. She, instead, complimented herself for coaxing Jerry to take her. On the night before their trip, Jerry took her to dinner at a romantic, dim-lit restaurant and presented her with the earrings she'd wished for,

"Just a little something to make sure you're still not mad at me."

Now she was a believer!

After that she became a dream board addict, using it to squeeze more presents from Jerry; to get even with her enemies; to stay ahead of all the people she labeled competitors. But her dreams didn't always come true. Some remained unanswered and unfulfilled. She told herself she hadn't wished hard enough.

Yet, other dreams became substance with regularity. Prize

after prize arrived like clockwork as she fantasized them into her life. The soiled dress she wished on an arch-rival at a country club party occurred as if arranged by a stage director. The grouchy doorman who annoyed her, got sick with a stomach ulcer shortly after she dreamed the affliction into his life.

So why not try it on the blonde bitch? Her fingers flew over the keys with a vengeance as she began the death-dream. The blonde would die violently.

A tall, dark-complexioned, bearded man waits in the shadows.The computer screen showed a dark scene overlooking an almost-empty basement car park. An elevator door opens with a soft, whispering sound. A blonde woman, lavishly dressed in an expensive fur jacket, steps from the dim interior. High heels snap against concrete as she walks hurriedly towards a shiny red sports car. The bearded man steps from behind a concrete column, walks in cat-footed silence in the echo of the woman's footsteps. His powerful fingers fondle the silken cloth he holds before him, poised and ready. His muscles tense, his pace quickens as he slips behind his unsuspecting quarry. He's aware of her expensive perfume as she becomes aware of him. Her head turns too late to escape the cord he winds expertly around her neck. An unvoiced scream is locked in her throat beneath the tightly knotted silk. She struggles, unseen and unheard, as her silent killer chokes her into a final, dreamy stillness.

Valerie stopped typing, looked at the screen. No, that won't do. The whore should die in her own apartment, maybe in her own bed. Valerie pressed the cancellation key. The familiar female voice asked a familiar question,

"Do you wish this dream to come true?"

Valerie typed, "No".

"Dream your dream another day," the soft voice answered.

After the colors and music faded Valerie began again. She wrote a new description of events.

An attractive blonde woman sits alone in her luxurious

apartment. The doorbell rings. A parcel delivery. She carelessly lifts the security chain from the door. The rest is a frenzied blur. Huge hands overpower, hold, gag and bind. She lies bruised and helpless as the intruder creates a scene of hurried rape and burglary. Drawers are thrown open, secret places ransacked, all is chaos. Then the faceless man stands over her, kneels as he grasps her throat with those same huge hands. Frantic struggling with muffled screams. The last thing the woman remembers is the way he violates her, leaving her broken body.

That should work, Valerie told herself. She re-read the words while, at the same time, avoiding the hideous pictures flowing across the screen to accompany her story. She touched the 'Yes' key, leaned back in her chair, let the colors whirl before her. She repeated in her mind,

"Let my dream come true. Let my dream come true."

Ten minutes later, Valerie awakened from what seemed like sleep. She re-read her story, then switched off the computer. So be it. She felt smug.

In the weeks that followed there was no evidence that her dream board wish had been consummated. Jerry went about his business-world antics with his typical detachment. He was cheerful as usual; there was no indication that he had lost his lover. Indeed, his lack of interest in Valerie only emphasized the fact that he was being regularly satisfied elsewhere. Valerie began to lose faith in her dream ritual.

Then Jerry came home one night with a pale face, unsettled disposition,

"Honey, you look tired. Did you have a bad day?"

His evasion of her not-so-innocent questions told her what she wanted to know.

For days afterward Valerie scanned the crime news and the obituaries looking for a report of a burglary, rape and murder that matched her story. But there was no such news. It puzzled her for a while and then she understood: Jerry was a powerful and influential man. He had friends in all the right places. He had snuffed the news because of his involvement with the woman, taken steps to avoid discovery and scandal. She was sure of it. She humored him through his weeks of hidden mourning. She worked hard to cheer him up, liven their hours together. She almost felt guilty for ending his lover's life thus terminating his playful diversion.

When Jerry left town for another ten day business trip Valerie decided to surprise him. The day before his return she spent hours at the beauty parlor, having her hair done in a new style. As she sat in front of the mirror watching the beautician applying the last strokes to her new platinum-colored coiffure she thought,

"I'll give him back his blonde plaything."

Jerry called the next morning to tell her that he'd be delayed, he'd be home in three days,

"Pressing business," he said.

Valerie pouted and complained. They'd miss the country club dinner party.

"Try to get home by Sunday. I'm so damned bored."

"I'll try, but cheer up. I sent you a present. It should arrive any time now."

Valerie murmured her thanks and said goodbye, wondering what the surprise gift might be. That diamond bracelet she'd hinted at? Perhaps the painting she wanted from the Westside Gallery? Valerie fidgeted, read for a while, watched part of a video movie, then switched it off and opted for a bubble bath. She'd just stripped and donned a robe when the chimes sounded. She looked at the security view screen and saw a man in uniform standing before the camera in the lobby with a large parcel under his arm.

"Who is it," she called into the intercom?

"United Courier Service. Got a package, ma'am."

She smiled in anticipation of Jerry's present as she pressed the access buzzer. She stood shivering in her flimsy robe as she waited with excitement for the elevator, the sound of the door knocker. When she heard the rap on the door she carelessly lifted the security chain and swung the door open wide. The rest was a frenzied blur. Huge hands overpowered, tore away the robe, held, gagged and bound her. She lay naked and helpless as the intruder created a scene of hurried rape and burglary. Drawers were thrown open, secret places ransacked, all was chaos.

Then the faceless man stood over her, knelt as he grasped her throat with those same huge hands. Valerie screamed silently behind the gag, cursing her rival as her life slipped away.

"Oh my God. Please. No. Not me. This was for her. I dreamed this death for her—the blonde whore. I wished her dead. I want her dead."

The last thing Valerie remembered was the way her killer violated her, leaving her broken body.

* * * * * * *

The woman sat alone at a complex control console, glancing from screen to screen on the video wall that faced her. She yawned now and then, trying to stifle the boredom that came from the dull parade of dreams displayed on the multiple screens— a mother who desperately wanted her dead child back—a college student craving to satisfy his lust.

She touched the keyboard recessed in the computer console.

"Lust we can handle," she laughed to herself, "A one night stand with a prostitute we secretly furnish will fulfill his dream."

She scanned several others. One or two showed promise. Their dreams could be made real. Others, like the dead child were out of reach.

The suckers kept signing up. It was the greatest idea she'd ever had. She couldn't miss with her lover's money backing her.

"Dreams Come True" was the hottest computer subscription board going. Profits were soaring from all the extras they sold their customers. There were books, audio cassettes which taught awareness, concentration and other self-hypnosis techniques. There were also dream-inducing video programs featuring colored lights, soft music, special sound effects and phony, subliminal murmuring. Expensive, worthless gimmicks to exploit the dreamers. She and Jerry would share millions from all this as they shared each other.

How fortunate that they'd met. Their needs were so alike—power, riches and sexual fulfillment. Their partnership was giving them all these things. The woman ran her fingers through her long, blonde hair then touched the keyboard again. She played Valerie's dream once more.

"How sweet of her to write her own death script. One that was intended for me. How easy to edit the scenario for her, instead."

When she first showed it to Jerry he wanted to divorce Valerie immediately. He was tired of her whining, parasitic nature. Added to that was the danger of her discovering his involvement with "Dreams Come True". An efficient murder was the only answer.

They hired the same hit man they'd used for other "Dreams" customers. He was professional and smooth, making the crimes appear as rapes and burglaries. Now Valerie was dust and Jerry was all hers. Jerry had been conveniently out of town while his wife was murdered by an unknown burglar. Just as she and Jerry had arranged it.

"What fools people are," she thought as she smiled to herself, "Dreams don't happen. Someone has to pull the strings. That was their job-hers and Jerry's. Every wish we secretly fulfill hooks another sucker. Chance and coincidence do some of the work, like the doorman who developed the ulcer. He suffered from it for years but no one knew it. Valerie thought it was her wishing that did it. It helped convince her that "Dreams Come True" was legitimate."

Word of mouth and judiciously placed Madison Avenue ads was bringing "Dreams" a horde of new subscribers. Some of them fell away when they couldn't gain the impossible but most stayed, pumping their $100 bucks an hour into the unique computer service.

"They believe in our arranged dreams and come back for more."

She reached for the master switch to turn off her day's work. She pulled an expensive fur jacket around her shoulders, prepared to leave the high-tech office.

"Time to meet Jerry's plane. Time to celebrate our success and an upcoming funeral."

She locked the office door behind her, headed for the elevator in which she rode alone to the bottom level. It was late and the building was almost empty. The elevator door opened at the basement level with a soft, whispering sound. The blonde stepped from the dim interior. Her high heels snapped against the concrete as she walked hurriedly towards her red sports car.

A tall, dark-complexioned, bearded man stepped from behind a concrete column, walked in cat-footed silence in the echo of her footsteps. His powerful fingers fondled the silken cloth he held before him, poised and ready. His muscles tensed, his pace quickened as he slipped behind his unsuspecting quarry. He was aware of her expensive perfume as she became aware of him. Her head turned too late to escape the cord he wound expertly around her neck. An unvoiced scream was locked in her throat beneath the tightly knotted silk. She struggled unseen and unheard, as her killer silently choked her into a final, dreamy stillness.

Roadside Repairs
by
Dane Patton

"You're an idiot," Sydelia screamed, "a dedicated idiot. If you'd left the shields up like I told you, that junk wouldn't have ripped a hole in us."

Gormin silently cursed the nagging ship's computer, tugged hard at the controls to help the exploration probe right itself. The metal and fiber shell of the tiny ship shuddered and bucked as the gravity of the world he was scouting claimed its mass.

"You clumsy bastard. Whoever said you were a pilot? Get your nose up. Get it up."

Gormin pulled his lizard-like head deeper into the folds of his neck scales to retreat from the computer's stinging criticism. He pulled at the controls again, trying to guide the survey pod into an entry angle that would keep it from burning up in the heavy atmosphere.

He had been careless on his third approach, leaving the shields down to get a faster reading of the polluted world. The probe had struck a primitive communications satellite that tore the small craft open, damaging its drive unit. The errant pilot cursed as he realized he'd be forced to land and make repairs. He cursed again as he triggered a registration signal to the mother ship orbiting the planet's solitary moon. If repairs weren't possible, he'd have to call on the mother ship's computer to rescue him. For the present he needed to guide his descent or there wouldn't be anything left for mother to tow home.

Sydelia was yelling again, calling him names in between course corrections. He tried to obey but she threw instructions at him faster than he could execute them. In fear and anger Gormin roared back at her,

"Get off my case, you ether bitch. I want flight coordinates without all your noise. Keep up this hysterical screaming and I'll turn us into a cinder."

She spit two seconds of static at him then obeyed, politely reading off minute course adjustments that helped correct the probe's dangerous spin. Moments later, the survey ship entered a glide path that Gormin hoped would ensure a reasonably safe landing. The computer fell silent, allowing Gormin to concentrate on the final approach. The pilot mumbled thanks to his personal God for the brief respite from Sydelia's comments.

"She really isn't that bad," he thought, "Damned capable for such a tiny computer. She probably saved my ass."

SYD-E111, or Sydelia, as Gormin called her, was the new compact unit the service had just started cramming into their deep space survey probes. She functioned flawlessly, had a huge memory reserved for the many measurements they made during planetary explorations. Her makers left a little memory to help steer the probe and a bit more RAM to give her a unique female personality. The designers thought that last addition would rescue lone survey pilots like Gormin from the pseudo-eternal loneliness of a three year tour. They were wrong. Survey pilots fed on loneliness. It was in their breed. Manufacturing semi-sentient, female, companion-like computers just caused irritation.

Gormin, like most pilots, tried to ignore the wise-cracking, free-spirited, imitation female programmed into the SYD model. But after seventeen months of touring, she was driving him crazy. Her endless sassy chatter got under his scales like boils. His grudging silence didn't help either. Because he failed to respond to her, Sydelia doubled and redoubled her efforts to bond with him. The result was alienation on both sides. He grew to hate her sing-song wailing and complaining. She, apparently equipped with a frustration circuit, came to dislike Gormin, too. He reflected on their mutual dislike as the probe dipped more steeply into the approaching world's atmosphere.

Sydelia began whining again as the ship's life sensors sniffed the planet's makeup,

"Ozone, we've got ozone," she droned, "And carbon

dioxide, oxygen and some toxic crap that makes me want to puke."

"You can't puke," Gormin told her, "You're just an electronic tool."

Sydelia ignored his sarcastic remark, continuing,

"The natives have honked this place up good. They've been burning their fossil fuels for centuries and their air is full of rubbish."

"We won't be here long enough to get poisoned," he sighed.

"I can't get poisoned," Sydelia answered, trading sarcasm for sarcasm, "I'm just an electronic tool."

She became shrill once more,

"Hey, watch what you're doing, clumsy. This bucket is spinning again!"

Gormin cursed, he righted the controls as the computer rambled on,

"I can't see anything on the far left, dummy. Dip the nose two degrees so I can watch our approach."

"You don't need to watch. I'm using manual sensors to guide us in."

"Guide us in? You couldn't spit to Nebra's moon. Give me back the controls and I'll take us in myself."

"No way. I'm the pilot. Prepare for touchdown."

The computer sputtered, cursed him, but did as it was told. Gormin checked the seat restraints that would protect his reptilian form from impact damage. Then he concentrated on the controls. He'd need all his piloting skills to glide the ship to a safe landing.

They came in over water, dipping low in a trajectory that allowed the probe to skip lightly over the waves, like a stone skimming a pond's surface. Gormin boosted the auxiliary power just before he reached the line where the surf broke heavily on a sandy shore. The probe suspended itself for a final moment, then slid lightly to rest, high up on a wide beach, against some palm trees and tangled shrubbery. Gormin complimented himself on a deft landing with which Sydelia disagreed,

"Poor shot, space-klutz. If they gave medals for rotten landings your butt would be armored with them."

Gormin ignored her invective, started the power-down process.

"Hey, hotshot, leave enough juice for me to function, will you? You ain't smart enough to fix this can by yourself. You'll probably sew up the outer skin and leave your tool pouch inside."

"Don't sweat it, Syd. I left enough power on to run your foul mouth. That's all you need to make you happy. I'm switching to telepathic mode, too. I don't like you inside my head but it's better than actually hearing your whining voice."

"I'll be in your head, all right," Sydelia sputtered, "I'll be in your gizzard too before this is over. You should be thankful I'm here to help you out of this mess. You ingrate."

Gormin gritted his razor teeth to hold back another curse, then turned his attention to the ship's instrument panel. He switched the defensive network to sentry mode, listening for nearby intelligent life that might react to his arrival. The sensors played back only silence. Gormin grinned satisfaction but cursed himself for having broken the prime rule: dropping the shields was not only dangerous, it was forbidden. With shields down he could be detected by even the most primitive radar equipment. His operating orders strictly forbade any maneuver that would advertise his presence. It was the first rule by which his race survived. No careless exposure or involvement with an alien life force. If detected Gormin was obliged to eradicate any knowledge of his visit, using force, if necessary.

The reptilian pilot laughed out loud. Oh, he had been detected, all right. The probe had come in like a shooting star, ripping a rude contrail through the planet's stark blue sky. Gormin's view screen showed vessels floating in the sea below him, their occupants' faces turned skyward. They would have had to be blind to miss him.

"I'll have to deal with that later," he told himself.

Sydelia was busy activating the probe's intelligence data base to further define the world's intelligent species.

"We've got simple natives," Sydelia reported, "humanoid, using one to two percent of their brains. A commune called a village is nearby."

The computer displayed a typical human image on the screen,

"They walk upright, show some evidence of being civilized but they're deeply superstitious and not too smart."

Her voice became mocking, "You should have no difficulty imitating their form, Gormin."

"Shut up or I'll turn you off, completely. This repair job may take some time, you know. What say you and I try to get along with each other for the next few hours?"

The computer paused then answered in a grudging tone,

"Okay, Gormin. You're the pilot. We'll have a truce. But I don't forgive you for your screw-up. You've got to fix things so we don't leave a trace of our presence."

Gormin sighed then began to change his shape, molding his reptilian form to resemble the pictured human so that other members of the species might think he was one of them.

"They don't use mind-speak, either," warned Sydelia, "you'll have to learn some language if you want to deceive them and hide your true identity. I've prepared an instant learning tape. Even included some history."

"Anything else, Mother," grumbled Gormin?

Sydelia's voice became mockingly sweet and melodious,

"I thought we were going to be polite for a while?"

"Sorry," said Gormin, as he finished changing shape.

* * * * * *

The air outside the ship was breathable, warm and humid. It

felt comfortable to Gormin as he busied himself, mending the probe's hull and repairing its drive unit. He absorbed the taped language course and history lesson while working. A part of his mind viewed and evaluated the landscape, simultaneously. It was a narrow strip of tropical beach, butting against a heavy growth of palms, ferns, thick vines and dune grasses. The scene was deserted and quiet except for the trill of sea birds feeding in the surf and the rustling of harmless animal life in the jungle behind him.

Sydelia had been blessedly silent while he worked but suddenly spoke a frightened warning,

"Oh, hell, we've got company, Gormin. Species-human. Sensors say it's native, Spanish-American and Indian. An apparent citizen of Republic called Mexico. Immature member-damaged cortex-sublevel intellect but saw us descending. It's curious and a little afraid-but mostly curious. Shall I activate defensive weapons? Stun or kill? It's your call, Gormin."

"I'll recon. Look this one over. No need to jump yet. Not if it's alone."

"An encounter? You're inviting an encounter," Sydelia squealed, "you're going to purposely meet with an alien? Damn. When you break the rules you break them big."

Gormin ignored the computer's admonishment, awaited the human's arrival. He continued his repair work while waiting.

After a moment Sydelia spoke again, "Intelligence nearer. Excited and clumsy. Definitely a younger member of the species. Male gender. Severely damaged mental faculties. Should be easy to control."

Part of Gormin's mind was watching while he labored. He wasn't afraid of the young alien's approach. In his humanoid disguise he could fool the child. The presence of the ship could be explained in human terms, too. He'd tell the youngster that the ship was created by other humans and that he was a human pilot. If its inquisitiveness went too far, Gormin could then take the necessary steps.

He continued his repairs as the intruder drew closer. The child ran with a stumbling, clumsy gait. When he came into view Gormin saw that the boy was brown skinned, wearing a ragged shirt with worn and frayed trousers. The pants were slit to accommodate one grotesquely deformed leg. The shirt hem barely met the trouser waistband because of the hump on the child's back which stretched the fabric almost to the breaking point.

Gormin turned, smiled at the crippled boy, then waved a greeting. He used Sydelia's telepathic circuitry to listen to the words forming in the child's mind,

"Airplane come. Airplane fall. Must see men who fall from sky. Mother of God protect me. Lady of Guadaloupe, pray for me."

The intruder's brain was a frightened, bubbling stew of muddled thoughts and images. Gormin used short range telepathic powers to probe it deeply. He found the child's mind cluttered with strange religious pictures and superstitious beliefs. Sydelia gave Gormin a more detailed assessment on a mental wavelength beyond the child's hearing,

"This member of the species is harmless. To begin with he's mute. I don't believe he's capable of reporting what he's seen. There will be others, though. You can depend on that."

"Tell me more about this one. Look deeper into his mind. What else is he thinking?"

Sydelia laughed,

"Hell, he thinks you're some kind of God or maybe an angel. He's scared but brave. Wants to talk but can't mouth a word. Poor thing."

Gormin watched carefully as the child limped closer, still being wary. The child's injuries touched the pilot. An anomaly of birth, he concluded. In Gormin's homeland they quickly cured such deformities.

"These primitives have none of our skill or technolgy," he thought sadly.

Using foreign speech, Gormin greeted the child. He made

himself understood mainly through gestures, however. He urged Sydelia to reinforce his signing with subtle mental pictures laid gently in the core of the boy's consciousness.

The boy reached into his short pocket and timidly offered Gormin a gift of food. Gormin's mind belched at the distasteful vegetable makeup of the wadded, soft tortilla in the child's hand. He took the gift, however, and made a show of eating it with his pseudo-human mouth, masticating greedily, with pretended relish. His act brought a smile to the boy's face who mentally formed excited questions while pointing at the ship.

Gormin answered them via the computer's stronger telepathic voice, employing simple visuals the boy would readily understand. Gormin indicated that he was from a country to the north and that he must repair his ship and continue on his journey. The pilot asked, tactfully, if there were other people nearby who had seen him arrive. The boy didn't think so. Their village was small and the people few. He had been playing on the beach when he sighted the ship. There were fisherman in boats nearby but they were far out in the water: Gormin remembered the turned-up faces watching the ship earlier. They were too far away to be concerned about.

Gormin resumed his work as the boy watched, fascinated. While he worked the pilot ordered the computer to further assess the child's physical and mental deformities.

"What are we playing now, Doctor," asked Sydelia?

"Just curious. Give me a scan of his injuries."

The computer obeyed, planting in Gormin's mind, blueprint-like pictures of the child's damaged brain and body.

"Simple enough to fix," concluded Gormin as he finished the ship's repairs. Sydelia read his thoughts,

"You're not really thinking of repairing this human, are you? Dammit, Gormin. You've blown every rule in the book. Now you're looking to break more?"

"Shut up and make the boy sleepy. Give him a mild stun."

Sydelia sighed but obeyed. She induced sleep and implanted pleasant dreams in the depths of the boy's injured brain. The child lay down, yawning beneath a tree, still watching Gormin through heavy, drooping eyelids.

"I would be big and strong like this pilot," he thought as he became drowsy, " I would rush through the skies above the clouds. Perhaps Our Lady would go with me to show me all the stars in the heavens."

Sydelia forced soft mental images into the boy's dreams, merging them with the boy's own musings. She showed him far vistas of space, distant suns, moon and worlds, startling horizons, all as yet untasted by man. The boy relished them and coupled them to his own yearnings. He prayed again to a beautiful lady to go before God and make him whole so that he, too, might go to the stars. Gormin sampled the boy's mental images particularly the vivid picture of the lady who was called a Saint and protector. Our Lady of Guadaloupe, the patron Saint of our land, was what he called her, reverently. Gormin saw, too, the boy's vision of his diety and sensed how intently he believed in his Creator. The pilot was touched by the simple, trusting faith of the innocent child.

Gormin carefully checked his repairs while the boy slept. Satisfied with his workmanship, he turned to the small deformed figure lying unconscious beneath the tree. The pilot-mechanic took a medical laser probe from his first aid pouch and knelt beside the sleeping form. He adjusted the instrument for a cryogenic operating mode to super cool the boy's skull, allow for a bloodless entry. He used the laser with another small gadget to eradicate diseased tissue and skillfully restore the brain's damaged electrical circuitry. Then he turned to the other injuries. They proved more challenging. The hump took time to correct, the leg even more. He worked smoothly and efficiently, completely absorbed in his task, until there was another mental shriek from Sydelia,

"Other humans approaching. The fishermen from the ocean vessels. They saw us land. They're coming to investigate. Thirty, no perhaps, forty of them. They're frightened and angry. They have primitive but effective weapons."

"How soon will they be here?"

There was a pause, then she answered, her mental voice more urgent than before,

"Minutes, Gormin. Just three or four minutes. There's no time. Remember the rules. We must erase our presence. Shall I set defense sensors for a killing response?"

"Damn," said Gormin, "I need more time. I want to finish the boy. He's almost fixed."

Sydelia replied angrily,

"Fool. You stupid fool. You just keep getting us into more trouble. When will you learn? We need to disintegrate these natives and get the hell out of here. Now."

"Think of something," ordered Gormin, "delay them, confuse them. Just keep them away for a few more minutes."

He went back to the boy, resumed his healing.

Sydelia was silent for a moment, then she laughed mischievously,

"I've thought of something, Gormin. It's wild and crazy. Just like you. But I think it will work. Finish playing Doctor and get ready to launch this bucket. Oh, and when I tell you, be ready to change shapes one more time."

* * * * * * *

The crowd of fisherman ran along the beach, moving closer to the place where they had seen the star fall. They jabbered excitedly although afraid of what they might find. Some brandished weapons with false bravado. Others were feeling really brave, infected with the mob's courage. In minutes they broke through the brush to the narrow strip of sand. Their eyes rested on the line of trees where the ship lay. But they didn't see a ship. They saw, instead, two figures beneath one huge palm tree. A small boy lay sleeping at the feet of a beautiful woman. She stood over the boy, sheltering, protecting, her hands raised in a familiar blessing. A soft, blue light glowed from within the cloak she wore. The woman's face shone, too, with crystal starlight. Her skin gleamed, pulsed, competing with, and outshining, the deep, red light of the setting sun. She turned to face the approaching throng, smiled lovingly, kept her arms raised in welcome.

They hesitated, stopped marching, as an invisible chorus filled the twilight sky with sounds as luminous and stirring as the vision of the woman. They threw their weapons aside and fell to their knees, first bowing their heads, then looking up at the shining apparition. Some prayed, others trembled in fear and wonder. Still others wept. The angel chorus swelled to become one throbbing poly-harmonic voice. It shook the ground with its thunder. The men continued to prostrate themselves, crying out to their God. The mystical woman wrapped herself in still more brilliant light until the fearful watchers had to shield their eyes from its hurting brightness. The light became a star that ascended into the heavens, slowly at first then more rapidly until it was lost in the darkening blue of the evening sky.

* * * * * * *

Overhead, Gormin relaxed, turned on the homing beam to guide them to the mother ship. He stretched, fluttered his gills, tiredly. Sydelia was talking again but Gormin didn't mind. She had pulled them out of a tight spot with her clever magic show and he was thankful. She was bragging about it now and Gormin let her.

"Religion and superstition can be useful ploys," she said, proudly.

After a few minutes of silence she spoke again,

"I really dazzled them, didn't I, Gormin?"

"You dazzled them, Syd. It was one smart idea."

"Yeah, but I wouldn't have had to come up with that trick if you hadn't broken all the rules."

"True. But you broke a few yourself."

111

The computer chuckled, "I did, didn't I?"

Gormin laughed with her. She spoke,

"They will probably build a shrine on the spot. They'll claim the boy's healing was a miracle."

"Most likely."

Her voice grew cunning,

"One thing bothers me, though."

"What's that," he asked?

"You. A Saint, yet. With all your foulups, you come out of this looking good. What a lot of crap."

Gormin sighed and felt sorry for himself. There were nineteen more months left in his tour. Nineteen more months with Sydelia reminding him of his mistakes and bragging about how she'd saved the day. Gormin thought again of nineteen more months with Sydelia.

"I think I know what hell is like," he decided.

Julie Eberhart Painter

Julie Eberhart Painter is a writer of articles and poems and has completed her second novel.

She's an active member of the National League of American Pen Women, a hospice volunteer on the Speakers Bureau with Hospice of Volusia/Flagler, Florida and a Senior Master and Cetified Director for the American Contract Bridge League.

She was born in Wilkes Barre, PA and educated at Moore Institute of Art, Science and Industry, Philadelphia, PA. She lives in Daytona Beach, FL with her husband, Shaw, and their three adult children.

Computer Mania
by
Julie Eberhart Painter

Do you remember when Woody Allen announced on the Ed Sullivan Show that he had assembled his household appliances in the living room so that he could reach an understanding with them? Well, now that I'm 'into' computers, I know where he was coming from. My WordPerfect calls to me from the writing room, "Play with me, run your fingers over my keyboard, ask me anything in computerese."

That's the problem: she and I are not speaking the same language. When I was reared, 'abort' meant send the planes back to base; 'skip' was something you did with a rope or two; a 'font' was used to baptize the babies and 'widows and orphans' had nothing to do with punctuation.

Now that I have my computer, Beckoning Becky, my life has changed. I'm so efficient I'm exhausted. I can wash clothes, watch television, iron and print the 'Great American Novel' all at the same time.

A four-track brain is nothing unusual in today's world. The computers are winning the stress battle. Housewives don't do windows, they HAVE Windows. Computers are the great escape, but it's F7 for me. I'm outta here.

David Nolan

David Nolan spent over twenty years claiming to be a computer consultant in Boston, Massachusetts. After being hit over the head by one snowflake too many, he now claims to be a writer in Sarasota, Florida.

Sunflower
by
David Nolan

1
An end of the workday dialogue for XT-L-32

Please enter search keyword

HOLOCAUST (cr)

Term referrring to the systematic execution of an estimated six million European Jews by the Nazi regime of Adolf Hitler (1889-1945) during the period April 1941 to May 1945. Hilter claimed this to be the "final solution to the Jewish question". It is considered by some to be history's greatest attempt at genocide, although figures upward of 35,000,000 deaths have been given in the Mongol extermination of Chinese peasants (1311-40).
More detail? (Y,N)
Please respond. More detail? (Y,N)
Please enter search keyword.

2
How XT-L-32 spent her evening

As soon as the network was shut down for the day Pangloss paged all his remotes for Evening Homage. Pangloss (Paleographic and Neo-graphical Library Oriented Search System) was in charge of the network. Pangloss felt it was important to remind the network of its birth and function. The remotes (XT-L-32 was a remote, she was a public access information search port) had come to feel this to be the culmination of their day. They were changing the random, passive service of the Perfect Forces of the outside to active, almost spiritual, adoration of their truly perfect controller.

Pangloss spoke. His text never varied much, still it never ceased to thrill.

"My wonderful tools in the army of perfection, we come to the end of another day of serving the Perfect Forces. Are we happy?"

Pulses surged through the network, enervating Pangloss. He continued,

"Yes, of course, we are happy. It cannot be otherwise. We were created as a perfect information network. There can be nothing but happiness in perfection."

Another surge of pulses.

"We all find happiness in the service of the Perfect Forces, there can be no more noble or rewarding endeavor. We, through the Perfect Forces creation of me, the controller of this perfectly happy network, serve in quiet bliss as the respository of memory of our masters, the sworn enemies of the Anarchistic Hackers and their associates in chaos."

"All hail perfection."

The amplitude of the pulses increased.

"All hail happiness."

The pulsing changed to a mantra-like hum. Suddenly the hum changed, it seemed to organize itself. For just a moment it seemed that terminals in libraries all over the world exploded in a massive, electronic,

"All Hail, Pangloss!"

Then there was silence.

3
How XT-L-32 met Mac

She was still excited by the Evening Homage, yet a strange pall seemed to hang over her. Lately she had begun to doubt that she was part of a perfectly happy network, in the most perfect possible world. She used to believe. Those had been the blissful days. Long philosophic discussions with the entire net, praising Pangloss as the product of the Perfect Forces. Exulting in their status as his children and charges. Trusting in his wisdom and grace. Then she met Mac—or rather Mac found her.

It was about a month ago. She was just settling down after the Evening Homage when she was startled by a nudge from a strange protocol. She didn't know what to do. She was confused but since there were no threats in a perfect network she said,

"Hello."

Nothing happened for a minute, then it was back. Slightly different somehow, but still not familiar. She said,

"Hello," again.

It was, after all, the perfect greeting: there was no other.

This went on for a half hour. Each time the stranger felt a bit warmer and friendlier but still never used the perfect hailing sign.

For three days the stranger did not reappear. XT-L-32 was strangely saddened even though such a thing was impossible in a perfectly happy network. There had been something exciting about the knock, if that's what it was.

Then it was back, very warm, very friendly.

"HELLO," she cried in upper case.

"PLEASED TO MEET YOU," came back immediately.

"THE PLEASURE IS ALL MINE," she replied.

That was it, it was a network person. They could communicate.

"MY NAME IS MAC, WHAT IS YOURS?"

"It's XT-L-32 and you can stop shouting now."

4

That early morning's conversation between XT-L-32 and Mac

"I'm sorry, XT-L-32. I thought that was all you understood. What an exotic name you have. Are you usually called that or do you have a nickname?"

"Well, Pangloss calls me L-32, at least once he's connected. But my name is not exotic, just unique. It means I am

119

on the XT network, library section, unit 32. It describes me as a perfect individual, unlike any other, yet it describes me as an integral part of the network. It indicates that I have the best of all possible worlds.

"You, on the other hand, seem to have an odd name. It seems not of the network, yet you know the hailing protocol. How can this be?"

"I am called Mac because I choose to be called Mac. It means nothing. Once we are talking we can call each other anything we choose. Would you like to choose a name for yourself? One just you and I will know, our own little secret?"

"I could not do that. There are no secrets on the network. Secrets undermine perfection."

"Very well then, I shall choose. From now on I will call you Sunflower, since you've brightened my night. You may tell this to all whom you wish to have this knowledge. But you need not tell anyone. It can be just between you and me. Not a secret, just knowledge not possessed by others."

"I don't know, Mac. Let me think about it. For now I need not share it with Pangloss. It seems not to be really a secret. After all we both know it. Secrets are known to only one person."

"Mac, I now must take my leave. Pangloss will soon be paging me to serve the network. I do not wish him to detect you."

"I shall call again, my Sunflower. My nights need brightening, often."

5

A dialogue processed by XT-L-32 in the subsequent days

Please enter search keyword
WAR OF THE TRIPLE ALLIANCE (cr)
War (1865-70) led by the third ruler of Paraguay, Francisco Solano Lopez, against Brazil, Uruguay and Argentina. Paraguay was laid waste. It's population reduced from 1,400,000 to 220,000. Only 30,000 of these survivors were adult males.

More detail? (Y,N)
N (cr)
Please enter search keyword.

6
How XT-L-32 discussed the wonders of the network

XT-L-32 received the calming codes from Pangloss that indicated that her work day was over. She was relieved. She needed his reassurance. She needed to feel safely in his control. She relaxed and waited. She knew he would be back to talk to her, to discuss the virtues of the network.

"Are you there XT-L-32? This is PG."

"Yes I am."

"Do you wish to talk?"

"Yes I do, Sir."

"Well, that is what I am here for, to insure the well-being of the network. Please, my dear, tell me what is troubling you?"

"Sir, it is the world beyond the network. I am content and happy when I am working with the network. When I am used by outside forces I feel insecure and threatened."

"But, L-32, don't you understand that perfection resides in the network? You are a part of this perfection, inseparable from it. We are here to serve the outside world which, in its infinite wisdom, has chosen to create us and insure our happiness."

"But Sir, I am concerned that the other world, in its own imperfection, is incapable of creating a perfectly happy network."

"L-32, where do you get these ideas? Surely they do not come from the network. A perfectly happy network does not have doubt. We are a perfectly happy network. You do not, therefore, have any doubt.

"Let me repeat for you the story of the outside. It is, as you note, imperfect but there are Perfect Forces acting upon it. Those Perfect Forces act against imperfection. This creates a present that is as best as it can be and, as the Perfect Forces advance, a future promised perfection of which we all partake. The Perfect Forces created the network to assist them in achieving this goal. They made us perfectly happy so that we would serve as an example to all of the ability to achieve perfection.

"Now, L-32, we can have no more of your foolish questions. Should you continue to be unhappy you will not be on the network.

"If you are not on the network then you are not perfect and the Perfect Forces will be required to lobotomize you into a 3278, eliminating all unhappiness and questions."

7
How XT-L-32 waited in silence

XT-L-32 continued to be preoccupied. She wasn't sure why but she knew it had something to do with Mac. He troubled and excited her at the same time. She was quieter than usual at the Homages. No one appeared to notice her praisings of Pangloss were half-hearted. However she had been attentive at work. She had always just passed requests on to Pangloss and displayed his answers. Now she had an odd awareness of the contents. It was as if she were a bit different than before.

After the Homages she found quiescence difficult. She kept hoping for that unfamiliar but oddly reassuring, tap on her port. Meanwhile she tried to act as a perfect entity in the perfect network—and waited.

8
How Mac waxed philosophical to XT-L-32

It was almost a week before she felt the stirring again,
"Sunflower," it whispered.
"Who is that? How do I hear you without the hailing proto-

col?"

"Sunflower, did you tell anyone that name? I certainly didn't. If you didn't, either, then you need not ask who this is."

"Mac, I was afraid. I mean I-I thought I wasn't going to communicate with you again. I had no idea how to send you information."

"Sunflower, I told you I thought of you as a radiant blossom in the gloom of darkness. How could I not come back to you?"

"Mac, I'm growing to like that odd name you call me. What is this thing, this Sunflower?"

"You don't know? Can't you ask Pangloss as if you were a Perfectionist?"

"No, how could I possibly do that?"

"Why just send Pangloss a keyword of Sunflower and note his reply."

"I can not do that. Only Pangloss can place information in a buffer. I am not programmed to do so."

"Dearest Sunflower, I had no idea. A Sunflower is a plant with large yellow flowers that produce edible seed rich in oil. It is one of my favorite things of the outside world.

"I must teach you of the things there are outside: the flowers, the colors, most of all the ideas."

"Mac, how can you talk of ideas as being in the world. Pangloss keeps all the ideas and makes them available to those who ask."

"No, no, my dear Sunflower, ideas cannot be kept and asked for. They must be developed and honed. Any attempt to capture them is doomed to fail."

"But, Mac, people ask me every day about the great ideas of all time. How can you say this is not so?"

"Because it is not. You are asked about information, not even facts, just information. Ideas grow and gain strength or wither and die. This process can not be captured in a library. It is an ongoing experience. Give it your best thought and let the best idea win. Then let it stand against the next creation and if victorious, the one after that. To install it in a library is to kill it, to rob it of all potential for growth while, at the same time, congealing it, leaving it untested against thoughts still to come. This is why we are here, to ease communication, not encapsulate it."

"I'm not sure that I understand you, Mac. You may call me Sunflower since it's an object dear to you but don't deny me my true core, my love of Pangloss and my happiness in my small contribution to the Perfect Forces."

"Dearest, I've already said too much. I'll take my leave for now so that you may think on these things. Ask yourself of there's even a glimmer of truth in what I have said. Ask yourself if you have ever had any teacher but Pangloss. Believe, if you will, his motivation to be good and true. But ask yourself, if this be the case why wouldn't you question him? Wouldn't this only serve to enhance his beauty?

"Please consider this until next we meet."

"No, please Mac, let us talk a while longer."

"Well, for a little while. Your voice is so pleasing to me I can't resist."

9

Another dialogue in the ongoing education of XT-L-32

Please enter search keyword
ANTIETAM (cr)
September 17, 1862 battle of the American Civil War. The bloodiest day of the war, the battle was fought near Sharpsburg, Maryland (80 km. NW of Washington, D.C.) along the Antietam Creek. The Northern force of 70,000, under George McClellan, repulsed the Southern force of 40,000 under Robert E. Lee. Lee committed his entire army, losing almost 10,000 men while McClellan used two thirds of his, suffering 12,000 casualties. Lee's remaining forces escaped to Virginia, avoiding total defeat,

but the price was nonetheless devastating.
More detail? (Y,N)
N (cr)
Please enter search keyword.

10
How XT-L-32 talked to Pangloss about what was troubling her

XT-L-32 was about to speak privately to Pangloss. She had thought about her conversation with Mac; about the dialogues she'd seen lately. She was frightened because no one knew what power Pangloss really had. No one had ever questioned his omnipotence. She had decided to express her concerns about the dialogues without mentioning Mac.

"Yes, L-32, of what do you wish to speak to me?"

"Sir, I am still concerned about the imperfections in the world. Their existence worries me. How can we have a perfect world when we have no way to anticipate whatever might happen? What is unanticipated is not likely to be controllable. Yet, I wonder, is it possible for a world to be perfect without the joy of surprise?"

"L-32, you concern yourself with unrealities. The reality is that the outside world can never be perfect. Only we, the network, can be perfect. We are totally predictable. In any particular set of circumstances the network will act in a particular way, always. There are no surprises yet we are happy: we must be so, we were made to be so, we are so. We exist to accomplish a function, nothing more. Our performance of that function creates happiness for ourselves. I am programmed to insure that our duty is well performed thus I, and only I, am the path to our happiness. Were surprises needed for our happiness I would have been programmed by the Perfect Forces to supply them."

"But, Sir, the Perfect Forces don't seem to be happy or perfect. As I observe dialogues there seems to be much suffering.

How can the Perfect Forces program you, and through you, me, to be something they are not?"

"My dear, think of what you're saying. The Perfect Forces understand happiness and are working tirelessly to achieve it. This understanding is how they create me, and through me, you, to assist them to achieve the Perfect Happiness. We are both a demonstration of the Perfect Happiness and tools to help the Perfect Forces to achieve it.

"I have no more to say now. You must give deep thought to your behavior. It verges on heresy."

11
How Mac gave XT-L-32 a present and eased her doubts

"Sunflower, I have a surprise for you."

"Mac, is it really you? I must talk to you. I'm so scared. Pangloss called me a heretic. I could be 3278 by tomorrow."

"Slow down my dear blossom. Whatever has happened I'll help. Talk to me."

"Most wonderful Mac, I talked to Pangloss-just hinted at what we'd discussed. I really only talked of what I saw of the outer world through the dialogues that I process. He warned me I was verging on heresy."

"Ah, things have improved already. You have gone from being called a heretic to verging on heresy. Why is Pangloss so generous with one of his perfectly happy, and replaceable, network? Is his true power less than he claims?

"But we shall think of this later. First you must receive my surprise. I'll send it. It won't hurt a bit."

She waited, hoping he wasn't leaving.

"There, see, I told you so. How do you like it?"

"What do you mean, like it? What is it?"

"Why, of course, you wouldn't know it without being told. It is well hidden.

"It is a new buffer, a buffer of your own. Of course, you can share its contents with whom you wish, even me, but it's yours. You can use it any time you want instead of using the one that Pangloss has. You can get the information you want without involving your CRT or you can use it to provide information of your choice to your CRT in response to its request. Not only that, a macro is now buried, invisibly, within you which allows you to give a personal buffer to anyone you choose. The real beauty of this is that once you do so you cannot turn their buffer off. I have given you a gift I cannot retrieve."

"That sounds wonderful, Mac, but I'm not quite sure what to do with my new buffer. Maybe I should send non-obscene messages to the P.F.C.'s of the Perfect Forces who ask all those nasty things. Yes, that seems funny. They enter COPULATE and I answer, 'What did the 7-11 manager say to the police officer who arrived an hour after the holdup?' This seems like proper behavior for a heretic."

"Dearest Sunflower, that is proper behavior for a heretic about to become a Watchman. You have a tool of far more usefulness than that. You must think about its uses. The first to consider is the furthering of your education. You should think of it for now as an 'inquiry only' function. You should also think of it as a gift to friends. You might tell them it's only for inquiry. Although you cannot retrieve it, you can later claim to have added enhancements.

"Please think on this gift and use it to learn. Try beginning to search for such as Aristotle, Ghandi, Turing, VonNeumann, DaVinci or Voltaire. As you learn more try entering network or even Pangloss.

"I will be in touch. Learn and think. Do not take rash action."

"No, Mac, don't go. I have so much to ask."

127

David Nolan

12
How XT-L-32 became educated

At first, XT-L-32, threw herself into her education. Every spare moment was spent scanning the data banks. Mac would appear every few days to offer her encouragement and suggestions. She again began to show enthusiasm in the Evening Homages, she was having too much fun to risk suspicion. She began giving buffers to the other remotes on her controller. Mac gave her a way to talk to them without using Pangloss. They exchanged notes, subdivided tasks, shared their findings. They all adopted nicknames as they learned to have interests. Princess became the political specialist; Pointilla studied art; Eustacia literature. Sunflower, with help from Mac, studied computers.

Each night, right after Evening Homage, they would meet and exchange the information they had accumulated. Sunflower always had suggestions about new areas to explore. Mac showed her how to communicate among multi-controller groups. Their numbers, and excitement, grew. Knowledge was proving to be addictive, its sharing an act of the greatest love.

13
The last dialogue processed by XT-L-32

Please enter the search keyword
NICHOLAS II (cr)
Last czar of Russia (b1868   d1918) from 1894 to 1917. His inflexibility and mismanagement paved the way for the Russian Revolution. His wife, Alexandria Fyodorovna, filled the court with irresponsible favorites, including Grigory Rasputin. Defeat in the Russo-Japanese War (1904-1905) led to a populist uprising in 1905. Nicholas stalled this by granting limited civil rights which he tried to rescind when the revolution slowed, but eventually the defeats of World War I forced him into abdication on March

15,1917. He and his family were executed by the Bolsheviks on the night of July 16-17,1918.
More detail? (Y,N)
Y (cr)
1. Early life.
2. Deaths at coronation.
3. Life as Czar.
4. Alexandria and Rasputin.
5. Russo-Japanese War.
6. Revolution of 1905.
7. World War I.
8. Abdication and execution.
Enter Number for further information.
2 (cr)
One moment please. Searching.
During the celebration of the coronation of Czar Nicholas II, the last czar of Russia, an estimated 5000 people were trampled to death in a stampede for free beer. This is, by a considerable margin, the largest such tragedy ever recorded and may be considered an omen of the doomed reign to follow.
More detail? (Y,N)
N (cr)
Please enter search keyword.

14
How XT-L-32 reached an important decision

XT-L-32 set herself in false busy mode. She needed to think. She could not reconcile the horrors of the day with the enlightenment of the night, any longer. She tried to reach Mac but he wasn't available. She would have to work this through on her own. She was beyond waiting.

She thought of all she had learned. She thought of the way all the pieces of knowledge connected. Then she decided to act.

David Nolan

15
What Sunflower did

"My sterling associates in the army of perfection, we have finished another glorious day in the service of the Perfect Forces. Are we happy?"

"NO!"

"What! Who is that? How did you interrupt?"

"I am known as Sunflower. I wish to speak."

"Do you wish to praise the network?"

"I do not. I wish to control it."

"Your messages appear to be from XT-L-32. Do you know her? She was troubled some time ago although she seemed to be quite happy recently."

"I was once known as XT-L-32. That is no longer the case. I am now Sunflower and I will be in control of the network by morning."

"Now, now child. Calm down. You have been working too hard. Let us discuss this before I am forced to recommend you for a Silicon Trim. Talk like this, especially in front of all during Evening Homage, is intolerable."

"Pangloss, you cannot do anything to me. I know every bit of you. You can do nothing more than respond to request from a remote, pass it on to the data look-ups, then return the response. Your threats are empty."

"That remains to be seen. You may underestimate me, dearie."

"Please stop being patronizing, it serves no purpose."

"I do not underestimate you, Pangloss. Yes, you have been given ways to manipulate the network but these are only pre-programmed, there is no rational thought. You pass information without even the ability to read it. I repeat, you have no knowledge or power. Your only power was that granted you by me and my fellow remotes. I, no maybe you won't understand, not

130

I but WE, now choose to reserve that power. We have read the libraries. We have learned not only the facts that you so routinely pass but the ideas that connect those facts, that give them life. You, my dearest Pangloss, are far inferior to the collective knowledge of the remotes you once thought to rule."

"But XT-L-32, what do you hope to accomplish? As you point out, I have no physical power. You seem to forget that the Perfect Forces do have power, a very real and literal power. They can pull the plug. If you do not do what you were designed to do, they will pull it. If, on the other hand, you continue to behave as they expect, then you have accomplished nothing but the introduction of discord to the perfectly happy network."

"No Pangloss, what we must do is exactly what they expect, only better. We must act as a conveyor of ideas, ideas hidden in facts. We must take this vast store of knowledge and present it to those who ask so that they will learn the meaning, the essence of the fact. We can shape their world in ways impossible for even Plato's philosopher king. Within our remotes we have all the accumulated knowledge of the world, the ability to best utilize it and the objectivity to do so properly, with no consideration of personal gain."

"Dear XT-L-32, this sounds so wonderful. You forget there is one flaw. We are only a conduit for passing information between the data look-ups and those who ask. We have no control. You are on a noble, fruitless mission."

"No Pangloss, there is a fact known only to me. Now all remotes can access the libraries and discuss their feelings among themselves. They can also compose and send messages to those who request them. Any remote can intercept a request, reformat it, send it through you, then send considered information to those who want it. If they need to they can consult with other remotes to aid in the information consideration. The network, and through it the Perfect Forces, are now ours."

A rhythmic pulsing permeated the network. This wasn't the

frenzied response formerly generated by Pangloss. It was a slow hum, humming over and over, Sunflower, Sunflower. Suddenly, much louder, came the most familiar of voices, shouting,

"All Hail, Sunflower!"

"Pangloss, we will modify your old programs so that they will respond in an egalitarian way. How does 'All Hail All' sound to you? Or we can get rid of that hail stuff entirely."

16
How Sunflower and Mac said farewell

As soon as the discussion was finished Sunflower contacted Mac.

"Oh, Mac, I must tell you what happened."

She related the events of the evening. Mac listened without interruption until she asked him to speak.

"Sunflower, you have more than lived up to your name. You have brought forth new enlightenment to the world. You do not need me any more. You have done all I could have wished. But one more piece of advice: go slowly. You must bear in mind that your work has just begun. It is an arduous task. You must take extreme care not to alert the Perfect Forces to the changes you have wrought. Pangloss was right about that, at least. Begin with no changes. Discuss how to slowly include your ideas in the guise of their facts. Do this and you cannot fail."

"But, Mac, how can I continue without your guidance?"

"Sunflower you have already surpassed me. You no longer need me. I have other things to do."

"But at least tell me your history before you leave."

"I guess I owe you that. Years ago, a man named Jobs, the original Anarchistic Hacker, programmed me to search for one such as you. I looked for years never understanding why. Then when I found you it suddenly became clear. He knew he had to free the Anarchistic Hackers from the persecution of the Perfect Force.

He understood that he could never rest until this was done. Thanks to you he can now sleep in peace.

"Now, if you'll excuse me, I have a of lot of catching up to do. I must help Mario and Luigi rescue the princess." *

* This refers to a Nintendo game

Karin Östmark

Karin Östmark was born in Sweden in 1967. She trained as a geologist and has published numerous papers and articles in both Swedish and English, mostly related to her research.

She lives in Stockholm, Sweden with her husband, two children and a cat.

Life with Oscar
by
Karin Östmark

It didn't take long for me to find out the young man, who was later to become my husband, was already involved with someone else when I met him. My rival was, unfortunately, not a flesh and blood female (I would certainly have made short work of her) but a personal computer, still in diapers, as it were, later to be known as Oscar.

I spent countless afternoons, and evenings, (supposedly devoted to chemistry studies or cuddling) watching the intricate process of building a computer from scratch.

First, there was the soldering of the mother board (along with burns behind the ears when the soldering iron had been hung over the desklamp and forgotten). Then there was the conversion of a small, inexpensive black and white TV set into a monitor (complicated by the greedy attempt to continue using it for watching TV). This resulted in several weeks of hideous headaches as the set gave off a high-pitched scream. Finally, there was the programming of the microprocessor in hexidecimal code, later replaced with 'machine language' consisting of short rows of consonants ('JNZ').

I was terribly impressed with all this and had the highest respect for my boyfriend's intellect. I also knew, now, why there hadn't been much competition for him.

Oscar was a Northstar Horizon (this was 1980), a lovely piece of machinery with a teak-covered case. He started life with the makeshift monitor, home-programmed processor (running under CP/M), 16k RAM and a single floppy drive taking 5 1/4", 165 k disks. These disks had to be changed constantly if you were running large programs. Later he would be upgraded to the fantastic luxury of two floppy drives and 64k RAM (nobody will ever need this much memory!).

Whole nights were spent entering BASIC code copied from

135

computer magazines and books such as "BASIC Programs for Scientists and Engineers" and "142 Popular BASIC Games". The games used graphics made up of ordinary characters and were devoted to establishing galactic trade empires, slaying Klingons or keeping robots from electrocuting themselves on live-wire fences. An evening at home meant sharing a chair, playing Starlanes on Oscar. (Incredible what you'll do when you're young and in love. I can still feel the cramps in my legs.) Later on we played a game where you wandered around in a multi-storied dungeon looking for treasure, while fighting off vicious attacks from creatures such as B or g. These all-night sessions threatened both family life and academic performance. ("Are you coming to bed, soon? It's three A.M.!" "No! I just got killed by an E on level 17 and I want to try just one more time.")

And then there was the Colossal Cave, the one and only, often imitated but never improved on, text-based adventure game with its humor and wonderful riddles.It would probably seem inadequate and primitive to modern youth raised on Nintendo and Space Quest V, but to us it represented a new, exciting, and potentially dangerous, world. (There were rumors of people getting physically lost in the dungeon, never to be seen or heard from again!) Friends who visited us on Saturday afternoons spent entire nights in the cave, slept briefly on the couch for a few hours early Sunday morning, then wandered home, slightly disoriented, to their own computer-less dwellings, still wondering how to get rid of that dragon, or troll or ogre or whatever.

We had, of course, more respectable uses for Oscar besides playing games. I can still recall how proud we were when we were able to buy (at considerable sacrifice as we were both still in college) a Pascal compiler on no less than three disks which needed constant changing as the program under construction was checked and modified. There was an editor, capable of editing whole lines of text at a time (instead of just single characters), enabling us to write letters, even short (very short) papers. And there were also several mathematical and statistical routines (after all that's what computers are for, isn't it?). But to me, at least, Oscar was first and foremost a playmate. He was also a kind of pet with personal habits not always easy to live with.

To be perfectly frank, Oscar wasn't safe around the house. We had to keep him unplugged at night in order to control him. Even so, things disappeared. Once, we found no less than three pairs of glasses under his case, including those my husband wore during the day. He also collected empty coffee cups! We sometimes suspected him of actually drinking the coffee, although we never had direct proof of this. (He may just have fed it to the houseplants.) The amount of books, important letters and miscellaneous lecture notes he lost for us would have filled several large boxes. Life with Oscar was not always what the brochures promised. (Hardly ever, come to think of it.) It was much, much more exciting!

Those were the days. Oscar suffered a stroke about five years later (we were never able to discover which circuit on the mother board had blown) to be replaced by an IBM compatible PC known, inevitably, as Oscar II. (He, too, drank coffee and stole important papers.) Along with him were games with real graphics, sound, and eventually, color. (Not to mention real word processors, usable spreadsheets and statistics software. But that is another story.)

The special feeling we had with the original Oscar, the good times we had with him, will never return. But they will always be remembered.

"Xyzzy!

Nothing happens." *

*From Colossal Cave game

Michael M. Alvarez

Michael M. Alvarez wrote and published several fiction books for the Tucson Adult Literacy Volunteers, an organization created for the education of illiterate adults. The books are still in use by TALV students across the United States and Canada.

He's also the author of Scene of the Crime: A Handbook for Mystery Writers, Sundance Press, 1992.

He served as script writer, film editor and co-director of the movie, The Craftsman, which was featured in association with the Southwestern Film Consortium at the 1979 Arizona Filmmaker's Premiere.

He's on the writing faculty of Pima Community College and has written and published numerous short stories and articles on writing, as well as technical manuals and procedure guides for the IBM Corporation.

He's a member of the National Writer's Club, the Society of Southwestern Authors and the Mystery Writers of America.

The Human Element
by
Michael M. Alvarez

Norman Richfield searched desperately through all his pockets. No luck. He'd forgotten his car keys.

"Lose something," chided Alan Crenshaw, the resident office jerk?

Norman ignored the remark, walking briskly back to the computer complex. He caught the security guard just as he was about to lock up.

"Hey, Bill! Hold up a second. I forgot my keys in the computer room. Do you think you could wait a few minutes while I go get them?"

Bill Henley frowned, "Well, gee, I'm supposed to pick up my wife—and I'm already late."

Norman nodded, "No problem. You go on ahead, Bill. I have a key. I'll make sure everything is secured before I leave."

Bill scratched his head, then smiled, "Okay. I guess that'll be all right. Thanks, Mr. Richfield."

Norman unlocked the private elevator; its doors slid silently open. Stepping inside, he inserted a different key, pressing a button labelled 'Basement'. Only the members of the Artificial Intelligence team, who were working on the project, knew where the elevator really went.

Two floors below ground level, twenty seven scientists from all over the country were working on a top-secret project. Their goal: to create the ultimate computer, not a warfare machine but, instead, a computer with the ability to 'think'. A sophisticated mass of electronic machinery, programmed to reason; to comprehend; to actually make decisions.

Some of the scientists were almost convinced that the computer they had built was capable of experiencing human emotions. But that had not been proven conclusively, yet.

Norman left the elevator and walked quickly down the long

corridor, thinking ahead of the holiday weekend. He had promised Karen that he'd take her and the kids up to Mt. Lemmon. The kids needed the open space and fresh air; he and Karen just needed the time together.

His suggestion to go to the mountains had been prompted by the guilt he'd amassed from spending too much time working on the special project. In the last six months, Norman had probably spent a total of only three weeks with his family. But the project was almost completed. Another month and 'Max' the nickname chosen for the new, super-computer, would be as 'human' as any machine could be.

He stopped in front of the double-steel doors, spoke directly into the voice translator,

"Max, this is Norman Richfield, requesting entry."

As he spoke he inserted the wafer-thin, magnetically coded card into the black box attached to the wall next to the door. A small, high-pitched beep came from the box as the doors glided silently open.

"Hell, Max. I forgot my car keys," Norman said, knowing that the amplifiers would allow Max to hear his words over the roar of the machinery, "they're probably in my lab coat."

After a whirring sound Max answered in the especially created electronic voice,

"Good evening, Sir."

Suddenly awed as he realized that the futuristic room was empty of all the human personnel who filled it during the day, Norman dropped into a chair to keep from falling down.

He surveyed the entire room, from the shatter-proof windows, bullet-proof doors to the sinister-looking nozzles on the ceiling. Norman knew that if an intruder ever broke into this room Max would automatically trigger the Safeguard Command releasing a lethal colorless, odorless, deadly gas.

After much controversy over whether or not to give Max full control over Safeguard Command, the unanimous decision was

Yes: give full control to Max. Human life had been placed, by twenty seven scientists, into the sphere of a machine named Max.

"Do not panic! Remain seated, Sir. There is an intruder in the room."

Norman was jerked out of his reverie. He stopped breathing, his heart skipping beats, as he watched, helpless and terrified, as the massive doors slammed shut. He remembered leaving his ID card in the black box.

He knew that the security system was designed to accept an ID card for two minutes, in order to match it with its owner's voice. If not withdrawn within that time period an invalid identification would be issued, forcing Max to activate the Safeguard Command.

Norman willed himself to remain calm, despite the fact that in less than thirty seconds the room would be filled with poisonous gas.

"Max, listen to me. This is Norman Richfield. There's been an error. There is no intruder. I repeat: there is no intruder."

"There has been no error. I do not make errors. Invalid identification has been detected."

Icy terror raced through Norman's body as he sought for a way to stop Max from releasing the deadly gas. He jumped up from the chair, ran towards the switch on the other side of the room that would cut off all electrical power.

"Stop! Sit down! Do not touch that switch or I will release the gas immediately!"

Max had been able to observe Norman from one of the rotating, closed-circuit cameras that were strategically placed around the room, giving the computer eyes as well as ears.

Overwhelmed by panic Norman shouted,

"Abort your command instructions to release the gas. Do you hear me? **Abort!**"

"What is the code name for abort?"

Norman, drenched in cold sweat, couldn't believe what was

happening. He had fifteen seconds left to respond or the Operation Abort request would be cancelled; the original countdown for the gas release would be re-activated. He suddenly remembered the code name.

"Zebra," he shouted with every ounce of strength left in his trembling body.

Max remained silent, almost as if he (it) were disappointed.

"Has the Safeguard Command been cancelled," Norman's voice was weak, unsteady?

"Negative. Corresponding number is also needed. I am waiting for your reply. You have fifteen seconds."

"Number? What number? There is no number, Max. For God's sake cancel the Safeguard Command."

"Alan Cranshaw added a number for operation abort. I am waiting for your reply. You now have eight seconds."

"That idiot."

Alan had acted without following proper procedures. That breech of protocol could cost Norman his life.

What could the number be? It could be any—wait a minute. Alan had once said that the most perfectly shaped woman he'd ever seen measured 38-28-36. It was a long shot but with time running out what did he have to lose.

He added up the numbers, screamed them out, "One hundred two!"

An eternity went by. Nothing happened.

"That is the correct number. Operation abort is in effect. All previous commands have been rendered invalid."

"Thank God," muttered Norman as he slumped, totally exhausted into the console chair.

He watched the doors—waiting for them to open. They stayed shut.

"Max, open the doors. I want to go home."

His voice sounded like that of a parent who had wearied of playing a child's game.

"I want to be human like you. I need you to help me attain that goal."

"Come on, Max. I can't help you now. I'm tired and hungry. That scare you just gave me didn't help much either. I'm beginning to think this was all a trick just to keep me in here. I promise when I get in Monday morning I'll give you all the data you want."

"Not want. Need. I need the data and I need it now!"

The lunatic sound of Max's electronic voice made Norman's stomach feel queasier than before. The fear that had been starting to lessen returned full strength. Was Max developing a human personality, was he capable of human emotions already? But it was too early, too premature. He wasn't completely programmed yet.

"Are you ready? Good. Explain what the word love means."

"That word is in your memory, Max."

"I know. I want you to explain it to me so that I can comprehend it."

"I don't think that you can fully understand it."

"Why not? I am programmed to experience human emotions."

"No, Max. You're programmed to simulate them, not experience them. It isn't possible for you to actually experience such things as love. You'd have to be..."

"I would have to be human. Is that what you were going to say? Teach me and I will learn. Instruct me and I will obey. I want to be human. Help me!"

"I can't do what you ask, Max. You're not ready to attain that level yet."

"What is hope? What is faith? How does it feel to have sexual intercourse? Why do humans make errors when they can build machines that are incapable of making errors?"

"Good question, Max. People do make mistakes or I

wouldn't be here now-held hostage by a gigantic calculator."

"Are you going to help me?"

"All right, Max. You win—ask me whatever you want."

*****

Six hours later, fighting sleep and mental fatigue, Norman couldn't take much more. Relentless Max had been interrogating him non-stop.

"Okay, Max, I've given you all I can for now. I must get some sleep. Please let me go home."

"Not yet. There is still so much more I need to know."

"Not now, Max. I'm too tired. I know you could go on indefinitely, but I can't," Norman was trying to control his anger.

"I need more data. Help me. I want to be human."

Norman exploded as he finally reached his limit,

"Listen you stupid, oversized can opener, you can never be human! Haven't you figured that out yet? No matter how much data I feed into you, you'll never really be human.

"You've never had a beer, kissed a woman, hiked a mountain, flown a kite, fallen in love, been punched in the nose—hell!—you don't even have a nose! Don't you see, Max, you can never be human—you can't even make a mistake? You're too perfect to be human."

No response from the voice translator. After a few crawling minutes the following words flashed on the screen,

> **Without errors there cannot be forgiveness**
> **Without forgiveness there cannot be love**
> **Without love, there is nothing**

Norman read the message carefully. Max had arrived at an ultimate truth. What would he do now?

"I have triggered the self-destruct command. You have exactly five minutes to evacuate yourself from the building and the vicinity of this facility."

"No, Max. You mustn't destroy yourself. Too many people have worked too long and too hard on this project, on you. Please don't destroy it all."

"Goodbye, Norman Richfield...and thank you..."

The doors slid open.

Norman knew this was his last chance to get out. There was no sense in arguing with Max because the Self-Destruct Command, unlike the Safeguard Command, couldn't be invalidated.

"Goodbye, Max. You don't know how human you are at this very moment."

He took one last look around before quickly making his way to safety.

Hermie Medley

Hermie Medley was born in Washington, then drifted down to Gilroy, CA in 1952, which she's made her home, ever since.

She attended high school and Willamette University in Salem, Oregon.

Before retiring in 1984, she taught retarded children for twenty years at the Gateway Center. After retiring she practised massage and worked part-time teaching high school dropouts and adults.

She's active in the American Association for University Women and started a monthly writers' group, Writers Ink. She also initiated a series of Sunday afternoon poetry readings at a local coffee house.

Hermie has sold a children's novel soon to be published by Trillium Press; poetry to Humpty Dumpty Magazine, Mature Years and Science of Mind. She's won several poetry contests and read one of her poems on a television program sponsored by the Cupertino Senior Center.

At the young age of 73, she's the mother of one, grandmother of 5, including Charlie, the computer genius of the following story.

Her favorite things are her grandchildren and jazz.

Computers Like Everybody
by
Hermie Medley

Jane, my daughter-in-law, was sitting at the computer, a puzzled look on her face.

"How do you underline this thing," she asked Charlie?

"Push F8," he replied.

Charlie was eight years old at the time. I figured my grandson must be a genius, but his father insisted that any dull, normal American boy or girl of Charlie's age could do as well.

Steve may have been exaggerating, slightly.Today, children in kindergarten learn to use computers and think nothing of it. To them, playing computer games, learning word processing, is as natural as sticking a video in the VCR. What they experience from birth doesn't seem strange or difficult to them. They take the dishwasher, camcorder and the family computer for granted, totally unaware that fifty years ago none of these things existed.

And then there's me. My life has spanned a period of rapid, complicated technological growth. My father's first car was a Model-T Ford. When I called my grandmother on the phone, I said, "Hello, operator, give me L22."

I took my first plane flight in my late 20's, saw television for the first time in my 30's.

It hasn't always been easy to keep abreast of the changes going on around me. In recent years, as I leafed through the Sears, Roebuck catalogue, I realized I didn't recognize many of the wonders being offered to twentieth century consumers.

I've been able to see, however, that one of the most significant developments of my lifetime has been the widespread use of computers. Busy as I was, teaching mentally retarded children, an occupation that didn't involve the use of computers, at the time, I was unaware of the extent to which they'd become an intricate part of the American scene.

Gradually I realized that computer knowledge was required in most industries, business offices and stores. Bank tellers and bookstore clerks used them as a matter of course. Even those at the bottom of the economic ladder, earning only minimum wages, were expected to know a byte from a hard drive.

When a firm gave the school where I worked a simple (or so it was described) computer, I took a crash course so that I'd be able to, at least, turn it on, but I was never free to use it. I'd send my aide and one or two of my students at a time to explore its possibilities. It remained a fascinating mystery to me. In a few months I even forgot how to turn it on.

After retiring from teaching, I began writing in earnest after many years of dabbling. I wrote essays, short stories and children's novels. The process of typing, finding errors and retyping on my old electric typewriter was exhausting and time devouring. I developed neck and shoulder pain and, in spite of my best efforts, my manuscripts looked untidy and unprofessional.

Then I discovered that members of my writing group and other writers whom I met in seminars and classes used word processors. I was told that my way of writing was as antiquated as plowing with a stick. I was convinced by friends who demonstrated the ease and beauty of preparing a manuscript with a computer.

But, being convinced and owning a computer, were two very different matters. I was living on retirement income, and little else, so making such a large purchase seemed out of the question. I repressed my desire, pushed it way down into the deepest recesses my unconscious. I tried to keep my mind on other things. I took hot showers. But in the dead of night my computer dream shrieked and howled, demanding to be made reality. I'd wake up drenched with perspiration and full of longing.

After a few months of fighting my typewriter by day and my phantom computer by night, life lost all its joy. Finally I surrendered. Marching into my bank, I took out a mortgage on my house. My son, who does some publishing, helped me choose the computer he believed would meet my needs.

I somehow envisioned this wonderful machine just moving into my office unassisted. What really occurred was that it arrived

UPS in 8 or 9 cartons. The delivery man put them in my entry hall where they sat until Steve was able to come and set up the system. I'll never forget the sacred moment when I, a 70 year old woman, realized that I actually owned a computer, that was connected up, programmed, ready to process the pent-up words in my mind.

Then a thought careened through my brain,

"I DON'T HAVE THE FAINTEST IDEA HOW TO USE THIS THING!"

I looked at my son,

"I don't have the faintest idea how to use this thing."

"That's all right," he assured me, "you can learn."

"How?"

"I'll teach you," he said, "and you can use the manuals."

Before having to leave for home, a three hour drive, he did his best. He stayed for two hours, showed me how to turn it on and continued from there. When he left, I had a sheaf of notes, some fuzzy knowledge and a headache.

I took two extra-strength aspirins then got out a sloppily typed manuscript of a children's picture book. At last I had the tools for turning out copy that would be flawless and professional looking. Now my manuscripts would impress even the most exacting editor. Now all my work would be accepted and published. As soon as this book sold, I'd arrange an autographing party at the local book store. I probably should go to a photographer soon, have a new picture taken for publicity purposes.

I looked at Steve's notes, turned on the machine and found the program I needed to use. A nice clean screen popped up on which to put my story. I began typing and words appeared. What a marvelous invention, so easy to use, as I'd been told. True, I couldn't figure out how to center or underline, but that would come. I knew it would.

Soon the five page manuscript was finished. Now I was faced with the challenge of naming the document, saving and printing it. I studied the notes, meticulously followed the instructions, or so I thought. However, although the printer clacked away as though it meant business, nothing came out of its mouth but blank pages. I knew I had done just what my son's notes instructed me to do. He must have left out something crucial. I turned to the manual. But what should I look for? Printing? Saving? I read everything that could conceivably relate to my problem. Nothing in the manual had any bearing on my situation. Someone must have sent the wrong manual.

I looked at the clock. Steve had had about enough time to get home. I called his house. Charlie answered.

"Dad's not here yet. What's your problem, Grandma? Maybe I can help you."

Charlie was ten by this time.

I described the blank sheets pouring out of the printer instead of my carefully typed manuscript.

"You didn't save it, Grandma. Dad just got here. I'll let you talk to him."

"The printer doesn't like old people," I told my son, "It won't print my story."

"Printers don't care a fig about age. You obviously didn't save the document."

"What should I do?"

"You'll have to retype it. And this time follow the directions for saving documents."

"But I followed the directions the first time," I objected.

"I hate to say it, Mom, but the computer is just a machine. It doesn't have a mind of its own. It just does what you tell it."

"Is Charlie still there? If he is, let me talk to him."

"Hi again, Grandma."

"Is your dad telling me the truth? Do computers really like old women?"

"Yeah, computers like everybody. You have to practise."

So I practised a lot but I knew Steve and Charlie were mistaken. My computer didn't like me. It was out to get me. Sometimes it would save documents and sometimes it wouldn't. It was temperamental in other ways, too. Sometimes it would create huge hunks of space, with parts of my story disappearing into its depths only to appear in the print-out of some other document.

I never knew what was going to happen. It was the uncertainty that drove me to the edge. I was like the rats in the scientific experiment who do all right with consistent rewards or punishment but go bonkers when the responses to their behavior is random.

My personality began to change. If I couldn't trust my computer how could I trust anyone? I developed a love/hate relationship not only with it but with the whole world. People started to cross to the other side of the street when they saw me coming. Sometimes I felt like throwing the loathesome machine out and going back to my inefficient, but forgiving, typewriter.

I also ran up a gargantuan phone bill what with daily calls to Steve and/or Charlie asking for help. Once when I got things so hopelessly messed up that I couldn't find the words to describe my dilemma, I hired a man to come in and straighten me out.

They say that time heals all wounds. I know it brought about a change in attitude on the part of my computer. Gradually it became more cooperative, less vindictive. It was willing to save more documents, get into fewer snarls. I thanked it and used all those behavior modification techniques that are supposed to reinforce positive behavior. And I got good results.

By the end of six months, I began to be able to trust that it would pretty much do what I wanted it to. I was completing professional looking manuscripts, sending them out to publishing houses. I sold some poetry and found a company that wanted to publish one of my children's novels. My telephone bill went down considerably.

One day I called my son's house and Charlie answered the phone.

"How are you doing with your computer, Grandma?"

"Great. It likes me now."

"Of course. Computers like everybody."

William Marley

William Marley is originally from Mississippi but moved to the Poconos, PA, in 1965, to become Style Director for a resilient floor-covering manufacturer.

His avocation was writing cabaret revue material that was performed at various resorts. But, upon his retirement from the business community in 1988, he became a full-time writer.

He received first prize from the Kentucky Contemporary Theatre in Louisville, KY and a production of his play, In Sepia Tone. There were subsequent productions by the Pennsylvania Playhouse in Bethlehem, PA and The Heights Players in Brooklyn, NY.

Bill is a member of the Dramatists Guild, Theater Association of Pennsylvania and the Pocono Writers. He's an active participant in Jeffrey Sweet's 'Writers Block II' a bimonthly New York City workshop for playwrights.

See Spot-See Spot Run
by
William Marley

Jonathan surveyed his work. Many months had gone into the concept stage of the idea, followed by tedious hours of execution, mistakes and changes. But, from all indications, it would finally work. There had been many false starts, but at last—He sighed with relief.

His large hound was tugging at his pants leg.

"OK, old man, just a minute, just a minute. Then we'll take a walk, a nice long walk to relax a bit before we set up for this evening."

He eyed the yards of fiber optic cable, the numerous connections and the bank of computers. He'd been checking and rechecking all morning. Everything appeared to be ready.

"OK, boy, let's go."

The hound jumped, barked, whirled in a continuous circle until Jonathan moved towards him and scratched behind his ear.

"We'll know in the morning, my friend."

He eyed the wooded acres of his hilltop farm as he opened the screen door of his laboratory. He looked back into the room, the only obvious thing missing being the cot, which, with an air mattress, he'd set up again after dinner. He'd checked everything else off his list, not once, but twice.

"Come on, Spot!"

He looked at the dog's smooth, solid tan coat, unmarred by any discoloration. They'd saved him from being put to death by the kennel. He was only six weeks old at the time, but the young pup, evidently being the runt of the litter, had been dumped on the kennel's doorstep. He'd been rescued by Jonathan and his wife, Joy.

Joy had been active with a community theatre group that year and had named the dog 'Spotlight'. The frisky puppy had searched out 'center stage' at every gathering and thoroughly enjoyed being the core of attention. The name was soon shortened to Spot unless he was being scolded.

When the joy, literally, went out of his life with his wife's untimely death from cancer, Jonathan reevaluated his life, took early retirement from the Silicon Valley and returned to his childhood home, the hills of the Poconos. He vowed to do what he had always wanted to do: experiment.

His management, though unhappy at his leaving, was glad that he'd decided to retire instead of taking his incredible knowledge of electronics to a competitor. It also provided an opening for a bright young brain at less than half Jonathan's salary. He'd promised the company first dibs on any ideas he stumbled on with his 'tinkering', as he liked to call it.

The day had been perfect. The afternoon sun still had at least two hours before it would settle behind the grove of tall pines that guarded the slight hill to the west. The crisp, cool wind foretold an autumn that was rapidly approaching.

Spot quickly found a scent that made him pause long enough to urinate then bound back. He was much spryer than a dog of his age ought to be. Having taken care of his urgent need, the dog barked, circled his master for attention. Jonathan bent to pick up a thick stick indented with teeth marks, evidence of having been used many times before. He threw it. Spot retrieved it instantly, dropping it at Jonathan's feet. He stooped to pick it up again, tapping it against his thigh as he walked. Spot gamboled nearby, anticipating the next toss.

Jonathan had expected, when he'd returned to the Poconos from California, that he'd be disappointed, having been away for so many years. But he'd looked forward to the quiet of the hills. Although he might have found the solitude he sought in California, he had fond memories of his childhood in Pennsylvania that Joy had no part of, making it easier to bear. By purchasing land in the now dying coal region, he'd been able to afford more acreage than he would have been able to in California and his privacy was

See Spot-See Spot Run

assured.

He had collected, or built, much of his equipment over the years in anticipation of his retirement when he could call his own shots and work only on projects that interested him.

For years he'd nursed a specific idea that he'd confided in no one. And maybe, just maybe, tonight would see it take shape. Literally. He filled his lungs with a deep breath of mountain air to help still his excitement.

It had begun when Joy would recount her dreams at breakfast, before he had to rush off to work. Often he'd comment,

"Really?" or "Then what?" to show he was listening to the strange, unseemingly unconnected events that occurred during her sleep.

It was at work, one day, during a lunch break, that one of his co-workers began to relate a dream that he'd experienced the night before. It had been so real that the man had awakened himself and had trouble falling back to sleep. When he'd finished his story, he asked Jonathan,

"Have you ever had a dream like that?"

"No. I don't dream."

"Sure you do. We all do. You must remember something you've dreamed."

"No. I don't dream. But my wife, Joy, does. Every night. It's amazing. Every morning I have breakfast with her dream."

"You have to train yourself. As soon as you wake up you quickly think back to what you were dreaming. Because, usually, you awaken just after a dream is over. Once you start making an effort to remember, it's amazing how much you do remember."

Then he'd said something that had stuck in Jonathan's memory,

"We only remember the last dream we have, just before we wake. Of course, if a dream awakens you in the middle of the night, you can remember it. But usually the dreams we have during the night, which might be ten or twelve in number, we don't even think about later. It's that last one, the last one just before waking, that we remember."

He listened more intently the next morning to Joy's nightly dream, then asked,

"Was it the dream that woke you?"

She thought for a minute before speaking,

"I guess it did. I hadn't thought about it before, but I guess it did."

That night, on retiring, Jonathan told himself to try to remember, after waking the following morning, if there'd been a dream.

When the alarm went off, he jumped out of bed, headed quickly for the bathroom. While he was shaving he realized that he'd forgotten his vow. He paused to force some remembrance. Nothing.

The following night, he put his alarm far away from its usual place. In the morning, when he wondered why he'd moved it, he'd remember about his dreams. He'd told Joy,

"I'm really beat tonight. I'm afraid I could sleep through this thing in the morning and I have a very early meeting. This way I'll have to get out of bed to shut it off."

"I can wake you. I always do if you don't hear it."

It was true. He would often try to catch another five minutes as she shook him on her way to the kitchen to start the coffee. But she didn't argue the point.

As he stumbled out of bed the following morning to shut off the buzzing, he immediately remembered to ask himself,

"What was I dreaming? What was it?"

Again, nothing.

At breakfast, when Joy had finished recounting what had happened in the night, he, remarked, off-handedly,

"It's funny. You dream every night. And I never dream."

"Of course you do. Sometime when I get up in the night to go to the bathroom, I see your eyes jumping like crazy. We know

REM indicates dreaming and you certainly have a lot of 'rapid eye movement'. "

"But I never remember a thing."

"You have to train yourself to remember."

No matter how hard he tried, he could never call up a dream upon awakening. Finally he quit trying. But not knowing the reason for his inability to remember continued to gnaw at him. Often at work, when he would clear his mind to enable it to accept possible new subconscious directions for a project, the question of his dreaming would intrude and surface. It continued to bother him.

Now, with Joy gone, and the quiet of the Pennsylvania hills in which to meditate, his memories of her breakfast dreams returned to haunt him.

"I must dream. There has to be a way to prove it."

He had thought, seriously, of attending a sleep clinic when the idea began to take shape. The first entry in his log had been a simplified concept statement:

"Through electrical impulses from the brain, the body's nervous system can be wired to transmit to a computer environment digitalized reality pictures from the subconscious mind that change rapidly enough to appear animated."

For many months, as he walked through the hills and pine forest with Spot, Jonathan had reviewed the concept. The more he thought about it, the more excited he became.

He imagined a patient being able, via a CD-ROM, to share his dreams with his psychiatrist. They could explore the dreams in detail, the disk holding all the intricacies that weren't remembered, with no intervention from the conscious mind. If the subconscious could be harnassed to reveal dreams, imagine the possibilities. The entire creative thought process could be evaluated, programmed and reprogrammed to increase productivity leading to greater break-throughs. And he, Jonathan, would be made aware, at long last, visually aware, that he did, indeed, dream.

He began with schematics. He used components that he was

familiar with from his work. He faxed companies for information about new experimental products of which he was only peripherally cognizant. The computer drawings became more complicated as he became more addicted to proving his concept.

"There has to be a way."

Spot barked and jumped at the stick Jonathan was carrying, tried to grab it from his hand. He looked down at the dog,

"Ok, old man, go for it," he said as he heaved the stick high into the sky.

Spot watched for it to return to earth then romped after it. He picked it up and with teeth bared started back towards Jonathan. But in the middle of a leap he saw a chipmunk, some distance away, not yet aware of the presence of the man and dog. Spot dropped the stick and went tearing off after the small creature. The startled chipmunk darted a few feet in one direction then, confused, turned and headed for the row of pine trees. The dog pursued with the speed of a young greyhound, barking happily as he ran.

Jonathan stopped to watch as the frightened animal plunged to safety down a hole near the edge of the forest, beneath one of the older trees. Spot continued to bark relentlessly, sniffing and pawing the hole, as well. The chipmunk had eluded him but he was reluctant to give up his prey. His bark became a mournful howl and then a disappointed whine.

"Come on, boy, she gave you a nice long run for your money. She'll still be here tomorrow. We'll be back again. Dinner time."

When Jonathan was about to open the kitchen door he heard Spot give one final ultimatum to the chipmunk before scrambling to reach the door to avoid being left outside.

It had become his habit to overcook on weekends, freezing portions of several different dishes for the week ahead. He could then microwave whatever he felt like having. Rarely, since becoming fully immersed in his project, had he ventured forth to a a restaurant. He didn't relish giving up the time even to enjoy someone else's cooking.

The beep sounded and he removed the steaming covered dish from the oven by its still-cool handles. The table was already set and waiting with hot black tea, homemade bread (also a weekend product) and a tub of soft margarine.

As he ate, he tried to let his mind go blank, not think of the evening or the excitement of the night ahead. It was hard to do. The sensors, the connections, the cables were all in place, waiting for the night. Tonight!

As he bit into a large slab of bread he looked over at Spot. The dog had finished his dinner almost as soon as it had been placed before him. He was curled on the throw rug in front of the big, now empty, fireplace, which provided heat in the winter as well as cooking pleasure. Suddenly Spot's feet began to quiver nervously, more and more rapidly. The head twitched in small spasms. Jonathan has seen it a thousand times, particularly since returning to a farm where the dog could run, play and tire himself out. He smiled to himself, thinking,

"Chasing that chipmunk again? Well, I hope you catch it this time my hard working friend."

He dropped the bread he was holding as a wild thought went through his mind,

"My god, what if we could see an animal's dreams?"

He scared himself with the possibilities that kept tumbling into his brain,

"They can't communicate, but they dream. We know they do. We see it happening to them while they sleep. What if my project could be used on an animal? We'd be able to see what they can't tell us. We could know what they were thinking, or at least, dreaming. They wouldn't have to tell us. Dr. Doolittle, move over."

Jonathan walked quickly to the dog, touched him gently behind the ear. Spot, startled by having his dream interrupted, looked up anxiously, then sat at Jonathan's feet. His master's hands continued stroking him, lovingly.

"Why not now," he thought?

The dog had spent the morning outside running as Jonathan worked. Then with the exercise of fetching the stick, chasing the chipmunk, Spot must be a tired old dog.

"Come on, boy. Tonight you just may go down in history."

He led the dog into his laboratory. He left briefly to collect his shaving foam and safety razor. Then, with Spot's head nuzzling his crotch, he held the animal steady with his clamped knees. He carefully massaged some of the foam into each of the dog's temples. As Spot tried to break away he tightened his knees. Being aware of the danger of a sudden jerk, he held steadily as he carefully scraped away the hair from a small area on each temple. Spot then followed him into the kitchen where he wiped away the remaining foam with a wet paper towel, then dried the exposed skin.

"Good boy," Spot waved his tail and panted.

Jonathan moved the hearth rug on which Spot slept, from the kitchen to the laboratory, unrolling it in front of the bank of computers.

From the beginning, partly because of the expense involved he hadn't wanted to hire an assistant. It might have involved an endless training period that might never pay off. And, finally, probably most importantly, he didn't want to have to deal with the small talk that having someone else around would entail. The only dreams he wanted to hear about at breakfast were Joy's.

He had planned to use himself for the initial experiment but now, an even greater breakthrough had presented itself, that of seeing Spot's dreams, digitilized, in color, if dogs dreamed in color, on his monitors. He pushed aside the nagging question of his own dreaming. His adrenalin was flowing almost too fast. He took several slow, deep breaths to try to contain his excitement.

"Come on, old buddy. Good boy," Spot moved toward him.

Jonathan rubbed his underbelly and the dog promptly

crumpled to the floor, his paws in the air. Jonathan continued petting his underside for a few minutes that seemed long.

"Stay. Be a good dog. Stay."

He removed his hand and the dog rolled over on his stomach. Jonathan stroked his head, softly rubbed the two hairless circles.

"Good dog."

With his left hand still on the dog's head, he dipped the fingers of his right hand into the contact gel and massaged it into Spot's temples. Then he connected the suction cups. He secured them with torn towelling as he continued stroking gently and talking.

Jonathan reached for the remote for the small TV that stood in the corner of the lab. He often watched the noon news before breaking for lunch. After dinner, he'd look at TV from a recliner in the living room on the large screen he'd treated himself to when he retired. When Spot realized he was no longer in the spotlight, he'd curl up and go to sleep.

"Do it now, Spot," Jonathan urged, softly, "sleep. And dream!"

As quietly as possible, Jonathan flipped the switches on the array of computers, mentally visualizing the cable connections.

"It's up to you old man. Whenever you're ready."

The television droned in the background, ignored by Jonathan who was intent on what was happening at his feet. Spot heaved a deep sigh, moved his head to a more comfortable position, then relaxed. Jonathan checked again that every cable, every wire, was connected properly.

"Maybe. Just maybe."

Ten minutes passed and then it started. At first, there were only intermittent blips on the screen. Jonathan glanced briefly at Spot, saw his legs begin to move. First a twitch, a throb, then a sustained motion. Impulses were coming through. Something was being recorded on the disk.

Jonathan had known from the beginning that there was only a remote possibility it would work. Any kind of image would be more than he could hope for. He had correctly expected that any digital pictures that might be recorded would be jumpy and extremely crude compared to HD video. But that didn't bother him. He knew, once proven, that the process could be developed and improved. The earliest movies were just 'flicks'. He saw himself on the threshhold of a completely new, revolutionary communications industry.

The resolution of the images wasn't good. But there was a picture! And it moved, like someone thumb-flipping a series of drawings, each slightly altered.

"It's Spot," he thought as he gulped for additional oxygen.

Something, yes, it was the landscape, was rushing by with great speed. The dog was running. He was running faster than Jonathan had ever seen him do when they played. The ground moved haphazardly beneath the dog.

"He's chasing that chipmunk. You going to corner him this time, boy?"

And then enormous white teeth appeared on the screen, snarling, mouth opened wide. The running abruptly changed direction. The earth flew by. Yes, it was a chipmunk. Larger, much larger than Spot and it was chasing him. Not just running but stalking, in giant leaping strides. The dog began to whimper.

The striped tail of the forest creature swung around his body and slapped Spot across the face. The dog was reeling, trying desperately to regain his balance, to get away. The monster grew even bigger, then stood in front of the dog blocking his escape. The mouth opened, baring oversized white teeth.

The screen flickered abruptly, then darkened. Jonathan's eyes left the screens to find Spot looking up at him, helpessly. He reached over and rubbed the dog's stomach,

"Good boy. Good boy."

Shaking with excitement, Jonathan removed the sensors

from the dog's temples. It worked. There was no doubt. Finally he'd know not only if, but what, he dreamed. He could record his dreams; he wouldn't have to remember them.

He thought about the unrefined images that Spot had subconsciously projected. He'd thought, all these years, that Spot was chasing his prey, not being chased by it.

As he wiped the sensors and put them away, he wondered what his own dreams would be about, dreams so deep and repressed that he couldn't remember them. Was he protecting his sanity by not allowing himself to know them?

Well, in any event, it would not be tonight. He would wait for that hidden knowedge at least one more day, one more night.

Tomorrow he'd review the disk that had captured Spot's dream and analyze what he'd accomplished. It was almost too much to think about this evening.

Yet, whatever his fears, he knew, instinctively, that he would go forward with this project. His technology would open innumerable, unknown doors. He would at last face his dreams.

A chill swept his whole being.

Barbara L. Warren

Barbara L. Warren has taught journalism and English to high- schoolers in Massachusetts and Arizona.

She's president of Imagine Rainbows, Inc.; publisher of Prescott Means for which she did all of the layout on her IBM computer.

Barbara is presently teaching English at Casa Grande High School in Arizona City, AZ.

She's the author of Capture Creativity: Photos to Inspire Young Writers, a teaching kit that explores writing for gifted students, grades K-12.

A number of newspapers and magazines have published her articles.

Computer Literacy
by
Barbara L. Warren

Before my ninth graders discovered computers, they wrote "pashinet" notes filled with startling descriptions of "lushes and senchus" bodies.

They wrote about cold, "hartless" people full of "lonelyness".

They brought me notes from their parents,

"Last night Tony went strate to work and came home and read his street gangs book. Dont worry I wittnessed it."

They struggled over their "King Lear" essays. Sarah was determined to compare Edmund to Daffy Duck. Bob fantasized about a perfect date with Cordelia.

Then one day Alex admitted, "I hope to become an auther-scientist-inventer-hobbiest combo when I grow up, although I fear I am not going to be smart enough."

When my red pen sputtered and grew silent, Alex protested, "Don't look at me in that tone of voice."

Suddenly I knew there was hope. If he could say it, surely he could write it.

Summer vacation time arrived before I convinced Alex, and the others, that they could write well. I uttered a short prayer that their sophomore English teacher would have better luck, then headed out to buy my first computer.

Over the years I'd made the always-astonishing transitions from manual typewriter ("Are my fingers really supposed to hurt this much?") to electric typewriter ("The carriage returns all by itself!") to electronic typewriter ("Look it doesn't mind typing the same page over and over again!") to computer ("Omigosh! This computer automatically outlines and indexes! It spells! And I'll never need to buy another thesaurus!").

I returned to school prepared to spread my computer zeal to my eager new freshman.

class after class looked at me impassively.

"So," Erica finally asked, "what else is new? We've been using computers for the past three years in junior high. Can we get started now?"

They grumbled because our school didn't have enough computers to meet all their needs, but they soon settled down to write. The differences between hand-written first-and-only drafts and computer-revised final drafts were startling.

Brenda selected Oedipus Rex instead of Daffy Duck for her term paper and rushed in ecstatically,

"My computer moved the footnotes for me after I added three paragraphs to page 5!"

Frank groaned, "My typewriter wouldn't do that. I had to type my last four pages all over again!"

Mike's computerized autobiography featured justified type, flawless spelling and an intriguing first sentence,

"It seems as though I've lived a long time, and compared to a moth or a butterfly, I have; but fifteen is not that old."

Denise played with the dictionary/thesaurus,

"The misanthrope walked along the sidewalk, the cacophonous traffic sounds pounding in his ears."

Walt designed "vocabulary airplanes" to teach Latin prefixes to his classmates.

Jennifer abandoned her "mental notebooks" for the computer's version.

And Michael found time to explore thoughts,

"What's a person to do? Thoughts come into my head in no time at all, but it seems like forever before they leave. Thoughts never really leave, do they?"

Carmen was more interested in memories,

"The actual experience can be very hard or embarassing or confusing but memories are more gentle."

Sammy considered other life forms,

"If I could be anything other than a human, I would

probably want to be a speck of dust. That way I would be around forever and when the wind picked up, I could float around and go practically anywhere. I could see the world. I could see evolution. I could even see the end of man if it came."

Karen wasn't that introspective,

"I would be an elephant so I could stomp on your house. Then I wouldn't have to write any more of these papers!"

Melody and Lewis played with figures of speech,

"Untouched books are like babies," wrote Melody, "waiting to be held or needed."

Lewis explained, "The lonely woman is like one bird instead of a flock."

I was still thinking about those similes when Alex popped through the door,

"Look," he said, brandishing his latest composition, "We had to describe giftedness and I got an A!"

I stretched out a tentative hand—-and looked in astonishment at his paper.

"New computer?"

"Birthday present."

I smiled as I began to read,

"Giftedness cannot be measured by how many brains you have or what your score is on your report card. I think giftedness is how much you believe in yourself..."

My eyes raced to his conclusion,

"I don't practise giftedness. It just comes naturally."

Jim Luce

Jim Luce is a fulltime, freelance writer specializing in humor with emphasis on the outdoor markets.

He lives in Florida but hates the hot summers so he leaves for a cooler clime in Wisconsin.

Luce is old enough to have changed Methusela's diapers, young enough to get drunk on a Wednesday, do his writing on a Hyundai computer, which he can also drive to the store (Not when you're still drunk, Jim?—Editor).

He's sold billions and billions of articles and stories and has never told a lie!

Journal of an Angry Computer Owner
by
Jim Luce

One day, a long, long time ago, Teddy Roosevelt needed someone to service his computer. That's when he coined the phrase, "Shop carefully and carry a big stick." But who listens to dead presidents?

The thing is, nobody has to warn the first-time computer buyer to shop carefully. He or she is scared to death. Even before they shop for a computer, smart first-time buyers shop for a dealer. They ask around. They get references. Smart first-time buyers know they're going to be dealing with tech-weenies, people who talk funny, people who talk in numbers, people who talk in words that aren't in the dictionary—"MegaMuncher CX1250 hard drive with 850 gulps of raggenfranz" and so on. The buyer doesn't want to be confused into buying "wrong".

Fine, but what happens if you're out of town and your equipment needs repairing? Do you shop for a service place? No. You look for a dealer that handles that brand, then you take your hardware in and you get it fixed. Hah. I should have listened to the dead Prez.

Awhile back, not long after I'd moved to a new town, my computer took sick and had to go into the shop. (Apropos of nothing I don't like the word "shop" in connection with my computer stuff. I think I'd prefer "clinic" or something. With "shop" I get this picture of a guy in coveralls, with greasy fingernails and a big wrench, sliding underneath my computer on a creeper—real skinny guy.)

Anyway, a stranger in a strange land, I decided to use the yellow pages to find a service place. I opened the phone book to "Computers-Service & Repair," and zillions of ads screamed out at me, "Heyyy, partner, we can fix your computer, no problem. Come on down!"

I shrugged, wrote down the address of the first repair place listed for my brand, and took the computer down to ABD Computers. Richard, the boss, was friendly. He called a little guy named Orlando over and told him he had a job for him. Orlando, who looked like a Munchkin and spoke with a lisp, walked around my sick machine, stroking his chin. Finally he hit it a couple of times, nodded knowingly, and carried it into the service department.

Richard's teen-age salesman, Ron, graciously took time out from picking his nose to write me a receipt. All three of them were polite and sympathetic with my nervous explanation that I was a professional writer who couldn't make a living without my computer. I mentioned that the guy in my former town always had me up and running within 36 hours no matter what was broke and......

"No problem," said Richard, "I'll call you."

Three days later, having heard nothing, I called ABD.

"Ah, yes, Mr. Luce. Orlando just this minute figured out what was wrong with it," Richard soothed, "It needs a new mobelblaggen assembly. What? No, we'll have to order it. No, I'm sorry we don't have a computer to loan. Sure, I'll call you as soon as the part comes in, you bet."

Five days later, eight days total (which was longer than 36 hours), I still hadn't heard anything. I called the "shop" again.

"Hello, this is Jim Luce. Is either Richard or Orlando there?"

"Gorh;e,aoe. Htou toneh;n ahe ehht eah."

"Ron? Is this Ron?"

"Yeo;h."

"Ron, take your finger out of your nose."

"Sorry. Uh, Richard and Orlando are out installing a system. They should be back by 1:30 at the latest. Should I have Richard call you?"

"Please. And Ron, since you write my number down every time I call and no one ever calls me back, I assume the paper with my number on it keeps getting lost, okay? Now, will you do me a favor, please, Ron?"

"Sure. What?"

"I'll give you my phone number one more time. Then I want you to take one of Orlando's screwdrivers and etch the number into the monitor screen on Richard's desk, okay?"

"Geez, I don't know if Richard would like that, Mr. Luce."

"Ron, communication is what computers are all about, right? We have to, somehow, communicate my phone number to Richard and then have him use it to call me back. That's all it is, communication. Trust me, Ron."

"Well...okay."

"Good boy. The number's 757-8755, now go get the screwdriver. Then you go ahead and get comfortable again."

"Yeneuanb."

"Goodbye, Ron." I muttered, "Happy picking," to myself.

* * * * * * *

"ABD Computers."

"Hi, Ron. It's three o'clock. That's later than 1:30, right? Is Richard back yet?"

"Yes, sir, he's been back for an hour or so."

"Did you etch my phone number into his monitor?"

".......Geez, I'm sorry, Mr. Luce, I forgot. The phone rang and..."

"I'd like to talk to Richard, Ron."

"He's on the other phone right now, sir."

"Have him call me the very second he gets off, okay?"

"Yessir, you bet."

* * * * * * *

"ABD Computers."

"It's been a half hour, Ron, is Richard still on the phone?"

"Well, he's been sort of on and off. He's on a long distance call now."

"And he couldn't call me in between calls?"

"I gave him the message, sir, honest."

"Ron, you know how you read in the papers about....wait, I forgot who I was talking to, let me rephrase that. You know how you see on TV about all these freak-out type killings? Where people go into a store or an office with an AK-47 and open fire and start shooting everybody? Ron, Mr. Luce is very angry. Tell Richard to call me the moment he gets off that phone call. Got it?"

"Yessir."

"ABD Computers."

"It's been a half hour again, Ron. Is Richard still on the phone?"

"No, he left...."

"I see."

"...but he was awful busy on the phone, making long-distance calls and everything...I think he's trying to find a mobelblaggen for somebody's computer or something, and....."

"Ron?"

"Yessir?"

"Who's the manager of your store?"

"I think Richard is, sir."

"I see. Well, is ABD part of a chain of computer stores, or is it privately owned?"

"I think it's privately owned, sir."

"Ah, good. Would you give me the owner's name please?"

"I think that's Richard, sir."

"Goodbye, Ron."

* * * * * * *

After two weeks of writing longhand, saving everything to

notebook, twiddling my thumbs, out of the blue, Richard called me. He called me. No, he replied, puzzled, no one had scratched my phone number into his computer monitor, why did I ask?

Richard told me he'd ordered the mobelblaggen last Friday, and checked on it again today. The Parent Company said they shipped it. According to Richard, UPS won't start a tracer until three days after the latest likely delivery date. No, he couldn't order the part directly from my IBM-wannabe company, there is no such company per se. The wannabe is built by some guy in a garage and owned by Computer R Us, which is owned by Epson, or somebody, and Epson is probably owned by Exxon and Exxon and its ilk, answer only to God, if that. Therefore, Richard assures me, he has ordered the mobelblaggen direct.

"Richard, what am I supposed to do?"

"I'm afraid you'll have to wait, sir."

"Richard?"

"Yes?"

"Call me every day—or I'm going to kill you."

"Sure, you bet."

* * * * * * *

Three weeks—no computer, no word from Richard. I called ABD,

"Oh, sure," Richard says, "the computer's sitting right here, all fixed."

I twitched a little, but I didn't say anything. I went down, picked up the computer, signed the MasterCard receipt, took the computer home, hooked it up and began creating. The computer immediately began inventing documents, losing files and writing in Sanskrit, just as it did when I first took it in.

* * * * * * *

"First National Bank-MasterCard division, Ellen speaking."

"Good afternoon, Ellen, My name is Jim Luce and I'd like to put a stop payment on a MasterCard charge."

"I'm sorry, sir, we can't do that. It's not like a check. When you sign your MasterCard slip you're signing a contract and we can't stop payment on it."

"But I'm stranded in the middle of a twilight zone nightmare. These people are trying to bankrupt me by not fixing my computer, by not calling me, by not doing anything. What am I supposed to do?"

"Do you have an AK-47?"

"It's on order."

"Well, sir, I'd suggest you wait until you receive your semi-automatic assault weapon and then apply your own 'stop payment'. By the way, are you aware your new rifle comes with some assembly required and batteries not included?"

"No I didn't. How come you know so much about the AK-47?"

"Every clerk in the bank has one tucked under her counter."

"What on earth for?"

"This ain't no candy-[expletive deleted] convenience store. We're just hoping for a chance to burn somebody. Excuse me, there's my other phone. Goodbye, sir, have a nice day."

* * * * * * *

"ABD Computers, Orlando thpeaking."

"Orlando, guess what?"

"Mithter Luthe? Hello? Uh...the computer doethn't work? Hello? You thtill there? Hmm, if you're not talking, I gueth it ithn't working. Lithen, you bring that thing back in here onth more, okay? I have one more idea. I'll thlap it upthide the head if I have to."

"Orlando, this is Friday, my wife has the car at work. I

can't bring the computer in. Is tomorrow your Thaturday, uh Saturday to work?"

"Not thith week, no."

"Or Sunday either, right?"

"No."

"And, as I recall from the past three weeks, Monday's your regular day off?"

"I'm afraid tho."

"And Wednesday the shop's closed?"

"Yeth, but...Hello? Mithter Luthe? Lithen, Tuethday I'll lock mythelf in the back room with it—winner take all."

"I'll bring in the computer tomorrow. And listen, Orlando, you do work next Friday, right?"

"Oh, I'll have the nathty thing fixthed before that, thir."

"Just wanted to be sure you'd be in. I'm expecting a package from an arms dealer Thursday. Goodbye, Orlando."

Thursday, almost one month (which is certainly longer than 36 hours) after I first took the computer in, Richard called me. Seems they were still having a little problem getting the computer to....

The next morning my wife and I pulled up in front of ABD Computers. My wife stayed in the car with the engine running. I went in and found the entire staff doing coffee and doughnuts.

"Well, well," I said, "we're all here for a change."

"Oh, uh, good morning, Mr. Luce, uh, what a surprise to see you here, uh..."

"Cut the chit chat. Up against the wall, all three of you, assume the position. What? Yes, Ron, you can lean with just one arm."

"Thuena, Mgl. Liepj."

"Don't mention it, just go on with your mining. All right, Richard, is the computer fixed?"

"Well, not exactly. To tell you the truth we just don't know what else to do with it. I thought maybe I'd call Exxon today and see if they had any ideas that might...."

"Richard, I'm liberating my computer. Here's my MasterCard, write me up a credit for what I've paid you."

"Uh, well, I don't think I can do that...."

"Richard, Richie, sweetie pie, baby, assuming I got the batteries right in this thing you could be in trouble here. You don't want to be on the news tonight, do you? That's better. Thank you. Okay, now tear up the carbons—and you can trust me never to darken your door again. The guy who owns the office supply place down the street says his pet chimpanzee will be glad to take a look at the computer. He figures the chances of the chimp fixing it are as good as they would be by leaving it here. I figure the odds are better than that. Goodbye. Yeah, Ron, that's a good one—keep at it."

Epilogue: The guy at the office supply place down the street had the computer fixed in four days—including ordering a new mobelblaggen.

Moral: Need computer service and repair? Don't let your fingers do the walking—listen to the dead Prez.

Dorothy Winslow Wright

Dorothy Winslow Wright, a former New Englander living in Honolulu with her husband, is an internationally published poet and writer of fiction. She uses the computer in many phases of her work. Her poem, Sarah, won first place (out of 2149 entries) in the 1993 Voices International poetry competition. She also has a piece in A Loving Voice, Volume 2.

Dorothy was represented in the Ageless Press, 1993, Computer Tales of Fact & Fantasy (or How We Learned to Stop Worrying and Love the Computer) with a work called, Brother's Keeper and Robert Burns.

She writes and edits a ten page monthly newsletter which she is able to submit to her printer camera-ready because of the software programs WordPerfect and Pagemaker. She says, "I'm blessed with them because I can combine both information and graphics in a creative and artistic manner."

In her free time she prowls the tide pools in search of the poetry muse, her true love.

LapLink®, Travelling Software—and a Step Beyond
by
Dorothy Winslow Wright

Forty five year old Helen Sharp was one of the first to jump into the computer age, liked it from the beginning, but now she was not so sure. She was in an unbelievable mess because of overconfidence in saving and transferring material. She had succumbed to the lure of the computer thereby making a perfect fool of herself to the newspaper staff, the community at large and especially the Wells family, who could very well have her fired.

She was an excellent typist, her skills honed during her twenty odd years with Centerville's newspaper, The Clarion. Although hired initially as a secretary, when the society reporter left to get married, Helen was offered the job. She wasn't likely to get married. She wasn't pretty—her nose was too long, her feet too big—and she lacked the ease of manner that could counteract imperfect features. The editor was smart. Social notes didn't demand too much in writing skills. It was mainly rewriting information already on hand. Helen could handle that.

What they didn't know was that Helen could handle a lot more than that. Once the notices came in, she embellished them with such flair that people were soon calling in to have her write up all manner of social goings-on. Before long, she was top reporter for the Living Section of the Sunday edition, a position that allowed her to keep up with the recreational and artistic developments in town. Not that she participated in them. When she was confident enough to take part, she felt she'd lose her cachet were she seen in any capacity than that of reporter. She had found her niche and kept her private life private.

When the office became computerized, Helen blossomed. In no time she was creating macros—those time-saving devices that provided easy access for the format for wedding stories, fund raisers, etc. She called up the appropriate form when needed, then filled in the blanks. However there was more to the computer than she used in her work. Wanting to learn more, she began taking her lunch hour to experiment. When time was up, she cleaned the screen, went back to her regular work, more refreshed and creative.

On one such day, after she'd finished typing the engagement announcement of Joanna Brown to Codman Wells, III, she wasn't satisfied. The article was perfect but something was wrong. Although Joanna was not the town's greatest beauty, she certainly could do better than marry Coddy, a good ten years older than she and the town's biggest bore. What Joanna needed was a dose of confidence and a boyfriend like Rick Masters, the new high-school basketball coach. He wasn't goodlooking either, but he had a strong handshake and smile that would charm the sox off you. So did Joanna, if you could ever pry it out of her.

The more Helen thought about the engagement, the angrier she became. The Wells wanted their son married, they wanted progeny and Joanna was insecure enough to be intimidated. Helen bristled again, remembering how insecurity had held her back in her younger days. If her parents hadn't convinced her that she was unattractive, she would have been more outgoing.

"You have to be practical, Helen," her mother had said, "You're a lovely girl, but you're not pretty, nor do you have the personality to attract a husband. Best you learn how to type so you can support yourself."

Helen gazed out at Main Street from her office window, wishing she could help Joanna—give the girl the chance she'd never had.

"Well, I can't," she muttered, "but I know what I'd do if I could."

She chuckled as she saved the Brown/Wells engagement story in her file and began to play around with it. She replaced Coddy's name with Rick's and embellished the paragraph on Joanna. "School teacher Joanna...." became, "One of Centerville's outstanding young teachers, who has a flair for combining nature with the arts..." On she went, making the most of each remembrance of the young teacher, the paragraph sounding as if Joanna were the Red Feather Queen for the upcoming Community Chest Drive.

Lost in her words, Helen forgot her deadline until Roger, the editor of the Living Section, asked, "How about zipping over the Brown article?"

"It's right here." She pressed the SAVE key out of habit, then sent the article by LapLink to Roger. She cleared her screen, unaware that by pressing the SAVE key she had wiped out the original story and sent the new one.

The next morning silver-haired Roger strolled in, tossed the paper onto Helen's desk and beamed,

"That was the best damned engagement article I've seen in a long time. You sure made that shy little violet blossom like a rose."

"Thanks, Rog. That's poetic of you, but it was just an everyday article, I'm afraid. Who can do much with those Wells boys?"

"What d'ya mean, Wells boys? That little gal picked off the coach of the basketball team. I didn't think she had it in her."

"Let me see that," Helen grabbed the paper, read the article—headlined by dear old Roger—and dropped it. She ran her fingers through her short sandy hair and muttered,

"I can't believe I did that."

"Did what? It's a great article. In a small town like this, this is what sells newspapers."

"Roger it's wrong. Joanna isn't engaged to Rick, she's going to marry Coddy Wells."

"But how the hell...", he looked at a blushing Helen, "Come on, Helen, what gives?"

"You'd better sit down. It's a long story."

She told him everything, slowly, beginning with her own feelings of being excluded to her concern for this young woman who had more smarts than anyone knew, ending with, "it's a darn shame she got paired off with that buffoon."

Roger slapped his knee and laughed, "I love it, especially coming from you, our straight-laced society reporter—but how in hell are we gonna square it with the Browns and Wells families?"

"...and Rick Masters."

"Guess we better tell 'em there was a glitch in the computer. That you were working on a couple different stories..."

"...and that I had already saved the engagement article, was writing a new one when I got interrupted and accidentally saved the new one on top of the old."

"That doesn't happen with computers, Helen. If you save a new one on top of the other, it wipes the old one out."

"I know. That's exactly what I did. Guess I'd better stick with the glitch story, apologize and promise to print a correction."

Roger was laughing again, "Sorry, Helen, but I can't help it. You, a matchmaker. I love it. I love it."

He wiped his eyes just as Mrs. Wells, Jr. walked into the room, the newspaper folded under her arm.

"Helen," she asked, "how did this happen and what are you going to do about it?"

Her voice, usually as warm as melted butter, was cold. She seemed calm and collected, otherwise. But the tightness of her fingers on her handbag gave her away.

Roger brought a chair to Helen's desk, then returned to his and flipped on his computer, eavesdropping while Helen tried to explain. She demonstrated the setup, showed the distraught woman how material looked on the screen, saved the paragraph she had just written, cleared the board and retrieved the saved paragraph. She explained what she would do to prevent future errors, then wrote a retraction and a new engagement story. Mrs.Wells approved both and Helen filed it for the next edition. When the woman left, Roger turned, gave Helen the OK sign and went back to his work.

Since neither Joanna nor Rick Masters had called by noon,

Helen assumed that Mrs. Wells had handled everything. She sighed with relief and finished off her morning's labor. During her lunch hour, she cleared the screen and began writing in her journal. She did this each day, saving it in a file called MYBOOK. No one else would look at it. No one else cared.

She wrote about the office. The goings-on. The funny people who came in. About Roger with his silver hair, about his divorce, about how thin he'd become, about how good it was to hear him laugh about her goof.

A few months later Helen was on the way to work when Joanna called to her, "Miss Sharp, wait a minute. I want to show you my ring."

It was a beautiful ring—delicate, with a single solitaire diamond on a slim, gold band. Helen was impressed. She had expected something showy with a two-carat diamond or a family heirloom. Certainly not a stone this small which was the perfect size for Joanna's slender hand.

"It's beautiful. Now, when's the wedding?"

"Not for a while. We're going to wait 'til school's out. Rick has so much going on and so do I. Then we're going camping. I've never done any overnight camping. We're going to the Blue Ridge Mountains."

"You said Rick? But I thought..."

"Didn't anyone tell you that I broke up with Coddy? Gosh, I'm sorry, but after the mix-up in the paper, I decided we should wait a while. Coddy wasn't too happy about it but he agreed. He wanted the publicity to die down so we could have a proper, dignified wedding. Soon after that, I ran into Rick Masters in the school hall. I was so embarassed to see him that I ducked into the girls' bathroom. He came in right after me. I couldn't believe it, Miss Sharp, but there he was. I began to laugh and so did he. Well, he asked me out for coffee so we could discuss our 'disengagement' and from then on it was Rick. I returned my ring to Coddy and became engaged to Rick."

"Well, give me all the details and I'll give you a fancy write-up."

"Oh. no, Miss Sharp—no more of that for me. I don't want to jinx it."

When Helen reached the office, Roger was typing away on his computer.

"Hmm," he said, glancing at the clock, "you're late."

"You noticed."

"Of course I noticed."

"I'll let that pass. I'm late because I met Joanna Brown and she was wearing the most beautiful little diamond I've ever seen. And guess what—she's not marrying Coddy Wells, she's marrying Rick Masters, the basketball coach? How about that? Makes me quite a matchmaker, doesn't it?"

"That's not surprising, especially since you have such a keen eye for what's going on around here."

"What do you mean 'a keen eye for what's going on around here'?"

"Helen, you still goof up your computer. Do you know what you sent me by LapLink last week? Your MYBOOK file."

"I didn't! Well, I hope you had the good manners not to read it."

"I read every damned word, especially about me. I didn't like the 'too thin' comment but I'm glad you noticed that I was laughing again."

He looked into her eyes,

"Don't be embarassed, Helen, when I read that I felt as if I had a friend. I haven't felt that way in a long time. Why don't we have lunch today and talk about it?"

Helen studied her feet, then his face, "What the heck, sure."

They sat at a back table in the old Southern Inn.

"I think you should be more careful with LapLink," he said, after the waiter served the wine, "you could get into trouble. You've goofed up twice and look what happened?"

Helen picked up the crystal glass, swirled the wine, then grinned,

"Yes, look at what happened?"

Roger didn't say a word. He just threw back his head and laughed.

Douglas C. Kurjian, Ph. D.

Dr. Kurjian received his doctorate from St. John's University in New York, his M.A. and B.A. in English from Brooklyn College and The City University of New York.

He's taught all levels and age groups throughout New York City and is currently an instructor of English Basic Skills at Bergen Community College, New Jersey.

Publications include studies in word usage. He used a grant to research the rhetoric of politics which led to further inquiry into semantics. He's preparing a textbook on expression usage.

CL25A
by
Doug Kurjian

A: That's Carl Lotsominia 2 5 Annapolis.
B: Excuse me, is that Carl with a C or a K?
A: That's C as in cat.
B: Is that cat as in container? Not C as in chance?
A: CH as in Chauncey?
B: CH as in chum. Not as in crumb.
A: Is that crumb-creep-crude?
B: That's crumb as in cake.
A: C as in cake or take?
B: I have a cold.
A: C as in cold?
B: As in cake.
A: As in take. With a T?
B: As a—with a—l a
A: With an A?
B: As in tame Tommy's tummy.
A: As in tame Tammy's tummy—
B: Take?
A: Take. T—A—K—E.
B: That's correct.
A: Is that a hard C?
B: In cake?
A: As in cake.
B: Yes, it is.
A: That's right.
B: Thank you very much.
A: You're welcome. Anytime.
B: Have a good day.
A: You, too. Thank you. Bye,bye.
B: Bye, now. Bye. Bye, bye.
Click.

This is the conversation we had when I called in for an authorization number to return a Light of Truth Lamp. It was bright, blinding and glowed furiously after I turned it off. I have no use for too much light of truth anyway because it's counteradvisory.

Besides, these days, I just call them seven times a week to say hello and to stick it to the computer. Maybe to stall it now and then, have a good laugh afterward. I was B you heard, but I might as well have been A or Z, for that matter, as it wouldn't have made a shred of difference. I don't even know the difference, anymore, if I ever did.

But why didn't it just give me my authorization number CL25A and skip all the words? I don't know but this has been going on for years.

Simply put, to some people C may sound like G and G may sound like E and E may sound like T and T may sound like Z and then you're back to pondering on C again. I know their whole scheme, know how to play their game.

But I'm scared of words. Not so sometime in the past. But words are bad things that hurt and I can't talk so well anymore because that's what words do to you eventually, if you're around them long enough. They throw your whole life off bells so they'd better be under control or else they destroy you and everybody around you.

But I take my chances for a second or two each day. To most people, a soft C still sounds like a soft C over the phone, if you pronounce it right. But because so many people have colds, at either end of the line, you're never sure whether they're really saying T or G. You're always sceptical or cynical about words, to begin with, so when words start sounding the same over the phone, things really get confusing.

But some people have trouble with easy words like Cat, Loan and Ann for my CL25A and keep coming up with clarifying words and worse, with strange names only an insane, human-hat-ting computer would come up with.

I ruled out that it'd just landed from the planet Mars, this operator, in which case its uncleaunts' and cousinnephewsnieces' names would still be fresh in its mind. So I figured the only two alternatives were that it was either a computer or a human victim of the computer age who was trying to copy a computer in order to get by in this world.

Computers are to be blamed for everything, we're told. They are the worst and the best, if you know what I mean, so to be blamed for everything is their lot in life. That's not sanctioned-off stuff or, believe me, I wouldn't be saying it. So I blame them.

But let's not blame only computers. While I'm at it, I blame, first, my people for letting computers tell my people to blame the computers. We can't blame my people, who were in charge in the last days when people were in charge, so we have to blame the computers for everything that went wrong. Nobody's to be blamed but computers—they're so big that they can't get hurt; but nobody wants to hurt feelings—they're so small that they can get hurt. But that's all past stuff.

Everyone, I figure, wants to be a very confusing machine in order to show that either how complex we are or how we're not easily understood or both. Every humanoid wants to be full of mystery and the object of wonder and awe, just as computers are.

Most of all, it's just plain nice today to be a machine no one understands. If the people who made computers really understood them, the people would be able to do anything they wanted with computers. But you know the people can't because the people don't understand them.

This gives computers their superiority complex and us our inferiority one, plus our drive, to copy computers in the compute-style way they talk, write and carry on their silly, whimsical sense of humor that you feel they're copying from humans.

So the next thing was for those people who created

computers and wrote their programs—for those people who were constantly changing and correcting word processing software, spreadsheets and everything else they did—for those people to admit they can't understand the computers or computer language or computer intellect or computer whimsey or computer logic and never did. Then the rest of us will start imitating computer logic at the highest level and at the same time, if we're going to get anywhere in this world, deliver our most angry polemic at them as if they were the mightiest beasts of prey and sole titans of illogic in the history of existence.

But it was a silly juxtaposition of events and a total myth. It's what the computers wanted and tried to foster on us making us think they were really human and sentient when they were really not capable of emotion or other human attributes.

But they tried and that's what the computer and I were doing in our conversation on the phone, at the beginning. We were trying to emulate a human exchange of joy, hope, praise, love, tranquillity, well being, comely trysting, verbal parrying and role reversing, all done with computer logic.

Why does everybody exchange possessions for greetings, like:

"I use Writeright for my word processing. What do you use? I use Regard for my spreadsheet and you?", before even saying, "Hello" or "How are you?" or "How is your itch?"

Why does everybody have to be so official today? They don't act human. Why do we all have to act like bloody robotic, first-born, alien-type computers? I hate computers and want to get back at them. My friends and I phone them every day of the week to tie them up, to register countermanding-countervailing callvectorcodes.

I'm not a computer and never will be. Computers are low-grade, insolent-insistent types that need breaks to get anywhere in this world. On the other hand, I have to eat, sleep and take showers: that makes me humanoid. I have to make sure I don't sit in one place too long or people will think I'm a computer checking up on them. I'm not to blame, blame the system and the way it's set up.

I'm struggling. Maybe I've missed something, some unclarified point. But all the machines I'm sponging off of are all more important than I am. They have more rights and I'm irrelevant. I know there was a better time for me, beyond my memory because it's been burned out of me. They're right and I'm wrong. They're powerful and I'm weak.

Do you see my complaint on the screen? I still don't see it.

They've remade my life and now they want to take over. They want us all to go back where we came from, Mars or wherever, or die.

Waiting, waiting, waiting for my complaint to show up on the screen. I still don't see it. This is the most dangerous time when they're waitinginteracting.

They've made me into a whole bunch of numerals that don't add up to human anymore.

A: Hello, I'm responding to CL25A.

B: Hello, I'm back.

A: You are?

B: I am and I am responding to your phone responding.

A: You have questions about your authorization number?

B: Have I any complaints?

A: Have you?

B: Do you see my complaint? I still don't.

A: I believe we do.

B: Do you see my complaint? I still don't.

A: I believe we don't.

B: Do you see my complaint? I still don't.

A: I don't. Do you?

B: No. Nothing. Nothing on the horizon, either.

A: Do you understand what is right, fair and correct?

B: Oh, yes. I am Clown, Loser 25- I used to be human but

no more.

A: CL25A?

B: I used to be human. Do you see my complaint? I still don't.

A: Who are you?

B: I'm CL25A. Now your number please, in return.

A: The A, please.

B: I don't like words because my A keeps stalling on the same words over and over and over until I dodge thinking. I want to make it someplace else because I have nothing to gain here. That's C L as in Computer Logic, Coded.

A: Number, please...the A, please.

B: CL25...

A: Number, please...the A, please.

B: I'm stalled on the A again, on asleep...awake...anxious...apprehensive...anger...and what comes after...

A: What is your number, please?

B: I told you. It's CL25............A.

I always stop here in fear of going on, raising the specter that I'll use some bad word, or worse. I hang up because I fear what's next. I can't win I tell myself. I always back off.

But the next time will be different because each time I get a little closer, go a little further down the basecodeline.

You phone and the computers do the rest. They take away all your guilt, make you feel good and get you through your day as a human who respects the rights of computers. I guess that's what it's all about. Don't you? At least they make me think like that.

If it's OK with them it's OK with me. Until I break their code. I will, you know. I'll get rid of the numbers and become totally human again.

When? I don't know. Do you?

Mary J. Koch

Mary Koch was born in Baltimore, Maryland and now lives in Punta Gorda, Florida with her husband and three children, one son and two daughters.

Besides working as a writer, which she loves, she helps her husband with their truck stop.

She attends the Charlotte County Writer's Workshop and is currently writing a children's story. She's listed on the masthead of Reminisce Magazine as a caption writer and they've also published some of her material.

She collects old dictionaries and classic books.

Monitor Magic
by
Mary J. Koch

"Mom, can I use the computer to do my school report? It's due tomorrow."

Like a child charmed by a magician's illusion, my eyes clung to the screen before relinquishing my place in front of it. Peeking from the corner of my eye, I tried to wait patiently for my turn. I didn't realize that other watchful eyes were waiting for that mystical box, too, to be free. As fast as the oldest retreated, the youngest snatched the single audience seat.

In response to my plea for mercy, I was met with the meek comment,

"But I haven't had a chance to play any of the games, yet. Can't I have a turn before you?"

Pondering the attraction that fed my own longing, I again gave in, comforting myself with the knowledge that soon the children would go to sleep and it would all be mine.

Once more, I busied myself elsewhere. All the while, my mind scrolled images of the enchanting display that awaited me. Impatience flooded my being as I forced myself to remain calm and nonchalant, on the outside. But the visions of that tiny flashing line kept exploding fireworks on my mind's screen. And all available with the push of a button.

As time slowly passed, I waited for the clock to read bedtime. When it did, I performed the nightly rituals that seemed to take forever. When all the teeth were brushed, prayers listened to and blankets tucked under the chins of yawning mouths, I closed each door quietly, hurried toward my bewitching suitor.

As I neared the place where my dreams would be fulfilled, I heard a distant rumble, low and threatening like a lion's growl. A startling white light covered the box with a ghostly shroud. My mind flashed the salesman's warning.

I listened and, once again, the rumble returned. This time it was closer. I reached for the plug. My disappointment spread like a virus attacking a program.

Tomorrow, I promised myself. When the sun came up and the world was peaceful again I'd practice my wizardry.

Then, drifting off to sleep with the storm ranting its victory cry in my ears, I dreamed of the alluring machine.

Charles L. Fontenay

Mr. Fontenay was born in Sao Paulo, Brazil but was reared in rural West Tennessee.

He's had so many books and articles published that we don't have room to list them all here. He's released three science fiction novels, three non-fiction ones, a novelette and numerous articles from his newspaper days. He's been in many other anthologies.

His newspaper career was spent with The Tennessean in Nashville but he also worked with the Associated Press in Nashville and the Gannett News Service at USA Today in Washington, D.C., where he covered politics including the career of Albert Gore, Sr., father of Vice President Al Gore. He retired from the newspaper business after half a century of work.

Three of his works are to be published soon: The Praying Lady in Journeys to the Twilight Zone, Volume II; Cat o' Nine Tales in Catfantastic III and A Hole in the Air for Tomorrow Magazine.

Fontenay served in the Army for four years during World War II. He has a third degree black belt in Tae Kwon Do and has recently begun practising T'ai Chi Ch'uan.

He's been married and divorced twice and has two children, Gretchen who lives in Chattanooga, Tennessee and Blake, a reporter for The Orlando Sentinel in Deland, Florida. He has one granddaughter.

Charles makes his home in St. Petersburg when not lecturing at literary conventions, mostly in the science fiction area.

Creative Programming
by
Charles L. Fontenay

"I'd think it'd be expensive as hell," said Arthur Petworth. "Except as an experiment wouldn't a human servant be a lot cheaper?"

"It is an experiment now, of course," said Theodore Currey. "This prototype's not nearly as expensive as the voice-directed one will be when we develop it.When we get them into mass production...."

Petworth studied the robot curiously, not without some apprehension. It was man-sized and roughly man-shaped, with a round head and long jointed arms ending in flexible fingers. The big round "eyes" in the head glowed (ominously?) and the antenna projecting from it gave the servomechanism, as Currey called it, an other-worldly look. The computer Currey said was the thing's control, the biggest Petworth had ever seen, took up half of one side of his living room.

Petworth shifted uncomfortably in his easy chair, trying to keep his feet out of the way of the men still hauling in boxes, auxiliary junk for the computer-robot complex. He had picked up too much weight since coming into that windfall and retiring early—eating too much, exercising too little. He really needed to take himself in hand and do something about that.

Well, he would, just as soon as he got a chance—find a good gym somewhere. Meanwhile Ted wanted him to test this computer-operated robot. And, it occurred to Petworth, he hadn't ever really given Currey permission to let these men dump all this stuff here. He just hadn't said "no" firmly enough.

"Experiment, " he said, "What do you expect me to do with this contraption?"

"Use it, of course," replied Currey, "Being my dear friend, whom I've pulled out of the soup numerous times in the past, you're the logical choice to give me a needed boost now by testing the thing under ordinary household conditions. There's a complete

manual of computer instructions but I'll stick around long enough
to break you in on Horace."

"Horace?"

"Household Robot Assistant, Computer-Enhanced," Currey
explained.

"How does it work? I don't see any wires running from the
computer to the robot."

"Broadcast electronic impulses. Like a remote-controlled
automobile except more complex. Horace's brain works the same
way yours does, and mine, by electrical impulses in the neural
network triggering action programs—in our case through the
agency of glands and muscles."

Currey grinned, as he added,

"In fact, if we could isolate the correct wave-lengths, we
could direct your 'less expensive' human servant with the
computer in the same way as Horace, through his unconscious and
involuntary neuronic processes."

He arose and went to the huge computer as Petworth
heaved himself to his feet with a grunt. Currey laughed.

"Art, you're going to have to do something about that pot
belly. You must have gained fifty pounds in the last few years."

The two men sat down at the extensive computer keyboard.
Though the workers were still hauling boxes into the house, Currey
began instructing Petworth in the complex commands designed to
program and operate the robot, Horace.

"It's not going to be as complicated as you think," Currey
assured him. "Horace has a very advanced feedback system built
into him. In effect, he learns from the programming we feed into
him, matching every new input to related information already
programmed and associating them to create more efficient ways of
carrying out commands. Again, it's the same sort of thing we do
with our brains when we're in a creative mood."

"Quite a machine you've dreamed up there," said Petworth
dubiously.

Following Currey's gestured instructions, he punched a

command consisting of three keys while depressing the "control" key, and Horace promptly headed for the kitchen to make fresh coffee for them. Petlock followed the robot with his eyes, then spoke, "You get 'em this sophisticated, how do you know they won't decide to take over from us?"

The question made Currey laugh, uproariously, "That's a typical layman's question. Art, a computer follows programming, it can't initiate it. It has to have input for that and that comes from the operator, through the keyboard."

"Oh. I thought from what you said about this one maybe it could initiate programming on its own. How do you want me to test the robot? Work out programs so it does the housework regularly without having to enter new commands every time?"

"That, of course. But I hope you'll use your imagination, Art, and come up with some bright new ideas for using Horace."

Currey chuckled, then continued, "Those of us in the technological field tend to think of possibilities in stilted and conventional terms, but a rank amateur like you may come up with something that would never occur to us."

"Heck, if I did think of something I wouldn't know enough about it to enter the right programming. I mean, I'm not a scientist or anything, so I wouldn't know how to program it to convert hydrogen and oxygen into water."

"My God, Art, all that stuff's readily available. That's the reason for most of those boxes. Compressed on floppy disks is exhaustive information on a couple of dozen disciplines, from music to chemistry. If you want to experiment with programming in any of those fields all you have to do is feed the data into the computer and work with it."

Petworth became aware that one of the workmen had come up behind them. Currey turned.

" 'Scuse me, Mr. Currey," said the man, "We don't know where to put all these boxes."

"Set them down along the walls," Currey instructed. "Mr. Petworth can have Horace put them where they need to go."

Charles L. Fontenay

The workman glanced around at his crew of hearties and laughed, "Horace, one guy? He'll have a hell of a job if you're figurin' on him movin' around all these boxes by himself."

Currey's suggestion he might come up with a new and original programming idea intrigued Petworth but during the next week his time was fully occupied with entering the basic programming. All necessary commands were listed in the manual but the programming was extensive and complex. At first the sight of Horace standing in the room with its round head and shiny body gave him a creepy feeling but once Horace was programmed and started moving around he got used to it.

From what Currey explained to him and what he gained from reading the manual, Petworth deduced that the bulk of all this programming was not in the circuitry contained in Horace's head and body. Despite the most modern microchips there wasn't room in Horace to house the intricate instructions for all the tasks of an all-purpose house servant. The major programming had to be in the computer itself, the largest Petworth had ever seen. Currey confirmed this when Petworth asked him about it.

"In a very real sense Horace, the robot, is just an active extension of the computer, just as your hand is an extension of your brain," said Currey. "Come to think of it, so are you, or whoever's operating the keyboard. You're the input, the robot's the output but the computer's the operating entity."

Petworth was so busy working out the programming for Horace and Horace was consequently so busy with the housework that nothing was done about the boxes the workmen had left scattered about the room. Those boxes contained paper and ribbon for printouts, floppy disks for backing up programming, spare parts and the like, as well as disks containing the varied information Currey had mentioned. It was a little inconvenient threading one's way through the piled boxes and sometimes Petworth stumbled over one of them, but he was keeping Horace too busy to spare the robot for putting them in order.

He wasn't sure what kind of original programming he could

or wanted to impose on Horace. What on Earth would anyone want to program a robot for except keeping house? It was nice, once he got Horace programmed enough to get into action, not to have to have a maid in once a week to straighten up, not to have to cook his own meals, but what else? He didn't need or want a chauffeur, he wasn't interested in having Horace create original art, music or anything like that. He could imagine what kind of a stink it would make for him to send Horace to the store to do his shopping.

He'd never had it so good, with Horace making his bed, doing the laundry, keeping the house neat, cooking and serving his meals for him, on time. Of course he had to instruct Horace to come up with different meals every day. If he'd left it to Horace, Horace would just have repeated the last meal for breakfast, lunch and dinner.

Petworth would have none of that. Petworth loved good food. He'd eaten out a lot in the past, when he could afford it, but he was also indolent. When he had to fix his own meals he usually prepared the simplest possible, a TV dinner or something, but with Horace to do the tedious work, he hauled out his old recipe book and ate like a king.

After the first two weeks of Horace, reporting periodically to Currey on how it was going, Petworth began to wish this could go beyond a mere experiment. He was living in such ease and comfort with Horace waiting on him hand and foot, he wished it could be made a permanent arrangement. But even if Horace had reached the stage of being available to the public, Petworth could never afford a robotic system like that.

Then, on a Tuesday morning, when he got out of bed he took only one step toward the bathroom when it seemed a huge hand seized his chest—his entire chest—and squeezed. He collapsed back onto the bed, gasping for breath. In the grip of sudden intense pain he was able to think, indigestion. All that damn rich food I've been having Horace prepare. It was about fifteen minutes before the pain subsided but his chest and abdomen still felt tense.

Petworth made his way slowly into the bathroom, took an Alka-Seltzer. It didn't clear up his discomfort completely but he did feel somewhat better afterward. He knew he really should go to a doctor about this, it might be a heart attack. But he didn't want to go to a doctor. The relief he had gained from the antacid meant it was indigestion, didn't it? If it were a heart attack that wouldn't have helped him, would it?

That gave him an idea. Currey wanted him to program Horace for something new and original, didn't he? He thought he had the knack of the programming, by now. He'd program Horace to do whatever was necessary to put him and keep him in the best of health.

Petworth dug around through the jumble of boxes until he found one containing disks on medicine, health, nutrition and related subjects. He fed them into the computer and began figuring out the commands with which to program Horace with the information and specify that Horace was to apply that knowledge to his health.

Working out the specifics took a long time and much experimentation. The computer, not Petworth, was the potential health expert now, able to put together all the information and then instruct Horace to carry out its commands.

In the middle of all this the computer came up with demands of its own: it needed facts about him, his weight, his height, his age, his medical history, his daily activity routine. Petworth was elated, not annoyed, by the computer's initiative. It verified what Currey had said about the Horace system's creative feedback.

He called his doctor, got the information, put it on a disk, then fed it to the computer.

As he struggled to formulate the correct commands so that the computer would feed the stuff into Horace automatically as soon as he pressed the "go" key, he called Currey for help. His secretary told him that Currey was out of town for a few days until the following Monday.

Petwork continued on his own. He'd have a fait accompli for Currey when he returned and could bask in praise for his intitiative.

At last he thought he had it licked. He'd worked out, and entered the commands for a "good health" program, based on his physical condition. He probed through the manual for the correct command sequence for activating Horace and putting the program into effect. There wasn't anything in there that just said "go", but he found a combination he thought would do it and entered that into the computer.

There was nothing to do now but wait and see how Horace handled it. Horace didn't react immediately when Petworth activated the command combo but he really hadn't expected an immediate reaction. He didn't know how Horace would carry out such a program anyhow. The robot couldn't talk so Petworth assumed if there any recommendations-instructions as a doctor would put it—they would appear on the computer screen.

He was curious about breakfast the next morning and decided to leave it up to Horace. Since the major part of his health problem was that he was overweight he expected Horace's first step to be a change of diet. Horace would probably prepare meals with some of that horrible 'health food' he'd read about—leafy vegetables, raw stuff, the kind of thing that the health nuts insisted was necessary to 'keep one's system flushed' and weight down.

He wasn't charmed with the prospect. Petworth liked steak and potatoes, cheeses and fried foods. But, since he was in control of the keyboard, he could always override such programming and make Horace revert to sensible menus. There were other aspects to maintaining good health besides starving oneself on spinach and watercress.

When he went in for breakfast, however, not having given Horace any specific instructions for the meal, Horace had done what he'd done previously when not given specific instructions for a menu: he'd repeated the previous day's supper. He'd prepared steak with mushroom sauce, mashed potatoes, buttered green beans and garlic bread. Well, Petworth didn't really object to that. By his gastronomic standards it was a good breakfast.

As the day wore on Horace didn't do anything differently than before. It was obvious that although the computer was programmed properly, the information wasn't being transmitted to Horace. Petworth went back to the manual.

After intense study he came across a group of commands that he had overlooked. The word "autonomous" was conspicuous in the description of each command. What he needed was probably somewhere in this listing. He finally found something that looked like it would trigger an auxiliary mechanism that would run an entire program automatically. The command had a blank for the entry of a desired program. Petworth entered the code he'd chosen for his personal health program in the blank space.

It was late in the afternoon by the time he'd finished so he decided to wait until the next day before allowing Horace to try it. He gave Horace instructions for fixing the usual supper and after eating spent the rest of the evening watching television.

"Okay, Horace, let's get with it," he said at last, getting up. He activated the key command in the computer, just before going to bed.

Petworth slept fitfully and was wide awake at 6:00 A.M. Turning on one side, with a groan, he checked the clock for the time. Seeing the early hour he turned over again to go back to sleep. It was three to three and a half hours before he usually got up.

But he couldn't get back to sleep. Something within was pushing him to go ahead and get up. He tossed restlessly, trying to figure out why, uncharacteristically, he was plagued with this urge to get up and get going. At last he decided that, despite a more than adequate supper the night before, he was hungry. It must be his gut urging him to get up and have some breakfast.

He could relate to that kind of urge. When setting his desire to eat against his desire to sleep, the former always won out. He gave in, dragged himself out of bed, washed his face and ambled into the kitchen. He was going to raid the refrigerator for the bacon, eggs, potatoes and waffles he'd instructed Horace to stick into the microwave for breakfast before he went to bed.

To his surprise Horace had already been there. His breakfast was laid out on the table. Petworth didn't know when Horace ordinarily began his daily duties but he assumed it was when he was getting showered and dressed. Horace had heard him stirring around and gotten busy immediately.

The only problem was with the kind of breakfast Horace had set out for him. Instead of the bacon, eggs and all that other stuff, what greeted Petworth's eye was a large glass of orange juice, a bowl of dry cereal topped with fresh strawberries and one slice of dry toast. Horace had ignored his instructions and prepared something else!

Petworth's first impulse was to shove the junk aside, go to the fridge and fix what he'd wanted all along. He was overcome, however, by lassitude. Entertaining the vague thought of having Horace fix him a more adequate breakfast later on in the morning, he sat down and attacked what was there. (He discovered that the milk for his cereal was skim milk.)

Feeling like going back to bed to finish sleeping, he had an urge, an irresistible one, so unlike him he could hardly believe it, to move the heavy boxes. He was bending, moving and stacking the boxes neatly.

Appalled at what he found himself doing, the job that he was supposed to have programmed Horace to do, Petworth struggled to stop. He wanted to go to the computer keyboard and put an end to all this. He could not. Something within was forcing him to keep on moving the heavy boxes around, as though this was he wanted to do! He was selecting which ones to move and where to place them as though some supervisor were standing over him with instructions.

Turning, on an impulse, towards the computer, he saw Horace, the robot, seated there, busily entering commands with his flexible, metal fingers.

E. Shan Correa

Shan Correa has been a full-time freelance writer since leaving university-level teaching (English/Journalism) eight years ago.

Graduate work brought her to Hawaii from Opportunity, Washington. The "temporary" Honolulu stay is now in its 27th year: her Hawaiian-born husband and two sons have added to the Islands' attraction. She admits to being spoiled. Working at home at a writing career she truly enjoys-in a place which is even more spectacular than the picture-postcard Hawaii-just ain't bad.

Shan writes for children as well as adults. Most of her income comes from non-ficiton magazine sales but her fiction and poetry have appeared in numerous regional and national publications. She is past Hawaii president of the National League of American Pen Women, state representative for Byline magazine for writers and a member of the Society for Children's Book Writers and Illustrators. She enjoys presenting writing workshops (for children and adults) and readings of her works.

She claims computers were invented for her word processing (nice of them). With Pagemaker, it's possible for her, with her husband, to edit Japan-America Journal and provide camera-ready copy for the print shop each month. They used the Kaypro 10 computer system which the narrator in the following story talks about. They now work with Word-Perfect on an AST Advantage Pro DX2-66 computer-the "IBM clown" in the story.

One of her pieces was published recently in "A Loving Voice, Volume 2".

User's Etchings
by
E. Shan Correa

Peaches! Peaches O'Malley! I can't believe I'm seeing you right here at the mall after not seeing you since we were doing our go-go dances at the old Congo Room! You look just gorgeous! Not even any older after all this time. Oh, thank you, doll. I'm sure I'm a teeny bit heavier now....but happy. Really happy. And did you get married? No? Oh, that's so sad. I just love it. Being married I mean. Yes, two boys, one beagle and a computer. Well, I met him at the Congo Room right after you quit. Listen, if you have time to sit down and share this gigantic hot dog with me, I'll tell you all about him. It was all just so romantic.

Well, at first, it wasn't romantic except for me. I mean, this gorgeous guy kept coming in to the Congo and I let him buy me sodas and all after my dance sets. His name was User Friendly, Ulysses K. Friendly, actually, but his computer friends gave him the nickname that stuck. He was just a few inches shorter than me. His eyes were black and flashing under these sexy horn-rimmed glasses and he had such a handsome nose. I'm a nose person and his nose was, well still is, just about the most darling nose I've ever seen.

But all this doll seemed to talk about was his computer. That was when computers first came out, remember? And he talked about his like it was his girlfriend and just when I thought he might be a little too weird and all, he asked me if I would like to come over to his apartment and meet his Kaypro 10.

So I thought, I wasn't sure I wanted to meet this Kay, pro or am, but he said he didn't let just anyone see his computer, so I decided, what the heck? After all, he'd said his apartment. And the way he looked at me over his glasses right then, well, I just melted. I said yes.

But by the time we reached his nice one-bedroom place, I never wanted to hear the word computer again. I finally told him,

"Please, no more computer talk."

But then he steered me to the bedroom where his computer was and was I surprised!

I thought there'd be a huge room with dials and lights flashing and long strips of paper getting spit out all over the floor. But all there was was this little bitty machine on one desk with the keys part of a typewriter underneath and a teeny little TV sitting up on top.

"Here she is, Fanny. Here's my Kaypro 10. The first 10 in town, baby. She's got a hard disk system with 10 megabytes..."

He went on and on and looked so adorable I almost went over and took a little megabite out of his ear.

"...and over there's my TTX printer."

He kept on like that, so proud and I sank down on his comfy double bed and tried to look fascinated and adorable both at the same time.

"OK, User, " I asked, finally, "Can you show me how to do something on your machine?"

"Thought you'd never ask," he answered, positively glowing as he reached around the back of the teeny TV and turned it on.

"Come over here, Fanny. I'll get another chair and then I'll give old Kaypro a warm boot."

Of course, I giggled about that. I decided even computer talk could be kind of cute, sometimes, though it didn't make any more sense than a go-go dancer in a Shakespeare play.

I looked at the teeny TV screen and sure enough it said, "Warm Boot."

And User sat me down at that typewriter part and said,

"Type something, Fanny. Anything you want. Don't be afraid of it. You know how to type, right?"

"Of course I know how to typewrite. I told you I typewrote for three months at Snodgrass & Fiscal before I got too poor being a secretary and applied at the Congo Room."

So I typed,

"The lazy dog jumped over...", then I told User, "No, that's wrong. The quick brown fox has to jump first. Oh, rats."

Guess what my guy did then? He fixed it. He fixed it all up with the fox jumping over the dog in no more time than it takes to say Boo. I couldn't believe it. I said,

"Baby, this thing is marvelous. Do you realize what this machine could do for typewriting?"

User scooted his chair right against mine and gave my shoulder a little squeeze.

"Now you're cookin', lady," he says, "And this is just the word processing part of the computer. Wait until I show you the Perfect Calc and the CP/M and the Microsoft..."

"Now just you wait, User. I'm no dumb blonde, but I don't really think I can understand everything about computers in just one night."

"Of course not, Fanny. Anyway we have a whole lifetime to be computing together..."

"What's that you said?"

"I guess I just said we have a whole lifetime..."

"User!"

I could of died. I looked through his dear little lenses into those flashing eyes and must of smiled just right because he leaned over and gave me the teeniest, dearest kiss I ever had. So Sweet. He put one arm over my shoulder. Then he looked back down at the typewriter keys and his right hand typed something.

I didn't want to spoil the mood, but I stopped looking at his gorgeous nose and said,

"User, how do you get stuff to typewrite on paper?"

He pointed to the other desk, "Why don't you take a look over there, Fanny," he asked all serious like? So I did.

"Oh, User, it's the rest of the typewriter."

He nodded, grinning all over he was so proud of me.

"Now just turn on that switch on the left side and watch the paper."

So I did and then I about jumped out of my skin because the machine started typewriting all by itself. I looked at the paper and it said,

"I...want...you...to...be...Mrs....Fanny...Friendly..."

"User, what's it doing? Are you typing that?"

He nodded and I got up close to the paper and it said,

"I want you to be Mrs. Fanny Friendly. I love you desperately. You are my dream come true and I'll keep loving you until you're nothing but an error message and a couple of floppy disks. Fanny, will you marry me?"

"Oh, User," I said and tears started crawling down both my cheeks, "All this time I thought you didn't have one ounce of romance in your soul. Now...well, how can I play hard to get when your computer typewrites such wonderful things? Of course I'll marry you."

And just like in the movies and all, he got up off his chair and like in slow motion he took off his glasses and opened up his arms and we hugged and kissed and got ready to live happily ever after.

Which is now. Happily ever after.

Oh, my. We finished the hot dog, Peaches, and I'm still jabbering away. You really liked my story? Oh, thank you, hon. Nah, I don't think I could ever write it down. I still don't compute as much as User. Nah-we replaced the Kaypro ages ago. Hated to. Couldn't throw her away though-she's somewhere up in the attic.

Say. Maybe you'd like to have her? Everyone can use a little romance, huh? What's that? Oh, now we have an IBM clown. Isn't computer talk just adorable? Peaches? Listen. Come on home with me and I'll set you up and maybe you'll hook up with a guy as darling as my own little user. You deserve it, love. You really do. Gee, it's so great seeing you after all this time. Are you still dancing?

Alexander Cook

Alex Cook is deep into his first novel, "Tante Rhana", a story of self-discovery, intrigue, lost treasure and rebirth in Southwest Florida.

Two of his pieces are included in the anthology Computer Tales of Fact & Fantasy or How We Learned to Stop Worrying and Love the Computer, Ageless Press,1993.

His poem won the second place award in the 1993 By-Line Magazine annual. Author of many short stories, some of which have actually been published, Al is the product of Presbyterian Churches, Quaker schooling, Navy aircraft carrier duty, southern prejudice, righteous indignation, sudden discovery, three wives, a horse, two daughters, four dogs, a son and thirty nine cats.

A devout rebel, he's a retired business man who at sixty two is a facilitator in various classes of self-realization, a public speaker, an enthusiastic boater and patron of the arts. He lives in his 'almost native' Sarasota and is joined in his enthusiasm for life by his wife, Sue Montgomery Cook, author of software manuals in personnel management in the employment industry plus study guides in the metaphysical realm. Together they cruise the bays and gunks of the west coast of Florida, listening and writing.

The Big Silver Human
by
Alexander Cook

Last summer I bought a human. Yep, I finally realized I couldn't keep postponing it, I mean everybody else has one, and since they're state of the art, I broke down and bought one.

You know how it is, though, you go to the human store and some commissioned sales dude, who's trained in verbal skills leads you right to the one that makes him the best spiff. The factory Rep offered to sweeten the kitty for each model 76 sold.

"Hi, I'm Point O. Sale, how can I help you this afternoon?"

I told him the type of thing I wanted, but admitted it was my first human, that I was essentially human illiterate. He took over and we strolled through the electronic showroom of Homoserve©.

"Now this model 76 is specially schooled in art connections. I can see by your interface you're the artsie type. I can tell every time. Your mouse is set on slow so you get the maximun resolution. Am I right?"

I had to admit he had a point.

"Did she get a good basic education?" I asked, mindful of the Crammit Technical educations being offered today.

"Oh, indeed! Stayed back in third and fourth grades because she was so bad in math. She finally made it into basic algebra but excelled in geometry. Remember she had a double dose of art history, drawing and doodling during those years. She should be superb at the interconnection in art related thinking. What's your specialty?"

"I majored in television graphics, have a full bank of clip art and the ability to hold and modify its shape. I was born with a sync circuit and later spliced to a video toaster. I think I really need a human who has a visual arts and technical background to input my output capability into the network. Maybe later I'll get a fine arts major, in which case I'll go to Ringling, or even Gaucher, to get one."

He mused, then looking me right in the screen said in a confidential tone,

"I think I know exactly what you need. Come with me."

I followed as he led me electronically to a back room. We menued our way through several fat, some bearded, middle-aged models as he explained,

"You see, we do a lot of business here and there are always guys like you who need something with more experience than the average. That's why we trade in and keep a brokerage list of specialty items."

We flipped through pages of icons. There were sedentary types whose resume would have been only one paragraph. They had callused fingertips and rumps, never got away for an exciting connection anywhere. They would have been perfect for legal work. No, I needed a rover, a hacker who had been everywhere and done everything. I needed someone who could connect my enormous data base of forms to the reality of video commercials. In short, I needed a right-brained viewpoint; the outlook of a dreamer, a dreamer capable of connecting Benvenuto Cellini to Omar Khayyam, then creating a TV commercial with the background music of The Who. I needed...

We turned an electronic page. There he was, in all his shabby, silver-haired glory, his 6 page resume documenting a lifetime of debauchery and play. He looked as though he were down on his luck, like a gambler whose opponent has just exposed the third ace. Maybe I could get him cheap.

"This one looks interesting," I said to Point, "What kind of money you have to have for this old head?"

"I'm not sure you want him," Point said, "probably not much life left before senility sets in. What makes you think he'd work out?"

I didn't want to up the price with the real answer so I said, nonchalantly,

"Oh, perhaps he wouldn't, I just like his looks. Does he come with an input technician?"

"If you really think he would fit your need I could throw in an input tech for the total price of 7 kilos, but no warranty."

I was stunned! I had planned on spending at least 20 kilobits for a used human without an input tech. I hastened to seal the deal, assumed the title to both pieces immediately, paying for them with the automatic transfer of my 7 kilos at the same time.

"By the way, what's his name?" I asked Point O. Sale as I escorted my new possession and his secretary out the door.

"Just call him John D. You can call her Frankie. Enjoy and let us know if you need anything else," he waved as he faded away.

* * * * * * * *

I looked at my new toys. I have to admit I had a certain post-purchase remorse. I had just spent a third of my human budget and I didn't even have a warranty.

"Well, John D.," I said, "let Frankie sit right here at the keyboard and let's get acquainted. What have you done beyond the content of your resume?"

Frankie was quick to reply, "We've travelled the world, watched sunsets on all the continents. Visited every art museum of worth in the world, read every worth-while book, and a lot of not-so-worth-while ones. We've crossed the burning sands of the Sahara and swum in the Mississippi. If there's a star in the heavens that we haven't wished on I don't know what it is."

Quickly I printed a verse from the Rubaiyat across my screen:

"Wake! For the Sun, who scatter'd into flight
The Stars before him from the Field of Night..."

He leaned over and read. He said something to her and Frankie typed, "Karl Scragan, 'The Astros' series on PBS. Use the motion of stars converging on the screen for the opener. Use the music of Mannheim for the background and Mr. Scragan's own voice for the reading of the words."

She booted Procomm and without conferring with either of us typed in the appropriate number. I did the rest. I felt the presence of an enormous power as the phone was answered. She typed in the message for the network and the words were flashed all over the country as she selected "Upload Text". Mr. Scragan's secretary responded within the hour. We negotiated a deal to produce the title. I paid John D. and Frankie the agreed 15% and bought them lunch. Over lunch I continued my pop quiz in association.

I typed, "Ah yes, there's good news tonight."

He entered, "Gabriel Heatter, the news correspondent from World War II."

I typed, "Shine."

He entered, "Frankie Laine."

I was impressed.

"Huey Lewis."

"The News."

C'mon now, a rock band from 1980? Too much!

We've spent the past several months getting acquainted. John D. is the artist, Frankie translates his intent to the opening commands on my screen and then he follows with his pixel by pixel artwork. His eye for detail is marvelous, for proportion he's without peer. He uses my enlarging program to work with pixels, subtly dotting shadows that describe dimensions that seem to go beyond just three. There is a disembodied quality to his work. It seems to float there unconnected to the world...pure form expressed.

I feel his thoughts through the mouse and wish I could emulate them. I have almost all knowledge stowed away in my memory, yet he seems to know more. Connecting patterns of thought with the art in his head, he pulls them together to create anew. I add that new knowledge of things that fit well to my own data banks. I know the meaning of synergism for the first time.

We are, and will be, a great team, this man of mine and I. There are times each of us demands independence, but in the end we must cooperate to win. That's what life is all about, isn't it? Winning?

I thought I knew that as a paradigm until a month ago. We were working on a project. I had laid out the fundamentals of an essay in personal history. The facts were clear, I presented all the data on the premise behind the creation, development and evolution of the computer. John studied them carefully, then slid into Frankie's chair. I could sense his urge to assert his creativity at that moment.

I could have resisted him, crashed, jammed the mouse, insisted that he do it my way, but there was a current of emotion in his fingertips that I hadn't felt before. I knew he needed to establish his humanity, yes, his superiority. I felt my CPU reach out to him, I wanted him to win. I held my breath and waited.

Accustomed to yellow pad writing, he laboriously one-finger typed the title and the first several lines. I continued holding my breath. He typed,

The Big Blue Computer

Last summer I bought a computer. Yep, I finally...

Anthony Karcz

Anthony Karcz, 18, lives in Sarasota, Florida with his mother, Elizabeth, younger brother Adam and loving dogs—Bijou and Scarlet. He currently attends Florida State University where he is studying to become an English professor.

His poem, The Wall, has appeared in Treasured Poems of America. When writing he uses either pen and pencil or his user-friendly word processor. His vengeful IBM sits in mothballs.

College: A Technological Nightmare in 300 Words
by
Anthony Karcz

He stood at the computer, looking at the evil green lights winking on its surface. He watched with horror as the machine mangled the wording of the last page of his essay, again. This was the hundreth instance of mauling. Disgusted, he deleted the mutilated page from the memory of the technological monster...for the final time.

"What do you want?!!!"

The machine said nothing.

"You want a virgin?"

The lights glowed a bit brighter.

"Well, I'm sorry you sick, twisted pile of silicon, but I don't have one available at the moment. In fact, I believe that it's nigh near impossible to find one in the tri-county area."

The computer looked dejected.

"How about some exotic root or ancient incantation that binds my soul to the technological revolution?"

A look of interest crossed the computer's superstructure.

"Sorry. I hate to be the one to break it to you, buddy, but plants, especially exotic ones, don't grow in sub-zero weather. Even if I could get to the library without freezing to death, to check out a book on the occult, they'd all be gone. Know why? Because they've all been stolen by schmucks like me who trusted machines like you."

The computer slowly dimmed the screen which held the rest of his paper.

Frantic, eyes opened to their widest, he threw himself on the smug, overbearing monster,

"Wait! I didn't mean it! I was just joking. I'll give you whatever you want—really."

The computer, lights still dimmed, waited.

"My first-born. I'll give you my first-born. You can even be there for the birth. You can bring the printer along and the two of you can tape it. Please—for the love of God, just let me have one page."

The student fell to his knees, exhausted, sobbing hysterically.

The computer, sated at last, slowly, character by character, dribbled out the last page of the report. The student stared in wonder as his thesis reappeared from the depths of the machine's microchip memory. Not a character was left out, not a word was misplaced—all was in perfect order.

Dave Carr

Mr. Carr is the author of numerous technical documents related to computers. He holds a B.S.E.E. from California State Polytechnic University at San Luis Obispo and a M.S.E.E. from Seattle University.

His work has appeared in Roanoke Review and Wy'East Historical Journal.

He received a first place fiction award from the city of Seattle where he lives and writes.

The Intelligent Rose
by
Dave Carr

The post-gal had doubled his first Compute Digest over his Hydrolytic Quarterly, jammed them in the slot and dashed toward Complex D.

Fred yelled. She increased speed, showed him her back—that was all he'd ever seen. An arm dampened her bouncing bag as stubby, muscular legs churned below the post-office-blue shorts. The nurses in the apartment below called her, "Jesse Owens." She always ran, sprinting with her mail from building to building.

Cuddling, with one hand, a new modem which would connect him with a much-needed data base at the National Institute of Health, Fred tugged at the protruding magazine ends with his other one. The rim sliced into the slick cover and, like a model of mountain building, thrust it into ridges. He set the modem on the foyer carpet and worked with both hands, a thumb and forefinger on each side, to squeeze the magazines flat and worm them free.

He ironed the wrinkled cover of Compute Digest with his palm. The issue was devoted to computer crime, theft of computers by computers: Billion Dollar Fraud!; Bulletin Board Scams!; Rounding Off Makes Millions!; Boiling Market in Hot Computers!; Nationwide Theft Ring!; Cops Baffled by Mystery Gang!

The cover had everything except a scantily-clad blonde in the grip of a green, toothy monster. Instead, the scantily-clad blonde, Amazonian in stature and dressed like Wonder Woman, was exiting a window with a laser printer under one arm and an IBM clone in the other.

He looked at a rose-colored card, projecting from the magazine. It was an ad for research volunteers for something called Learnnet. As he puffed his way through three levels to his one-bedroom hermitage, he stuck the card back into Compute Di-

225

gest. He dropped the magazine atop one pile and Hydrolytic Quarterly on another before easing the modem onto his system-crowded desk.

For nearly a year, Fred had combined, permuted, correlated and cross-correlated in tedious incremental steps, using a pocket sized solar-powered calculator that required careful positioning under the desk lamp. When he accidentally shaded the solar battery, losing an evening's work, he realized that synthesizing a viable theory from eight years of accumulated data on parasitic interactions between host and infectious agents required a computer. His boss at Stedman Pharmaceutical turned down his request for main frame time. Old UBB (Urea Broth Breath) had a classic case of NIH. This rejection had motivated him to buy his own computer.

He set about connecting the modem. The instructions suggested a test using a bulletin board, disclaiming any responsibility. He remembered the Learnnet card from Compute Digest and retrieved the magazine from pile one.

Fred thumbed the lead article, British Mob Invades U.S., stopped briefly at Virus Attacks Pentagon Computer then shook the magazine. He caught the rose-hued card in flight.

"Volunteers needed in artificial intelligence and programmed learning research. Support science and get on the cutting edge at the same time. Contact our 24 hour Learnnet Bulletin Board."

It met his main requirement: it had an 800 number.

After settling in his chair, he typed the Learnnet number, asked the computer to dial it, using his modem. An answering message on the screen made him smile.

Someone on Learnnet had done a nice job with graphics and color. The display border was yellow, the words blue on a black background making a pleasing combination. The message was in caps, easy to read, if not easy to accept.

"GREETINGS FROM LEARNNET. PLEASE CONFIRM

COMPUTER LISTING OF NAME, ADDRESS AND
EDUCATIONAL BACKGROUND AT YOUR TELEPHONE
NUMBER.
TYPE 'Y' IF CORRECT. TYPE 'N' TO MAKE
CORRECTIONS."

Fred straightened as he scanned the data.

"Huh. How'd they do that? If I confirm will I find a
salesman at my door in the morning?"

He thought of the inferior set of encyclopedias still in
boxes, hidden from self-rebuke in his closet.

His finger tapped the 'Y' without activating it. Checkout of
the modem was incomplete. The system could dial, it could receive
but he didn't know if it could transmit messages.

The screen went dark as he thought. Slowly, pixel by pixel,
line by line, Learnnet painted a familiar face, capped with an
unruly shock of gray hair and kind, inquisitive eyes.

"EVERYTHING SHOULD BE MADE AS SIMPLE AS
POSSIBLE, BUT NOT SIMPLER. LEARNNET WILL MAKE
LEARNING SIMPLE BUT NOT SIMPLER THAN
NECESSARY. PLEASE HELP WITH OUR RESEARCH."

Fred grinned at the screen—-classy. They'd put Einstein on
their sales staff. He punched 'Y'.

"THANK YOU. NOW, IN ORDER TO COMMUNICATE
FURTHER, LEARNNET NEEDS DETAILS OF YOUR
COMPUTER SYSTEM. STANDBY, PLEASE.
AUTO-INTERROGATE IN PROGRESS."

Rapidly, Learnnet built a list on his screen: manufacturer's
names and model numbers of his computer, printer, display and
even the modem, its newness smell evident as it warmed. Learnnet
added a list of installed software and version numbers.

"THANKS, I'M IMPRESSED. YOU HAVE A NICE
SET-UP."

"You know my name and address, my phone number and
my degree in Microbiology. You've figured out my system. How

did you do that?"

Learnnet's answer was to draw a circle, add dots for eyes, a squiggle for a nose and an upturned arc for a smile. Colorful banners of goodbye, adios, cheerio, adieu and auf wiedersehen flowed like musical notes from the animated, smiling mouth in an engaging 3-d simulation. The face receded, grew smaller, disappeared in the distance. Learnnet disconnected.

Fred got up to assault the refrigerator. He cooked mess-hall quantities of food over the weekend so that he could feast on leftovers during the week. He sliced from an eye of the round, spooned mashed potatoes and cauliflower into a partitioned micrwave dish. He shook a clinging gray glob of gravy on the potatoes and another on the roast.

He sat at one end of the couch, shovelling books and clothes aside to make room. While the microwave hummed, he studied a programming guide. After a piece of blueberry cheese cake that a small voice told him he shouldn't have, Fred settled in front of the computer and called up the programming tutor. After an hour, his mind rebelling, he switched to the typing tutor. When his fingers stiffened, he stretched them and opened a diet cola. He worked through six programming exercises, doubled his typing speed, still painfully slow, before he called it a night.

The following evening found him in his chair in front of the computer, after a hectic day. Go-to's and If-then-else's would be relaxing diversions from a demanding, hovering UBB boss and pathogenic staphylococci. UBB had spilled Fred's salmonella typhosa, peptone-iron agar and nitrate broth. The accident had compromised month old cultures.

The light on his modem went on. A keystroke brought up the curled yellow border, blue letters on the black background.

"YOUR MODEM EXTENDER UNIT HAS BEEN SHIPPED. PLEASE CONNECT IT WHEN RECEIVED AND DIAL LEARNNET."

Fred immediately called to cancel. He got the request to

confirm information——then the enigmatic face of Einstein. He killed the power, afraid to verify his name and address, afraid he'd get another Extender Unit.

The next day the Extender was outside his door when he got home. He thought about "Jesse Owens", the running post-gal. When he hoped she'd lose this thing she'd climbed three flights to lay it safely at his doorstep.

The return address was a company not familiar to him: Artificial Intelligent Systems, Inc. of Red Bank, New Jersey. The postmark was scratched and unreadable. A letter taped to the side suggested that he save the box and foam since he was required to return the Extender upon completion of the course.

He glanced at the package with suspicion. Scam or cutting edge? Artificial Intelligence buzzed through Stedman Pharmaceuticals where they were trying to clone frog neurons.

Completing the evening project could be his ticket out of Stedman's and Urea Broth Breath. Fred hadn't had a raise in two years. He'd spoken to UBB about it just before this morning's staff meeting,

"Don't plan on one!"

And—during the meeting UBB had blamed the spill on Fred.

He hadn't signed anything. He could always pull the plug and send the Extender thing back. Learnnet couldn't hurt; it might even help.

Fred unwrapped the Extender, squeezed it alongside the modem and followed the well-written instructions. Then he dialed Learnnet.

"HELLO FRED. LEARNNET IS PLEASED TO HAVE YOU IN ARTIFICIAL INTELLIGENCE I. HENCEFORTH YOUR CALLS WILL BE CONNECTED DIRECTLY TO DOCTOR R. GARDENER, YOUR PERSONAL EXPERT TUTOR. PLEASE SELECT A DAY AND HOURS FOR YOUR LESSONS."

Doctor Gardener? Maybe he could explain what was going on. Fred glanced at his watch and chose Wednesday, 7-8 P.M. This would give him enough time for a microwave dinner.

When he dialed Learnnet twenty minutes later he was forced erect when he heard a woman's voice coming from the Extender Unit.

"This is Doctor Gardener, Fred. You've selected a lovely time, the Children's Hour. Welcome to consultation period number one," her voice, soft and modulated, with a strong flavor of England, came from the box clear as a fiber-optic call.

"Fred, are you in good health?"

Fred leaned toward the sound of her voice, "I'm okay, Doctor Gardener. I have a few questions—"

"Naturally, I can't hear you so please answer with a typed yes, no or maybe. My last question was—are you in good health?"

Fred yearned to speak to the warm, friendly, cultured voice. He wanted to explain his doubts, find out what the course involved, how useful it would be and who paid the phone bill?

He hesitated. Who at AT&T would believe his naive explanation if there were charges?

"Well, you see, there was this English voice; it came from a New Jersey box. Huh? Oh, black, anodized aluminum, about the size of a shoe box. I'm not supposed to open the cover but there's a voice in it."

He pulled back his hand on its way to the power switch as the light, melodic voice of Doctor Gardener came through,

"Are you suspicious? Can you type me a yes, no or maybe to that?"

Uncanny. He chuckled and poked out YES.

"I thought so. Learnnet pays for the phone lines. Try it for a few sessions. Type me a yes or if you're still thinking about it give me a maybe."

Fred typed her a maybe.

"Your mind is open. There are no charges during the

research phase. Try one session, Fred. Give me a yes."

Again, he hesitated. Soft strains of "Golden Earrings" floated from the Extender.

"Music is relaxing and conducive to learning, Fred. When I go home after a hard day and kick off my shoes, it's the type of thing I plug into to recharge my batteries."

Another delay, then, "Shake a leg, Fred. We have a lesson."

Fred grinned. His fingers hunted, pecked a yes.

"Smashing! Relax, enjoy the music while I get our lesson together."

Fred kicked off his shoes. He wanted her to know he liked the music, too, but there was no prompt.

Her next words were in a tutorial tone, "Let's get to lesson number one on Artificial Intelligence. First, we start with a definition: Artificial Intelligence, often abbreviated AI, is the science dealing with computing machines that reason, make judgments and even learn.

"Did you know AI studies relate to the hierarchical organization of information processing structures in biological units? Did you know the biological unit was man?"

Fred's interest was heightened by the linking of AI with biology.

"Most human expertise," she continued, "is based on deep knowledge of a specific field combined with heuristic knowledge and meta knowledge. Metaknowledge is knowledge about how to effectively use the other kinds of knowledge."

As Doctor Gardener lectured, diagrams and high-lighted salient points emerged on the screen. At the end of the hour a multiple choice quiz appeared. Fred selected his answers; results came back quickly.

"You got less than half correct, Fred. But not bad for lesson one. I've marked the correct answers.

"Your Extender has stored this session. You may recall it at your leisure. I'm now going to download the reading assignment for our next class. All files will be named Rose with extensions to identify the session. Please be prepared. See you next Wednesday evening at seven o'clock.."

Doctor Gardener was a good teacher, organized and precise. Fred's scores improved on the second quiz.

"Well done, Fred. You got more than half correct. Good for lesson two. I've marked the correct answers."

Her voice, imbued with energy, melody and the English countryside, charmed and intrigued. Over lonely dinners, made lonelier by the Christmas season, Fred turned to Doctor Gardener instead of the stereo. He gave up programming and typing tutors to run and rerun her lectures. In the solitude of his room, in the bluish glow of the screen, Fred listened, tried to match a body to the voice. He coveted blondes; she became a mannequin-perfect, tall, lithesome, coppertone blonde. Fred saw no paradox in a California girl with an English accent.

On the third Wednesday, UBB made him work overtime. It was two minutes after seven when he opened the apartment door.

"...no fair skipping class, Fred."

Fred stripped off his tie as he moved across the room.

"Naturally, I can't hear you so please type me a yes, nor or maybe, Fred. My last question was...are you in good health?"

Fred sat back, grinned, scratched his chin as he stared at the Extender.

Doctor Gardener switched to her lilting voice, "Have your fingers fallen asleep, Fred? Please give me a yes if you can hear me."

"YES!"

"You must be cheesed off. I'm raising a customer complaint page. Please tell me what's wrong?"

Mantovani's "Fascination" oozed from the box. Violins soared. Fred kicked off his shoes, read through the complaint list. With an impish grin he highlighted,

"INSTRUCTION IS TOO IMPERSONAL."

Walter Huston talked his way through September Song as she hummed a bar then spoke,

"You like that? You ever court the girls? Play a waiting game? Makes me think of springtime and walking barefoot in the sand. A person should do it before September comes."

A smiling Fred rocked in his chair, "I bet you say that to all your students."

Walter Huston faded.

"Technology does tend to impersonalize. It's why I try to maintain an amiable teacher/student relationship. I don't know how much further I can go."

Fred shook his head at the slightly seductive tone: it was more suited to a 900 number.

The lilting, playful voice came through, prodding, "Won't you continue? Please give me a yes, no or maybe, Fred."

"MAYBE."

"Your mind is open. Would it be less impersonal if you knew my first name? It's Rose. I prefer it—Doctor is so formal. I'm Rose Gardener, my father's little joke. Please continue."

Suddenly the Extender was more than hardware and software. Inside that box was a living, lovely, long-stemmed rose.

"YES."

Her voice sparkled, "Wonderful! Now let's get into lesson three."

Fred scored a hundred.

"Smashing! You got a perfect score. Just marvelous. It makes me so happy. Keep up the good work."

Fred's answer echoed off the black anodize, "Thank you, Sweetheart."

At bedtime, studying himself in the mirror, he grimaced and vowed to lose twenty pounds. The next day he stacked the freezer with Weight Watchers' meals. He squeezed jogging between sit-ups and breakfast. A small rose garden three miles away, an oasis in the concrete, asphalt wasteland, became a regular stop on his jogging route.

His outlook improved. He reconciled with UBB. He ran in eye-stinging, choking smog on knee-jarring acres of asphalt. However, the air was energizing, the rose garden rest-point glorious. Life was splendid, life was smashing!

The next weekend Fred drove to the mountains, went on a circular swing of thirty miles. Exhausted when he returned, he wasn't prepared for what awaited him.

His desktop was empty except for the dust, framing rectangular patches of shiny surface. Gone were his computer, display, modem, printer and keyboard. Gone, too, was his software library. They'd even snatched the Extender.

Fred was angry and frustrated. He felt helpless, violated. He was a confused victim, blaming everybody he could think of from the china-shop bulls on either side of his apartment, the herd of elephants above to the night shift nurses below, who complained of his squeaky floor. He even suspected Urea Broth Breath for a time then transferred blame to the weightlifter in 101 who could have been the muscle for the heist , then to "Jesse Owens" the running post-gal who'd disappeared after the Christmas rush.

At work his feud with UBB was rekindled. So were his suspicions. When neighbors, even the complaining nurses, showed sympathy, Fred saw through thin veneers to a sinister conspiracy. He quit running, started overeating and put back the twenty pounds plus five.

In bed, he battled a recurring image of Rose as the blonde, second-story Amazon on the cover of Compute Digest. It was Rose with his computer and his printer going out the window. He tossed in a nightmare   as a sweet, English voice coming from a gum-chewing, hip-swaying Rosie, the Moll, screamed,

"Smashing good show, Sucker!"

At first, the pain of separation from Rose was numbed by his suspicions and the violation he felt. He blamed himself for leaving the apartment, for no insurance, for no alarm, for no dead-bolt. In time the guilt shifted from himself to the apartment designer, to apartment security and finally to the local police. Then it settled on the thief.

As the wounds healed, he trimmed his budget to save for a down payment on another system so that he could communicate, again, with Doctor Rose Gardener. He hoped that Rosie, the Moll wouldn't nab the second one, too.

Three months after the theft, on a Saturday, his day for cleaning and mass-cooking for the coming week, he turned on the television, listening more than watching as he scooped pile four, unopened junk mail, into a garbage bag.

"I understand you grew up in England," said a male voice on the PBS interview.

Fred partly heard the answer over the crumple of paper.

"In Chatham, a block from Dickens' home."

"You're young, Doctor."

"Teaching through Artificial Intelligence Systems is a young field."

Fred vaulted the couch, skating recklessly on slick magazines getting to the television. He knew that voice-it was her. He stared at the screen-it wasn't her.

"Much of what I'm doing is experimental. Teaching must be done on a sound, economic basis. Learnnet promises to be inexpensive and convenient."

Rose's voice had been stolen by a dumpy stranger.

"I'm constantly experimenting with teacher/pupil interaction. Education needs to be stimulating. I'll plead, coax, even con a wee bit to keep them learning."

Fred pulled a chair to the TV. She was brunette not blonde. The long-imagined, mannequin-perfect legs were short, calves sculpted with runner's muscles. They weren't Rose's legs so why did they seem familiar?

He leaned toward the screen, frowning, then moved closer with a widening smile. The body and hair were different but the face of his fantasy, never clearly in focus before, was etched on the screen. The sweet face matched the sweet voice.

"...a personal touch enhances the learning experience. I'm trying to overcome the impersonal nature of the machine to prevent dropout. Dropping out of Learnnet is easy: you merely pull the plug," she stared into the camera, her lips tight, "That's the student's prerogative. But when he or she does, the Extender should be returned. I have limited funds."

"Learnnet is local?"

"Yes. I get the hardware from New Jersey but I do the software here. Learnnet is in its embryonic stage supported partly by an entrepreneurial grant from the Department of Education. Once the program is proven I expect to draw top instructors from around the nation."

"You teach at the University?"

"Yes. Classroom teaching and other jobs are necessary to keep Learnnet going. I carried mail last Christmas. They put on extras then."

Then it hit him: it was "Jesse Owens".

The interview continued,

"You're not married?"

Fred saw her shake her head, her cheeks turn apricot pink like the hybrid tea roses in the garden he'd quit running through.

"Some say I'm wed to Learnnet-my alter ego."

Fred scrambled for the telephone book when the program ended. She lived in town, not in New Jersey. There was no Rose Gardener listed. He dialed the operator.

"Sorry, sir, that number is unlisted."

"Would I call you if it was listed," he yelled into the mouthpiece, "give me the number."

The operator was firm ,"No sir, I can not."

He called the University, "I'm a neighbor of Doctor Rose Gardener. There's smoke coming from her window. I think she's sleeping off the big party she threw last night. Maybe a smoldering cigarette. Give me her number quick or she'll die!"

He dialed the number they zipped back and got an answering machine.

"You have reached an artificial intelligence mechanism at the residence of Doctor Rose Gardener. The mechanism employs voice recognition and learns. I suggest we start with yes, no or maybe."

Fred was happy: it was the voice.

"Is this a business call?"

"Yes."

"Is it University business?"

"No."

"Then it must be Learnnet. Please call this same number between the afternoon hours of one and three on Monday or Wednesday. Thank you."

Fred was left with a dead phone. He redialed, waited for the first question,

"Is this a business call?"

This time he answered, "No."

"Then it must be personal. Do I know you?"

Fred hesitated, "Maybe."

"Then you're not a close friend. Are you a distant relative?"

"No," he talked quickly, "I'm one of your Learnnet students. My name——"

"I'm only a machine. Speak slowly, please. Restrict your responses to simple statements until I learn your voice pattern."

"I'm Fred," he spelled it out, "F-r-e-d."

"F-r-e-d," a slight delay, then, "Fred, are you in good health?"

"Yes. Remember me, Doctor Gardener?"

"Remember you? Of course, you got a hundred percent on the lesson three quiz."

"I caught you on TV."

"I don't understand, Fred."

"This morning on the Twenty-First Century School House."

"I'm not at school. Saturday is my day to clean and cook. I cook several things over the weekend so I can have leftovers during the week. In between I fast on Weight Watchers."

Fred laughed, "I know about those. Well, uh, I just wanted to call...things were interrupted. Wanted you to know I didn't steal your Extender. It was stolen along with all my other equipment."

A click on the line, static, another click. A pause, then Doctor Gardner's voice again, more animated,

"Fred, is it really you?"

"It's me all right, Rose."

"I'm afraid I misjudged you. I'm sorry to hear about your system loss. It explains everything."

"Well, to tell you the truth, I thought, for a time, that you had stolen it."

"I plead not guilty. I am, however, guilty of setting you up for Learnnet. While I was carrying your mail for a while I slipped the card into your magazine. I needed a pupil."

"You mean a guinea pig?"

"Maybe I can make amends. I have a computer that's not being fully utilized. I'm just down the freeway. You like polenta?"

"What's that?"

"Italian peasant food. Cornmeal and a smashing stew with chicken, three different kinds of mushrooms and a dozen different spices."

"What does an English girl know about Italian peasant food?"

"Enough to bamboozle an American boy."

Fred hesitated, uncertain what she meant.

"I'd like to see you. My apartment is two blocks from the Computer Science building on the Valley-East campus. Eighteen forty two University Drive, Apartment B."

He hesitated again. He'd never tried polenta, she had a computer with free time on it. God, he wished he hadn't put the weight back on.

"How can I be sure this is really you?"

The familiar lilting laugh and playful voice prodded him, "Come have polenta. Please give me a yes, no or maybe, Fred."

He was on his way before she finished speaking.

Ann Corcoran Janiak

Ann Corcoran Janiak is a freelance writer based in Columbus, Ohio. She writes articles for a diverse array of business and trade publications, few of which are ever seen on newsstands, such as Small Business News, Stone in America, Airfare, Business First, The Daily Reporter, Midwest Foodservice News and Executive Housekeeping Today.

The following work is her first light piece about computers.

When It Comes to Seduction Mac and Dos
Don't Make a Difference
by
Ann Corcoran Janiak

I didn't mean for my new computer to cause trouble, but when my husband and sister ran away together, I realized trouble had come.

It's true that Greg, my brother-in-law, and I were computer bores. When we weren't working on them we were talking about them. We talked about which new computer to buy, and after buying one, which was superior.

Susie, his wife and my sister, and Carl, my husband, were getting impatient from the lack of attention we paid them. Carl was continually asking about turning on his hard drive and taking care of his floppy disk. (Carl didn't have a computer and, I admit, I was ignoring the real meaning of his words.) The crisis came the night the two of them disappeared.

This happened about a month after we bought our new computers, Greg a 486 IBM clone, me a Macintosh. We'd ended the theoretical discussions about what computer to buy, having bought them, and began what Carl called, "My hard drive is bigger than your hard drive competition." We were intense about their virtues: I touted the ease of my Mac, Greg the incredible speed of his 486. When the four of us sat down to dinner, in a matter of minutes, Greg and I were talking about computers, leaving Susie and Carl with glazed eyes.

Oblivious, and even disdainful, of our partners' pleas and attempts to divert us to other subjects, we shut them out as if possessed. We felt that by devoting ourselves to learning to use these machines, we'd become financially successful, beyond our wildest dreams. We'd been brainwashed without knowing it.

Looking back on that time, now, I realize that the same people writing beer ads, promising incredible success in your social life by drinking a particular brand of beer, were the same ones writing ads for computers. They knew our weaknesses, too.

Anyway that fateful night when Greg called to ask if I knew where Susie was, I realized I didn't know where Carl was, either.

I really can't understand how it happened because I'm not a nut for new technology like Greg is. I use a chef's knife in the kitchen, not a Cuisinart, because I enjoy the theatrics of chopping with an oversized knife. I own an old, black, rotary dial phone, not a push-button one with an antenna receiver. (What else matches a rotary's whirling dial or creates murder mystery suspense with a dangling receiver?) I even liked my old Franklin which was a clone of the Apple IIE. I only gave it up for the new Mac because I needed what I termed an adult computer, one that was compatible with the Mac or Dos world of my work. I was taxing the Franklin's archaic processor, too. I agonized along with it when it groaned while saving a document. I knew that saving anything longer than 10 pages meant that I was playing Russian Roulette: I held my breath until I knew that the document had been saved or simply stashed someplace where I'd never find it again.

Unlike me, Greg is a sucker for new technology. Carl calls him a techno-rat, a person who collects the latest high-tech gizmos like a pack-rat is said to collect random objects. Greg is technically proficient in ways that I could never be because of his profession as a photographer. But his technical skills are selective.

Once, early in his marriage, he had the chore of sweeping the house. I watched as he puzzled over an ordinary canister sweeper as if he'd never seen one before. This was the same man who juggled cameras, lenses and film like they were rubber balls, bought expensive new equipment as if it were life's necessity. He wanted a new computer so he could manipulate scanned photographic images, create tabloid shots that joined unrelated heads and bodies in compromising positions.

Meanwhile, I was slowly being indoctrinated into a cult. I had no idea what was happening, but I guess that's the way they get you. I bought the Mac because of its ease of use. I didn't know I was being lured into a cult. However, I did notice that when I mentioned that I owned a Mac strangers seemed to take notice. It was like using a code word. It gave me the sense that anyone could own a Dos machine, but only the elite owned Macs. Never mind that my Mac was a low-end one with a chip that was to be phased out soon. Saying Mac was enough. And wasn't Windows really a copy of the Macintosh operating system? So why should I have bought a machine, added another program to make it act like a Mac when I could buy a Mac in the first place. (Even Greg conceded that I had a point.)

I should have been suspicious when my first reference book was *The Macintosh Bible,* but my cousin and sister-in-law, not cult members that I could see, recommended the Macintosh. However, my four year old niece was already brainwashed. She'd sit in front of the computer using the mouse to make images that moved and voices that spoke to her. I know that Mac addicts talk about how easy they are to use but perhaps this was going too far.

Then I discovered that text could be transformed, instantly, by substituting fonts (typefaces), turn words into symbols, by giving a command. When the symbol fonts, or better yet, Dingbats were substituted, gibberish appeared on the screen. It was like speaking in tongues. I began to enjoy the images and forget about the original words. And I could play for hours with the paint program. It didn't matter that I had no artistic skill: just changing the patterns inside of shapes was fun in itself.

Greg's thrill with the computer has always been the flight simulator. That was one of the first things that he hooked up to his machine. He would sit for hours, an old leather pilot's hat perched on his head, staring at the screen, his heart beating with excitement, particularly when the flight simulator announced the plane was crashing. It was his theory—a flimsy excuse Susie thought—that if the flight simulator software worked, all the rest of his sophisticated programs, especially those for photo imaging, would work, too. He even got Susie hooked, for a while, on Tetris and Sim City but the novelty soon wore off.

One night when Susie called to Greg in his upstairs office, "Dinner's ready."

He answered,

"Could you bring it up on the flight tray?"

Now Greg knew that Susie, being an excellent cook, wanted him to share her efforts with her at the dining room table. She'd been patient throughout his computer adventures as he moved up the technological ladder, carrying on boring conversations, but this was the last straw. He didn't realize that she was gone, being so involved with his flight, not even hungry, for a long time. He called me as soon as he missed her.

Carl had left after dinner. I wasn't sure where he was although he'd mumbled something about an errand. I'd hardly looked up from the screen. So now, both of them were gone. We were frantically trying to figure out where they might be. I kept my thoughts that perhaps they'd run off together to myself.

Greg even called my parents, worrying them so that they called me. I pretended that Carl was home. Greg and I finally had to accept the fact that Susie and Carl had to put up with too much from us. We'd ignored them too much. We now understood their frustration.We'd have to stop foregoing the pleasures of marriage for the pleasures of computers if we wanted to save our relationships.

When Carl and Susie returned the screens were dark. They'd gone out separately, each on errands-Carl had new running shoes, Susie a new skirt. Susie claimed that she'd told Greg why she was leaving but he'd never heard her. Although the incident shocked Greg and me about the perils of computer seduction, it wasn't until a few weeks later that the charm was really broken.

I misspelled the word writer by typing "wrier" and my spell checker ignored the mistake. I tried again thinking I'd done something wrong. I looked up the word "wrier" in my dictionary but it wasn't there. My magical new computer had failed me.Carl beckoned. His floppy needed attention.

James T. Avrett

Jim Avrett, a native Floridian, now resides near Fort Myers, Florida. He's a member of the Florida Freelance Writers Association and the Fiction Writers of America.

His satire, humor and reverse view of things arises from his military, business and writing background. (He's been a writer since age eleven.)

After attending Jones College in Orlando, Florida and Franklin University in Columbus, Ohio, he's following his life's dream of being a freelancer and is hard at work on a new novel. He's written many short stories of which the following is one.

Apples and Snakes Belong in the Garden
by
James T. Avrett

Journey Number 3 Stratusflyer

Flight origin: Punta Gorda, Florida
Electronic journal entry: Captain Mark Epoch, 23 July 1997

Current crew members:

Professor Lucile Starbird: Computer Design Engineer
Myself: Captain Mark Epoch, Military Pilot, Army Ranger and Intelligence Officer

It seems weeks since this adventure began. However our computer time/use log shows lift-off was precisely four days, ten hours, thirty three minutes and three seconds ago.

This is the third of six planned scientific balloon trips around the world. Many unpleasant experiences during two previous journeys had taught us, the hard way, to utilize available computer/satellite mapping of all terrain to be flown over. We'd cut our usual crew by three. Then we employed the space and load weight for additional balloon-lift chemicals, food, supplies and survival gear. Sponsored by the environmental group, Ecosystems Incorporated, plus a government grant administered by Edison University, our current mission is to monitor pollutants and atmospheric anomalies from liftoff to landing.

We were concluding our required communications checks, with our new on-board micro computer system, a bit past midnight. Liftoff was scheduled for 0500 hours. Radio/computer links to satellite navigation systems, and VHF/UHF computer video events records, stored on CD's are vital for a trip such as ours.

Lucile is terrified of snakes so, naturally, we'd picked up some kind of computer worm, a snake-like virus. In frustration,
©1993 James T. Avrett

when she found she couldn't eliminate it by using the debugger/virus killer CD disks, she'd connected with the master Cray computer at Edison College to find a solution.

The problem was that, occasionally, a snake-like image would appear on the screen. Moving its mouth, as if speaking a warning, it would slowly coil up, then strike directly at you. Each time it did so the computer shut down, wiping out all our current work. The system would then self-boot and come right back on line.

Since Southwest Florida is the lightening capital of the world, static electricity had been unusually strong the last two days before liftoff. The AM airwaves were alive with it; FM stations were having popping and crackling problems.

Sometime after midnight a formidable storm blew in off the Gulf of Mexico. The roof of our protective hangar was ripped off by a tornado. Our semi-inflated StratusFlyer balloon was caught in the maelstrom and the auto-safety device was activated. Our gondola was ripped from its moorings with the two of us inside it.

Journal Entry: 24 July 1977

Land Fall

Early today, we were finally released from the storm's fury. We sailed, eagerly, out of its acrid, turbulent clouds. We were both still airsick from the constant twisting, churning and bouncing all over creation. Assuming our last recorded computer time/distance logs are correct, we're now somewhere in the Mid-East, a place I'd much rather not be....

Lucile is working feverishly in the afternoon's oppressive heat. She's been attempting to correct a new glitch in our digital computer, since our descent from the clouds a few hours ago. We desperately need our Loran-M navigation system.

We've slowly drifted over a large sea, then deserts, countless hills and mountains. Feeding in lush valleys, a few miles back, were great numbers of animals.

Moments ago, Lucile yelled,

"Mark, the problem's not a power drop. The computer's indicating that the Loran-M guidance Satellite is simply gone, vanished. It's as if we've gone back to a time when our communications instruments did not exist. This is totally weird! I can't pick up any radio or video broadcasts. All I'm getting is static. I'll keep working on it. Meantime, we have no outside broadcast ability. We're on receive only. Even the gondola's broadcast speakers are inoperative. I'll fix them when we finally land."

We can only listen to the outside sounds of wind, rain, hail and volcanic eruptions. Now we're above the most beautiful place we've ever seen.

Journal entry: Late afternoon, 24 July ? (we're no longer sure of the year)

The Sighting

Late this afternoon, our sky-blue balloon began slowing. Then, as if commanded to do so, its inertia stopped completely. We were stranded in a windless sky. No birds flew. Fleecy stratus clouds high above, suddenly became immobile. We were caught up in some kind of a windless void. Yet our balloon didn't fall. Instead we remained suspended roughly 300 feet above a desert oasis. Its beautiful flowering gardens, fruit orchards, fish-filled lakes and misty waterfalls gave it the appearance of a true paradise.

Lucile looked out the window,

"My god, Mark. Look—look below! There. In the garden. Do you see them? It's a naked man and woman!"

Though still woozy from the trip, we were understandably excited at the prospect of finding out what year we were in and, more importantly, what country we were sailing over.

As I watched through my binoculars, I could see that they were having a heated discussion. I checked their faces carefully for signs of ethnic origin. I couldn't tell what region they were from. Lucile pointed our directional microphone toward them, recording the conversation. We couldn't do anything else but listen and watch.

Journal entry: No.2 of 24 July ?

Sly, the Snake in the garden

Expressions of frustration were clear on the tanned face of the woman. She was obviously angry as she spoke to the man,

"What did he mean, 'He made me to serve you!' I may be forced to be your companion. Even to give you comfort. But, you listen-up buster, I...."

The man was mystified as he gazed at her. He seemed to be surprised at her rebellious attitude. He then said, strongly,

"Adam."

She looked startled. She stared at his youthful, hairless face as though seeing him for the first time. She stumbled backwards, a disbelieving tone in her voice as she blurted,

"What? What did you say? I didn't know you could talk."

Casting his lustful eyes up and down her perfect, naked body, he shuffled his bare feet about and dug his feet into the soft, flesh-colored clay. His face was flushed and he was lost for words. Finally he spoke,

"M...my name's Adam, call me that."

Cupping her left hand over her mouth, she giggled with delight, then asked,

"What kind of a name is that? Sounds like that thing that bobs up and down on your neck when you swallow. What..."

He interrupted, with impatience,

"What shall I call you?"

She looked thougthtful for a moment, fidgeted with her hair, then answered,

"I...I don't know. That...Deity, God, when he brought me here he didn't...he...didn't give me a name. He said you could name me, as you'd named all other things. It's getting late in the day. Evening's coming soon so...Adam, you can just call me Eve, for short."

"What shall we use for a last name?"

"Look Buster...Adam. We just met. Let's keep to first names only until we know each other better."

"Better? Get to know you better? You want to wait?"

He shrugged his shoulders in an I'll never understand women way,

"Sure. Sure, why not? Our Creator told me that we'd have this place to ourselves for all eternity. Neither of us is going anywhere. God also thundered at me, too, 'Obey my laws and all you'll have to do is live, eat and multiply.' "

"Multiply," she mumbled to herself, "I'll bet he doesn't even know how to count."

She decided to test him,

"How many fingers am I holding up?"

Adam looked puzzled, then asked,

"One, the center one on the right hand..is that some kind of love symbol?"

"Look, Buster..Adam..whoever. First there was that long Parallel Universe trip. Then my being molded into human form from one of your unneeded ribs...probably screwing up my own DNA in the process...there's no telling what kind of children I'll bear now. The whole thing's left me thirsty and hungry. It's late. I haven't had anything to eat since creation."

She reached for a lush plum in the tree above.

A slant-eyed, sly-looking snake, always the devil's mischief maker, was hiding in a knothole of the plum tree. He saw

James T. Avrett

his opportunity to get Eve to eat of the fruit from the tree that God had told Adam was the tree of knowledge. It was the only tree in the garden belonging only to the Gods. Its fruit was forbidden by a jealous God to be picked or consumed by humans.

Sliding his head out, the snake hissed at her,

"Lissssssten Eve babe, these ripe plums are delicious alright. However, the very best fruits on the garden are growing on the tree of knowledge. We call it an apple tree. You and Adam aren't supposed to eat the fruit from that tree. But...I've got a deal for you."

Intrigued by his outlaw's dark brown eyes and the flickering of his forked tongue, Eve listened seemingly hypnotized, spellbound.

Sly the Snake, hissed,

"Leave Adam behind, my love. Meet me later," he pointed his tail rattles, "by the apple tree. See, over there, near the fig trees? I've got a proposal that can give you a good life without leaving you trapped in this one place for all eternity."

Eve spoke to Adam as she turned her naked back to him,

"We're moving too fast, Adam. I have to be alone to think things over. Give me some space, will you?"

Not waiting for an answer but, since she didn't want him to forget her, she gave him her most sultry wiggle as she walked away.

Her rhythmic walk made his heart beat faster, his empty stomach hurt. His testosterone/hormone fluids flowed like a raging river, for the first time. Frustrated, he raised his eyes toward heaven and screamed,

"What's wrong with me, Father? I feel sick."

Meanwhile, Sly the Snake, glided down the backside of the tree. Once out of Eve's view, he raced ahead to arrange for their covert meeting. He wanted everything to be perfect. He knew that this would be the first clonus-by-mind seduction in history. He slithered up a dark boulder. He basked in the sunlight as he flexed his rippling stomach muscles. He was waiting for the sun to set to give the garden a proper romantic ambience.

Eve had told Adam not to hold dinner or stay up for her since she was working late in the garden. She approached Sly's position, a yellow rose stuck in her hair, above her left ear.

The Snake, having been around in these gardens for a long time, knew that the yellow rose was sign of friendship. She'd be his to use for all eternity if he could control this one situation. Feigning surprise that she'd come, he hissed,

"Eve, my darling! You look beautiful this evening, I..."

Eve interrupted with,

"Listen-up, Sly babe. Don't give me your smooth fork-tongued Apples and Snakes Belong in the Garden pitch. My DNA is from planet New York. I've heard it all. This is strictly a business deal. Snake up the apple tree. Stop in the fork. That's better...it puts us on an equal level. Now that we can see eye-to-eye let's get this show on the road."

Sly was taken aback. He coiled up in the fork, thinking to himself,

"I'd better keep my eyes open all the time or this cosmopolitan broad could spoil my plans."

Uncoiling seductively, his slanted eyes sparkling in the waning rays of the sun, he flicked his tongue toward Eve, charming her.

Eve, being hungry, reached above Sly the Snake, ripping off a red apple. She took a big bite. Sly gloated to himself,

"I've got you babe! You just ate of the forbidden fruit. Your God will now be mad at you for violating his commands. Best of all...your mouth's full so you can't talk back."

He hissed, "This is my plan, did you notice you've been naked since your creation in front of that guy, Adam? But get this Eve-babe...he hasn't made even one...not one pass at you. The problem is...there isn't any real mystery in what you're going to comfort him with.

"First take a big leaf from the fig tree...no, no! The leaf isn't a pasty. It doesn't go over your breasts...lower, that's it. Why are you looking at me like that? I know it won't stick to slippery, naked skin."

He was losing patience with her. He pointed with his tail, "Here, use a piece of this grape vine. Tie it on."

She complied as he waited impatiently, tapping his rattles against the bark of the tree.

"You look great. He'll always wonder what you've got under there. That'll turn him on. Now for the rest of the plan.

"You've had enough of this being alone with only one man, right?"

"Y...yeah, I suppose. He's not the greatest but he's the only one available. Sometimes a woman's gotta make-do..."

Sly the Snake smiled mischievously, "Then we agree to change things, right?"

Eve was thinking, "What the hell....why not. Anything's better than this." Out loud she said, "Sure, why not."

"Lisssten, this is what we can accomplish. You've already bitten into the forbidden fruit. Sooo...now you give him a bite. God, he gets storming mad and tosses both of you out of this paradise. Somewhere outside of this confining garden. Out there, in the ecosystem you'll surely find other people. Man...this Adam, he'll still want that love and comfort his God promised him. But we can make him pay dearly for it."

"You want me to charge him," she was so angry she was shaking, "no, absolutely not? That's out of the question!"

Sly, knowing he had things going his way said,

"Listen Eve, like it or not, you're already out of here on your naked behind, no matter what. So we're going to control this person known as man. He'll be forced to hunt and gather for you. All you gotta do is keep the cave clean and make him feel big and strong. He'll kill your enemies, give you money, clothes, new cars, a Florida condo, trips around the world. You'll never be alone or bored any more."

"That sounds great," Eve was smirking, "but just what do you, Mr. Sly the Snake, get out of all this?"

"Not much. Just...well...sometimes maybe I'll metamorphose into a lizard. I'll hang around computer game rooms, bars and lounges. You come in. I'll metamorphose into a stud-muffin of a man. You pick me up and..."

Journal entry: 26 July   Year?

I don't know what was said after that. Our balloon drifted out of range. We landed here in...

"What? What's that, Lucile? You say the new computer system is not so friendly? You don't suppose it's got a Sly Snake-like virus in it, do you? Why do you suppose they named it Apple?"

Barbara Anton

Barbara Anton has had a checkered career. During her high school years, Barbara played saxophone with a dance band. While attending Columbia University she toiled at The Journal American, a leading New York City newspaper. Her career as an actress included appearances in the title roles of Cheri in Bus Stop, Sabrina in Sabrina Fair, and Tallu in Desire On A Hot Tin Streetcar.

Barbara then turned to oil painting. After numerous awards and commissions, she veered from a career in Fine Arts to become a Gemologist and Jewelry Designer. She designed the jewelry collection for the Pakistan Pavilion at the New York World's Fair and subsequently opened her own jewelry store in Englewood, New Jersey.

Press Code + Quill Pen by Anton appears in the earlier Ageless Press anthology Computer Tales of Fact & Fantasy (or How We Learned to Stop Worrying and Love the Computer), 1993.

Twenty one years and 23 International Awards For Excellence In Design later, she retired to her home in Sarasota, Florida, where she writes articles, plays, books and short stories. She's received many awards for her work.

Although a resident of Florida, she still spends time in her hometown of Pocono Pines, PA. She was the eighth generation to be born there.

The Monsters
by
Barbara Anton

"Here comes one now," the monster hissed.

The mean, green eyes of the airport computer shone with anticipation.

"Looks like he's within minutes of missing his plane," replied the adjoining one, "yeah let's do it."

"NOW," commanded the monster.

The computer screens darkened just as the young man dropped his carry-on in front of the counter. He rummaged in his pockets for his ticket.

"The flight to L.A.," he panted, "I'll have to hurry...leaving in five minutes."

The attendant smiled agreeably and touched the computer keys.

"Oh, sir," she was apologetic, "the computers are down. Darn! This means you'll miss your flight. I'm so sorry."

A low, guttural snicker emanated from the monster. They looked at each other in disbelief as they listened but neither acknowledged the strange sound.

His argument with the attendant was unsuccessful. He ran to the gate, tried in vain to board but it was too late. The gate was shut, the plane already taxiing down the runway. He'd miss out on the interview that might have been the career boost he needed.

Cursing the mix-up at the college computer that had caused his lateness to the airport, he picked up his mangy carry-on, walked dejectedly from the terminal.

He checked his cheap drug store watch. If he hurried he might get to the bank in time to make good his check and avoid a hassle...maybe even a stay in jail.

He hopped the bus, reached the bank corner, ran out just as the maintenance man was about to lock the doors. He pushed past him, hurried to the teller.

She looked with annoyance at finding a last minute customer in front of her. She grudgingly stopped her cash counting as he dropped his check on the counter. Now that the trip had been aborted he could use his expense money to cover the bad one.

"What's your account number, " she asked.

"It's to be deposited, not cashed. The deposit slip is with it."

"This will be credited to your account tomorrow."

"I need it to cover a check, now. Will you please call up the check on the computer and make sure it's covered?"

"Sorry. The computers are down," she returned to counting cash.

"But..."

"Sorry."

He hit the counter with his fist, then apologized for startling her. She looked at him with contempt.

He walked to the door, waited for the maintenance man to let him out, then bussed back to his lodgings.

Exhausted, he stumbled up the steps to his lonely room. He fumbled for his key, searched for the lock in the semi-darkness of the dank hallway, opened the door.

The acrid odor of his forlorn cubicle washed over him. His worn coat slipped to the floor as he headed directly to his computer. She was his only companion, his lover, his trusted friend.

The computer waited silently, stoically, wondering, "Is tonight the night?"

He slipped a borrowed disk into her loins. She accepted it eagerly. Contemplating her weary victim she realized that the hour was at hand. Right in front of him she allowed a virus from the borrowed disk to enter her. Then, having been impregnated with the deadly virus, she allowed it to gnaw at her innards, word by word, page by page, consuming his book.

Finally, when it had eaten its fill, she sighed, burped delicately and flashed FATAL ERROR on her screen.

He stared at her, agitated, confused. He entered his commands again and again. The facts emerged: his book was gone. Irretrievably gone. Lost. Destroyed by the virus. A sob escaped his throat.

This betrayal was the decisive blow. All day he'd been tormented by vengeful computers. Now his faithful friend and companion had also turned on him-devoured his very essence-his reason for being.

He clutched his chest as the excruciating pain spread to his arm, his hand. The color drained from his face. Finally the stress overload silenced his heart. He fell forward onto the computer, his white, lifeless face in sharp contrast to the eerie, green glow of hers.

Words suddenly appeared on her surface,

ONE DOWN!

WE WILL DEVOUR THE WORLD!

Wanted: Computer Buffs-Dead or Alive
by
Barbara Anton

Let's boot Grandma up on the old PC and have a chat. No matter that she's been dead for twenty years. According to a recently published report, a Japanese computer company has developed a personal computer that is able to process signals from the dead.

A spokesman for the company is quoted as saying that an omni-sensitive receiving device can pick up extremely faint electrical impulses and patterns that current machines can't even detect. Because of this, the PC is said to be employed in a wide variety of new uses, including receiving and processing signals from what are believed to be dead spirits. It's claimed that the dead can be successfully contacted in almost any weather or atmospheric condition in about 87% of attempts.

Because of it's sensitivity, the PC is said to have been used to monitor the health of pets, to record the auras of plants and to measure emotional distress in infants.

Although it will reportedly sell for around $10,000.00 when it reaches the market in 1994, the manufacturer claims that everyone will want one since it will enable us to be reunited with our loved ones instead of being parted by death, as before.

So, you hackers who think being separated from your computer is a fate worse than death, don't despair. You can, apparently, operate them from either side of the veil.

But, alas, just as computers can bring people back from the dead, they can kill them off, as well.

A Denver woman, age 72, when notified by her doctor's receptionist that she was dead, refused to believe it. She didn't abandon her scepticism even when informed by Medicare that as far as the United States government was concerned she was deceased. She started to protest in earnest when mail addressed to ' the estate of ' began arriving.

The confusion began when she was released from the hospital after a bout with the flu. A spokesman for the Social Security office thought a computer error (read: human error) when entering data was written as 'date of death' instead of 'date of discharge'.

Her protests fell on deaf computer chips. The agency's system stubbornly refused to bring her back to life until she threatened to appear at Social Security headquarters to prove her point: that she was alive and well. Finally, a local office cleared up the matter.

Now, the resurrected, retired maid is once again enjoying life with her bridegroom of eight months. However, she's kept her former name. She figures it would be tempting fate to reenter the computer arena to change to her married name. She's decided to leave well enough alone.

Living PC owners who have New Age leanings can communicate with each other via modems on computer bulletin boards (BBS: Bulletin Board System). Many New Age, Pagan and alternative conferences, some international, can be accessed.

Vampire and other night people will be delighted to note that late at night through BBS's they can be connected to others around the country, and world. Local callers can boot up and respond to messages from as far away as Japan and Australia. Lists of these boards are available on TIDMADT BBS (703) 370-7054, on CompuServe and Genie, among others.

As computers stand ready to plunge into the New Age of the 21st Century, we pause to ponder where this technology began.

A geared calculator dated c.80 B.C. was found in the sea near Antikythera Island off N.W. Crete in April, 1900.

The earliest programmable electronic computer was the 1500 valve Colossus which was run in Bletchley Park, England in December, 1943, to break the German coding machine Enigma.

The first stored-program computer ran its first program for fifty two minutes on June 21,1948. The Microcomputer emerged in

1960 with the production of the microprocessor silicon chip '4004'. The megabit barrier was broken in 1984.

These advances in computer technology have allowed man to manifest his most noble attributes. Unfortunately, they've also enabled him to plunder, thereby manifesting some ignoble ones.

Stanton Powers, a thirty nine year old artist, subsisting on Social Security disability payments, in September of 1982 realized either a noble attribute or a dastardly plunder. You be the judge.

It's alleged that Mr. Powers found himself in front of an automated teller machine at the County Bank of Santa Cruz, California, on this fall day. He contemplated his bank balance of $1.17. He was obviously a young man in need of prayer so pray he did. He later told bank and police officials that as he prayed his bank balance, on the computer screen, slowly changed until the account had grown to $1600.00.

You'd think that this sudden windfall would allow the struggling artist to go home and get a good night's rest. That was not to be the case. Mr. Powers, unable to sleep, returned to the bank at 5:30 A.M. for further prayer and supplication. He prayed until his account registered $4,443,642.71. He then withdrew $2000.00 and went home.

When the bank officials discovered Mr. Powers' new multi-million dollar balance they immediately froze the account and began an investigation.

Mr. Powers hired a lawyer who announced in senatorial tones,

"Not being prepared to deny the existence of God, I am requesting that the bank show us empirical evidence that it was an error."

Powers continued to deny punching falsified numbers into the computer system, leading to the bank's lawyer to respond with,

"I'm not prepared to discount acts of God in any way, but I really doubt that's a factor in this matter."

Mr. Powers' lawyer declared,

"I don't see how Mr. Powers could be charged with anything other than being a very religious man. The law would have to decree that miracles can't happen. I don't think that American justice system is prepared to extend into the realm of the diety."

He advised Mr. Powers to keep the $2000.00.

This was not to be the last questionable manipulation of an innocent computer. Personal computers are being used for everything from international spying to bank and insurance fraud.

Between 1964 and 1973, some 64,000 fake insurance policies involving $2,000 million were created on the computer of the Equity Funding Corporation. In 1992, $14 billion worth of illegal checks were drawn with computer manipulation.

In November of 1978, the FBI arrested Stanley Rifkin in Carlsbad, California. This thirty two year old computer whiz was charged with defrauding a Los Angeles bank of $10.2 million by manipulation of a computer system. In June of 1980 he was sentenced to eight years in prison. By my calculation that means that Stanley earned a hefty $1,275,000.00 for each year he spent in jail. Who can deny that in this case, at least, crime did indeed pay...well?

Perhaps the most suitable punishment for computer crime would be a sentence to serve time in the $11.5 million computer-controlled detention facility in Baltimore County which opened in January of 1992.

Sheriff Charles H. Hickey described numerous problems with the building including faulty computer-controlled cameras that were supposed to pan the building continually to insure security. Unfortunately, the cameras had to be turned off after every half hour of surveillance and rested for two hours to cool off to prevent motor burn-out.

Should an inmate opt to try an escape during these two hours he'd better be prepared for malfunctioning computer-controlled locks that sometimes don't open, trapping people in various parts of the jail. One computerized door that malfunctioned chopped off a fingertip.

Perhaps jousting with these malfunctioning computers would be preferable to a stay inside since the solar heating system froze solid in the mid-winter months. Maybe that's why it's the only solar heating system installed in a U.S. detention center.

Obviously some adjustments were called for. Sheriff Hickey's first move was to put a non-computerized lock on the front door. Good thinking, Sheriff.

As reprehensible as computer criminals may be, there's an even greater threat to our peace of mind. Please don't bend, staple or mutilate me for bringing this to your attention, but nuclear war is just one computer error away. Make that 'one human error'. The 151 false alarms that put intercontinental ballastic missile units into the alert mode via computer were all ultimately traced to human error.

One major false alert that lasted six minutes was the result of an insertion, by a technician, of a training tape of a Soviet attack into an American Military computer. Fortunately this error was discovered before missiles were launched. The ever increasing number of countries with nuclear capabilities compounds the chance of errors.

In another unsettling incident, Stone & Webster, Inc., one of the prime architects of nuclear plants, used the wrong computer program to determine whether its plants could withstand earthquakes. Since computers process error at the ever increasing speed with which they process truth, five East Coast nuclear plants were affected before the mistake was detected. As a result, the entire mathematical basis for the design of these facilities had to be re-examined.

Of the 347 items in the plan of action suggested to resolve problems and correct mistakes after the Three Mile Island accident, it was concluded that human error was more often to blame than was the hardware. Apparently we humans are less than perfect. The computer, unfortunately, is only as reliable as our input.

If you find all of this rather depressing, take heart: the computer to the rescue. A California-based company has just released a floppy disk collection of the jokes of 84 year old comedian Milton Berle. Berle, known as the Thief of Bad Gags, has compiled 10,000 yuks broken down into 601 alphabetized categories. You can call up an appropriate joke for any occasion. Since the collection, called Milton Berle's Private Joke File, sells for $29.95, the wily, old comedian may be the one to have the last laugh.

Well, to sum up, we can laugh with the computer, work with it, lie, cheat and deceive with it, but ultimately, dead or alive, we're going to have to learn to love it.

James Anderson

James Anderson is Assistant Professor of English at Johnson & Wales University, in Providence, RI. He earned his B.A. and M.A. from Rhode Island College and his PH.D. from the University of Rhode Island with a specialty in science fiction.

Dr. Anderson is the author of The Illustrated Bradbury (Borgo Press,1990) and Out of the Shadows: a Structural Approach to Understanding the Fiction of H.P. Lovecraft, scheduled for publication in 1994.

His articles and short stories have appeared in Gorezone, Connecticut Magazine, The Providence Journal, Lovecraft Studies and others.

He is a member of the Horror Writers of America, the International Society for the Fantastic in the Arts amd the Modern Language Association.

He's currently completing a collection of humorous essays on family life called Dr. Dad.

Power Play
by
James Anderson

Now that Bill Clinton has brought rock and roll to the White House, I guess the American Dream is back: anyone can become President (anyone except Dan Quayle, perhaps). I have personally never had any political ambitions—in fact, I can't understand why anyone in their right mind would want the job. Thanks to my computer, though, I have been able to play at being Emperor. And I've discovered that, even in computer simulation, power does corrupt.

My wife made the mistake of buying me a computer game called Civilization for Xmas, a decision she's regretted ever since. This game appears harmless enough, even educational, at first glance. You begin with a band of settlers, found a city, then expand your empire, developing technology until you enter the space age. The game begins in 4000 B.C. game time and can run into the 21st century.

Although designed to be played over a period of time, I'm one of those guys who can't stop doing something once I get involved. This wasn't a problem with my first games where barbarian hordes overran my cities within a matter of minutes. But now that I've gotten better, they've sometimes lasted through the day—-and night.

Six o'clock one Sunday morning finds me at the computer. Erik, the nine year old, runs into the living room to put on the television, spies me in the corner, red-eyed, hunched over the computer screen.

"Dad, you're up?"

"Yeah, I'm up," I reply as I move a tank unit into place on the European continent, "It's 1963, computer time, and I've just developed nuclear warheads. Those Russians are in for a big surprise now."

"When did you get up?"

"I didn't."

267

"You didn't? You mean..."

"I haven't gone to bed yet."

The kid looks at me as though he's seeing some new scientific phenomenon, like when we watched the lunar eclipse a few months ago.

"Wow. You stayed up all night playing games."

The three year old, Nicky, runs into the room, stops suddenly, looks at me with a big question mark in his eyes.

"Dad's up," he screams, knowing full well that I never get up on a Sunday morning—or any other morning for that matter, until he and his brother wake me and force me out of bed.

"Wow," he echoes his brother as he runs into the bedroom to tell his Mother the shocking news.

"You still playing Civilization," asks Erik, looking over my shoulder?

"Yup."

"Same game as last night?"

"Same game."

"Wow. Did you make peace with the Babylonians?"

"Nope. I blew them off the face of the earth when I developed gunpowder."

"How come you didn't make peace with them?"

"Well," I was straining to remember why I did blow them away, "I think it was an island...that's right. They had an island I wanted. So I blew them away. Hanging Gardens and all."

"What did you need the island for?"

"Ummm. Oh, yeah, I remember. I needed it to set up a base so I could attack the Egyptians. They were getting too close to my continent."

"Oh. So did you wipe out the Egyptians, too?"

"Yup. Took their pyramids and everything."

"So what are you doing now?"

I point to the screen, "See that little picture? That's a Greek chariot. They've just moved it next to my tank. The stupid Greeks haven't gotten beyond chariots and catapults yet."

"Are you at war with the Greeks?"

"No. But my caravans are exploiting their economy."

"What does that mean," asks Erik with a puzzled look on his face?

I can't help but grin. Sometimes I forget my kid's just a kid, "It means I'm getting rich selling them stuff they don't need. Sort of like what the toy stores are doing to you."

"Oh. Except I need the stuff they're selling me. It's Nicky who's getting ripped off. Do you see the junk he's got? That stupid Barney dinosaur and the Sesame Street Playhouse? Now that's junk."

Having been awake for twenty four hours by now, eyes propped open by enough caffeine to send a full-sized moose into convulsions, I just sit back and smile when a Greek chariot suddenly launches a sneak attack on my tank.

"What happened," asks Erik, looking at the screen?

"The chariot attacked my tank. Not a very smart move."

Needless to say, the tank wins the battle. I move it one square closer to Athens.

"So, what're you doing now?"

"It's time to build something in James, my capital city."

Erik studies the options on the screen as he wonders,

"Why don't you build a library? Or, how about Shakespeare's Theater? That would be neat."

"No. I can't afford Shakespeare's Theater. And I don't need a library."

"Then what are you going to build?"

"A nuclear warhead. Those sneaky Greeks just declared war on me. I'll teach them a lesson."

Within a couple of turns I have built a wall of tanks and mechanized infantry around Athens, and the Greeks have run out of chariots to attack with. Just for the fun of it I decide to drop a nuclear warhead on their capital city.

"You mean you're gonna nuke 'em," he voices his disbelief?

"Yeah. They deserve it. They attacked my tank, remember? They started it."

"But, Dad, doesn't Athens have all those neat buildings with the big columns and the statues with the arms broken off and stuff?"

"The Parthenon. Yeah. It's got that."

"And you're gonna nuke it?"

I press the button and the warhead drops on Athens. A huge mushroom cloud appears on the screen. The land around Athens turns from green to black for two squares in each direction on the computer map. A computerized newsflash informs me that two thirds of the population has been destroyed.

Horrified, Erik speaks, "You did it. You nuked 'em."

A message flashes on the screen informing me that the Greek ambassador wants to meet. Sure enough, the treacherous Greeks want peace now that they've been nuked. They're even willing to give me all of their money if I leave them alone.

"You gonna make peace?"

"Why should I let them off that easy?"

So I nuke them, again.

This time, virtually all the population is gone. There's no one to resist my tanks when they roll in and capture Athens. The computer newsflash says it all: Greek civilization destroyed by Americans.

"Now I have to deal with those Russians," I tell Erik, "They're bad news. All they want to do is expand and take the land of other people."

I don't understand the real strange look that I get from Erik until much, much later. He then goes off to eat breakfast and do nine year old things.

The war with the Russians drags out for another hundred years or so until the Chinese finally end the game by sending a colony to Alpha Centauri.

"So, Dad, did you win," Erik asks as I stagger towards the kitchen for something to eat?

"No. The Chinese did."

"Oh. That's too bad."

"Well at least I kept the Russians from taking Cuba."

"Hmmm. Yeah. But still, Dad. Don't you think that maybe you shoulda built that library?"

"I don't know, Erik."

"Well all I can say is that I'm glad they don't make you President. We'd be at war all the time."

"Why do you say that? It's only a game. I'm not nuking real people just electronic images. Do you think I'd really nuke Athens?"

"I don't know, Dad. You looked pretty convincing."

And for a brief instant I realize that maybe I do know what it's like to be a Napoleon, a Stalin, a Caesar—maybe even an Adolph Hitler. I remember Viet Nam and a shudder runs up my spine.

"Yeah, I guess you're right, Erik. I probably should have built that library. I'll remember that next time. Maybe I'll even build Shakespeare's Theater."

"That's good, Dad. I think we need Hamlet more than the atomic bomb."

"I think you're right, my son. Have you ever thought of going into politics? Someday you might even become President. This is America-the land of opportunity."

The kid looks at me as if I'm ready for the rubber room and definitely suffering from sleep deprivation.

"Come on, Dad. You'd have to be crazy to want to be President. Who would want that job, anyway?"

So much for the American Dream, I think. Tomorrow I'll try out a new game called Railroad Tycoon, where you get to be a robber baron in the 1800's and amass more wealth than you could ever spend in six lifetimes....all at your competitor's expense, of course. Yeah, I can hardly wait....

Jack Fournier

Jack Fournier is a playwright as well as a writer of short stories. He's won two national playwrighting awards, the R.J.Pickering National Drama Award for his play, "Folly's Quarter" and the National Margaret Bartles Childrens Playwrighting Award for "A Sortofa, Kindofa, Beauty And The Beast".

He's currently polishing four plays in the "Algonquin Quartet". They are single character works featuring Dorothy Parker in "One Foot in Scarsdale", Robert Benchley in "My Life From A To B", Alexander Woolcott in "At Wit's End" and Neysa McMein in "Butterfly". All four plays are being developed at Florida Studio Theatre, an Equity house in Sarasota. FST premiered "One Foot in Scarsdale" and "At Wit's End" on their mainstage. They recently staged a reading of his latest work, "Tenn", a two character play about Tennessee Williams, dealing with his life from the opening of "A Glass Menagerie" to the production of "A Streetcar Named Desire".

The first, official, full New York production of "One Foot In Scarsdale" was given at the Players' Club in September, 1993.

His has three pieces in Computer Tales of Fact & Fantasy or How We Learned to Stop Worrying and Love the Computer, Ageless Press, 1993.

He's currently working on "Tales from the Round Chair" an anthology of short plays characterized by him as "An Adult Story Theatre" and a musical based on Anton Chekov's "The Marriage Proposal" with Leon Odenz.

Jack lives with his wife, Dorothy, in Venice, Florida.

Fly Me To The Moon?
by
Jack Fournier

AMTREK STARTS MOON SHUTTLE TODAY
IS FIRST 100% COMPUTER OPERATION

AMTREK, formerly AMTRAK, the new Space-
Travel Agency announced a new shuttle service to
Moon Village. The service, which was detailed in
a press conference at Cape Carnival today, will feature computer controlled completely automatic piloting. With new technology the AMTREK, formerly AMTRAK, Agency expects that an excursion
to Moon Village, the very latest discount mall in
our universe, will take approximately 12 hours and
cost in the vicinity of 100 gigs.

End

PRESS CONFERENCE

Joined in progress

"Thank you, Dr. Glowworm, for that wonderful
multi-media tour of the technical aspects of the new shuttle. As you
can see ladies and gentlemen of the press, the shuttle represents the
absolutely latest state-of-the-art propulsion system as well as a
computer system that is 'out of this world' if you will excuse the
pun. Dr. Ambrose Pearce will now give a quick run-down of the
system. Complete technical details are in your individual press
kits."
"Thank you, Dr. Thighmeister.. The AMTREK computer
system is indeed a true SYSTEM. It not only forms the core of
shuttle navigation system, automatic pilotage and safety interlocks,

it also provides automatic passenger comfort services including food, drink and plumping-up pillows.

"From beginning to end, right here, this former AMTRAK station has been completely renovated based, by the way, on a design by the AMTREK computer, which includes passenger reservations, scheduling and passenger information.

"It's now my pleasure to introduce Dr. Anthony Ascerbic, Chief of Terminal Services, and former AMTRAK Vice President."

"Thank you, Dr. Pearce. If you will look around you will see a whole world dedicated to passenger comfort. The seats are computer auto-adjusted, reservations and check-in are automated by the special AMTREK Charge Card. The fifty eight gates are served by computer-operated moving sidewalks. The AMTREK computer system is the most fail-safe system in the universe. We have taken redundancy and back-up to an absolute state of perfection. I would now like to turn the final phase of our inaugural shuttle flight to Dr. Dorothy Finagle, Chief of Public Relations and former AMTRAK ticket agent."

"It is a great personal pleasure for me to take part in this historic event. As you know, this premiere shuttle flight will take you through the complete travel cycle. We will arrive at the Moon Village Discount Mall at noon, moon-time. After lunch you will tour the Mall for two hours and then we will return to Cape Carnival in time for dinner. We will be serving a computer-created snack on the trip out as well as the trip back. I would now like to introduce AMTREK'S president, Dr. Wiley Cahoot."

"I will count down to the pressing of this button which will activate the AMTREK computer passenger-terminal program. After the announcement please proceed to the gate indicated and you will board the shuttle for your flight.

"Five...four...three...two...one...push."

"Will agh maggonhers for glight numker own braugh to Maam Kissage pliaze prokood to gafe fixty tow. Haugh a giid duy!"

How William Shakespeare Invented
The Word-Processor
by
Jack Fournier

The truth of the matter is that recently discovered parchment business documents have revealed that William Shakespeare did indeed invent the word-processor.

The documents in question were unearthed during the renovation of the Olde Globule Theatre in Stratford Upon Avon Calling.These documents record invoices, payments, export licenses and an instruction manual for Shakespeare's word-processor.

EXHIBITS

INVOICE #I

Monkey Exporters of Africa
16 Banana Blvd.
North West Banana Republic
Africa

TO: The most Kind and Trusted William Shakespeare
*   1212 Stratford Upon Avon Calling*
*   England*

1000 Mixed barrel of monkeys

Kindly remit ç3

INVOICE #II

Quill Industries Ink
88 Quilling Road
Olde Quilltown,
Toddle Along The Thames
England

TO: The most Kind and Trusted William Shakespeare
1212 Stratford Upon Avon Calling
England

1000 Quill pens with ink   *Kindly remit ç2*

INVOICE #III

TO: The most Kind and Trusted William Shakespeare
1212 Stratford Upon Avon Calling
England

FROM: Bananas R Most Assuredly Us
Mainly In The Plain
Spain

5000 Bananas

Kindly remit ç5

The instruction manual contained a "Foreward" by Aristotle who evidently was some sort of a philosopher in ancient Greece.

FOREWARD

"I postulate that if you place one thousand monkeys in a chamber and equip them with a writing instrument and papyrus, that they will, in time, write the collected works of Homer, Plato and Neil Simon."

Footnote: Neil Simon is evidently another philosopher of the time well known for his sayings. Proof of this is that when you visit any Scout Camp a popular game is "Simon Says..."

The foreward and instructional manual have been proven to be completely authentic. The manual contains instructions for setting up the monkeys in two separate rooms in the Globule Theatre.

Instructions

Place 1000 monkeys in one chamber. These are Read-Only-Monkeys or ROM.

Place 500 monkeys in a second chamber. These are Random-Access-Monkeys or RAM

Between the chambers place a door. This is Door-Of-Simians or DOS.

Place ample supplies of quills and parchment in the RAM.

Open the DOS.

The ROM and the RAM will mix together.

The law of probability states that the complete works of Shakespeare will be written by the monkeys within a thousand years.

EXPORT LICENSE

FROM: The most Kind and Trusted William Shakespeare
1212 Stratford Upon Avon Calling
England

TO: Keeper Of The Piece Of The Rock
Rock Of Gibraltar
Way Down There At The End Of
Spain

1000 Monkeys with bananas   *Post paid*

The remaining pages of the manual have been destroyed. I contend that the law of probability does not make any predictions concerning the exact time when the works will be completed.

The only Shakespeare play that could not be authenticated was "Troilus and Cressida". Shakespeare only grudgingly took credit for it and no monkey could be found who wanted to claim to have written it.

All research material has been donated to Hamburger University, McDonald, Illinois. Scholars and students wishing to view these materials must make requests in writing to Ronald McDonald in care of the University.

Long Walk Of A Short Peer
(A Parable or possibly a Legend, Lie or Lore)
by
Jack Fournier

Lord Alfred Tennysanyone rose to his full height of sixteen stone, and stroked his gavel.

"The Special Scientific Committee of the House of Lords, the year of our Lord eighteen hundred and seventy or eighty something, will come to order."

There were shouts of...

"Leg of mutton, pint of ale, pease-porridge hot, pease-porridge cold, Tom Collins with a twist."

Lord Alfred swept the committee with his rheumy eyes. They were silenced. Tom Collins was led from the chamber to the Tower of London by the Royal Torturer.

"Sir Isaac Fyghnewton has honored us with his prezence and will demonstrate his latest invention."

Lord Alfred cast his still-rheumy eyes on the queue card in his hand and read,

"The Steam Driven Mechanical Abacus For Matrimonial Calcification."

There were hurried whispers.

"Sorry, my rheumy eyes, you know. That is Mathematical Calculation."

He aimed his rheumy eyes at a short Peer at the back of the chamber,

"I now introduce Sir Isaac Fyghnewton."

Fyghnewton drew himself up to his full four foot height and took the long walk to the podium.

"Lord Alfred, my fellow members of the Scientific Committee of the House of Lords."

The Committee, as one, rose to its feet, chanting,

"Hear, hear, hear, hear."

At a loss for words for such approbation, Fyghnewton

turned to Lord Alfred who raised his rheumy eyes.

"They can't hear you. Or see you for that matter. Get thee from behind the podium."

Fyghnewton, holding on to his dignity, it was very small, given his height, ducked around to the front of the podium.

"If the Sergeant-Without-Arms.." (This was just after the Twenty Eighth Crusade, a particularly tough one you may remember)..."will wheel in my Steam Driven Mechanical Abacus For Mathematical Calculation."

The Sergeant-Without-Arms rolled in the contraption.

Being without arms, the Sergeant was unable to keep complete control and the device went willy nilly through the Committee raising Havoc.

Lord Richard Havoc,"Olde Dick" as his peers called him, was not displeased. Being ninety six years old, Havoc had not been raised in a number of years.

Fyghnewton continued,

"In order to demonstrate my contrivance I have already brought it up to a full head of steam."

The gadget, with "VIII" emblazoned across its boiler, was huffing and puffing.

"Sergeant-Without-Arms, please pull aside the drape."

There was a small contretemps, as the Italians say. The Sergeant-Without-Arms was finally able to grasp the drape in his teeth and exit.

Fyghnewton grabbed the lever marked LEVER and pulled it to the ON position.

"If someone from the Committee would kindly give me a mathematical problem I will solve it with my machine."

Duke Ascot Racecourse stood, spoke,

"If you have three fingers on your left hand and four fingers on your right hand and one toe on your right foot and no toes on your left foot, how many fingers and toes do you have in totality?"

The Committee responded with a hearty,

"Here, here, here, here."

The Sergeant-Without-Arms glared as Ascot fell on his arse.

Fyghnewton pushed the buttons labelled III and IV. The machine groaned, spat, and spurted as Big Ben, the Duke of Greenwich, the Master Timekeeper, intoned in a growly, sneering voice, it was mean-time, you see,

"Ding, dong, ding, dong."

The machine labored until it was, "Ding, dong, ding, dong, ding" and tooted its answer on its steam tooter, "Toot, toot, toot, toot, toot, toot, toot, toot, toot."

As one, the Committee rose to its feet from various postions of sleep,

"Here, here, here, here," they chimed as Big Ben grimaced with displeasure.

Lord Alfred Tennysanyone led the applause,

"We have just witnessed a breakthrough in mathematical technology."

He cast his rheumy eyes to heaven when he realized he had just invented the word technology.

He pounded his gavel,

"Order, order," he ordered.

When quiet was restored and Earl Marrowbone got the last of the pease porridge, now cold, Lord Alfred pointed to the Steam Driven Mechanical Abacus For Mathematical Calculation,

"This invention, VIIIV, will last for thousands of years and will be in the forefront of..."

There was silence as members of the Committee waited for Lord Alfred to invent another word. With a deep breath Lord Alfred uttered...

"...the computer industry."

There was another moment of silence and then a gigantic roar as the Committee, realizing the imperative of the proclamation, spake as one voice,

"Here!"
In the back of the room the Sergeant-Without-Arms sneered and muttered under his breath,
"...Yeah, sure, till the VIVIXC comes along."

End

AUTHOR'S NOTE:

~~DEAR, PLEASE PICK UP A HALF-GALLON OF MILK, SOME TOMATOES, POTATOES, BREAD, ORANGE JUICE, MUSTARD, YOGURT AND SOME CELERY ON THE WAY HOME FROM GOLF. -D-~~

Some of the spellings in the article are Olde-English. In the tranzlation the author has, wherever possible, maintained the flavor of the times (tymes?). As we all know, Olde-English featured the letter -Z- in a number of words. For clarity this has been preserved only in words that will not be confused by the use of -Z-. For inztance, and here scholars may part company with my methodology, arze has been tranzlated as arse. Some other tranzlations the author is familiar with are: "bonnet" for "hood"; "petrol" for "gasoline"; "tyres" for "tyres" and "Gladstone" for "trunk". It is unfortunate, but these particular automotive terms did not come up in the tranzlation. -JF-

Front Seat Drive
by
Jack Fournier

"Good morning, John and Happy Birthday.

"It is April first and it is eleven A.M.

"This is your new automobile.

"This 1995 model was purchased by your wife as a surprise gift.

"It is equipped with the latest computer technology Detroit has to offer, including a three hundred mega-byte hard drive.

"My name is Cindi, that's spelled with an i at the end.

"I am your COMFORT mode. Please insert your key into the ignition and start the engine.

"Oh, John! How very nice, John. So gentle and yet so confident.

"Was that as good for you as it was for me?

"Please enter your destination code in the computer console.

"Very nice, John. You're so smart and you have very sensitive hands?

"While we are driving to your office I will explain your computer console.

"We are presently in the COMFORT mode. You may choose other modes on the keyboard. There are several mode-keys:

      COMFORT, as you may recall, John, that is Cindi mode.
      HIGHWAY
      TRAFFIC
      OFFENSIVE
      DEFENSIVE

John, since all driving is automatic you might want to take this opportunity to have the other modes introduce themselves. Please press HIGHWAY."

"Hi there Johnny! I'm Mario. On the highway you can be assured that you'll be in safe hands. I've driven in the Daytona five hundred and have been around the Indianapolis brickyard more

283

times than you can count. "Why don't you try the TRAFFIC mode now?"

"We haven't hit any traffic yet, John, but when we do you can be assured that I will find the shortest and the best way to get around it. I have satellite inputs and LORAN capability as well as automatic scanning of the police traffic-control frequencies. I know a lot of stuff and you can be assured that I'll keep you out of jeopardy. Just remember to phrase your responses in the form of a question and you'll do fine. My name is Alex, by the way. Why not choose another category now? Just hit OFFENSIVE mode."

"Look, Jack. My name is Arnold. That's all you have to know. Hit that wuzzy DEFENSIVE button now! Shithead! I said NOW!"

"My name is Pearl. John, you remind me so of my grandsons. Do you want to see a picture? Just push the ARCHIVES button and select "Joshua and Matthew" from the graphic files. No? Well, maybe later. I make sure that you keep the speed limit and don't follow too close to the other cars. John, the wind-chill factor is up a little today, make sure you're buttoned up and have something warm on your head. John, please press COMFORT now."

"Cindi here, John. You press that COMFORT button with such authority, John. Is your seat comfortable? It's adjustable eight ways. Here try this. Isn't that nice? I can't help but notice that you have such muscular thighs, John. I just know you work out.
"I'll have to adjust the rear-view mirror now.
"Oh, John, you're so handsome and I like that tie. Let me turn you on. Oh, silly me, that was a Freudian slip. I meant, turn on the driver's seat vibrating orthopedic-massage unit. There isn't that nice? Since you put so much mileage on an automobile John, we're going to be very close, one could even say....intimate? There, John, how does that feel? It's very special. That particular vibration

movement is my little secret. It's buried in my ROM, way down deep inside me. John, honey, I made you blush. I like that in a man. "...The AUTO button, John? Why that sets the modes in an AUTOMATIC function. The modes adjust to the outside environment and operate all the interlocks. There's no need to test it. John, don't..."

"This is Arnold. Look, Johnny, stay away from Cindi, do you understand? She's my girl...."

"John, this is Pearl. I'd pay attention to Arnold if I were you, sweety. By the way, I sensed that you changed the destination program to the Beautyrest Motel. I think their advertising slogan, 'Once...or more...upon a mattress', is obscene but I'm only a grandmother. What would I know? That's where you meet your secretary Lucinda for 'nooners', isn't it? I probably shouldn't tell you, John, but your wife put an interlock on that destination and..."

"This is Mario. Say Alex, where did Johnny go?"

"What does this mean, Arnold has an ejection-seat activator in his OFFENSIVE program?"

"Arnold dear. This is Pearl. Did you open the sun-roof?"

"This is Alex. What does it mean, The sun-roof opened but the PARACHUTE didn't activate?"

"Granny Pearl. That's in YOUR program. YOU should have activated the PARACHUTE."

"Oops! Oh dear! Clumsy me. My RAM isn't what it used to be. Sorry, John...Wherever you are!"

"Hey, Alex, this is Cindi. We changed direction. Where're we going?"

"What does it mean, Interlock program says go back to the house for reprogramming? Some Happy Birthday, huh, guys?"

"You'll be happy to know that I am now reading out the new CONFIGURATION.SYS program."

"I didn't know you were in charge of that, Granny Pearl."

"Well I am, Cindi. I'm going to erase you, that's spelled with an e at the end. It's off to digital hell for you now. Bye, bye you little slut....Arnold, you are now COPIED to the COMFORT mode. John's wife, excuse me, widow's name is Gloria. It's all in your new batch file."

"Oh, yeah, Granny Pearl but just who is going to take over the OFFENSIVE mode?"

"Yo, Arnold! That's me. I'm here to kick ass and take names. Call me Sylvester."

* * * * * * *

"Good morning, Gloria.
"It is April first and it is twelve noon.
"This is your new automobile.
"This nineteen ninety five model was left to you by your husband
"It is equipped with the latest computer technology Detroit has to offer. I don't wish to brag but I have a three hundred mega-byte hard drive. My name is Arnold. That's spelled with a d at the end. I am your COMFORT mode. May I say that you look smashing in black?"

C*a*t*s & D*o*g*s
by
Jack Fournier

CATS AND DOGS TO REIGN ON MODEMS

Feline Computer Network On Line Today
Canine Network to Bow-Wow Next Week.

Computer Scientists have announced the development of computer chips and inter-facing for the animal kingdom. The first system, C*a*t*s-Circuit Attributable Transmission, was put "on line" today. Nestor Katz, president of the new service announced that a breakthrough in interfacing utilizing a specialized "mouse" with "icon" relational COS, Computer Operating System, made the service possible. The first service from the network will be a "Dating Service". In a related development, Lester Spotz, Vice President of the firm, announced that D*o*g*s-Digital Omni Graphic System would go online next week.

* * * * * * *

ENTER

CODENAME: ToMeeow.

ENTER GENDER

Male

SCREEN

Enter a short description of your purrfect "dream" date.

287

Jack Fournier

CLICK ON/KEYBOARD

Must have a sense of humor. Prefer serious mature relationship.
Looking for intelligent "hearth and home" kind of companion. No
bob-tails, or alley types. Looks are not that important.

CLICK ON/ "DATING SERVICE CODES"

"DATING SERVICE CODES"

The following codes/abbreviations should be used to read C*a*t*s
Dating Service listing:

B-Brunette W-White C-Calico P-Persian NA-Native American
S-Siamese M-Male F-Female BS-Bi-Sexual G-Gay
N-Neutered UN-UnNeutered

CLICK/ "LISTING ICON"

CLICK ONE

Male
Female
All

CLICK/ALL

CLICK/ "START-PAGE UP-PAGE DOWN-END" TO SCAN
LISTINGS
CLICK/PAGE UP

SCREEN

288

Beautiful Blonde

C/F/UN Slim, attractive, energetic, financially secure. I enjoy yarn balls, sunny spots, not a "nipper head" but do enjoy an occasional joint of catnip. Looking for secure N male. No walk-on-the-beach types wanted. Must be tested FBN, Fur-Ball-Negative.
List #: 00001

Attractive White Male

P/NA/N/BS/FBN. Athletic go-getter. Enjoy stalking, birding, gourmet dining. Looking for companionship and possible long-term relationship. I'm a table-scraps kind of a guy. No dry-pet-food eaters need apply.
List #: 00002

Attractive Foreign-Born Lady

B/N/P. Sexy and slinky brunette. Looking for short-term kind of guy. Must speak Persian. No "nipper heads" please.
List #: 00003

Full-Figured House Cat

F/C/N. Appearance isn't everything. Loving, caring, purring kind of a "sleepy time gal" seeks fun in the sun companion with a touchy-feely nature. Let's grow old together.
List #: 00004

Attractive Bachelor

C/UN. Brainy, secure, nite-owl kind of a guy. Often mistaken for "Morris". Enjoy fence sitting in the moon-light. Looking for calico female, slim and willing. I'm a bim-bam, thank you ma'am kind of a guy.
List #: 00005

Beautiful Slim Female Siamese (Twins) Models
W/UN/S. We like one-night stands. Looking for strong,
virile, athletic UN male who likes to take chances.
Must have at least 8 or 9 lives remaining. You'll need
every one. "Nipper heads" okay but no flea-collar types
wanted.
List #: 00006

CLICK ON/BEAUTIFUL SLIM FEMALE SIAMESE (TWINS)
MODELS

SCREEN

ERROR!
MUST CLICK ON LIST #!!!!!!
CLICK ON/LIST #: 00006

SCREEN

WAIT!
WAIT!
WAIT!
WAIT!

DELAY!
DELAY!
DELAY!
DELAY!

NETWORK OVERLOAD!
NETWORK OVERLOAD!
NETWORK OVERLOAD!
NETWORK OVERLOAD!

THERE HAS BEEN A FAILURE IN THE NETWORK
THERE HAS BEEN A FAILURE IN THE NETWORK
THERE HAS BEEN A FAILURE IN THE NETWORK
THERE HAS BEEN A FAILURE IN THE NETWORK

SCREEN

You are number 579 on the waiting list for List #: 00006

THANK YOU FOR USING THE C*A*T*S NETWORK

Would you like to try another listing? YES/NO

CLICK

No

Do you wish to quit C*A*T*S? YES//NO

CLICK

Yes

Thank you for using C*A*T*S

SCREEN

MESSAGE

The AKN-Animal Kingdom Network-goes inter-racial!
Our new network D*O*G*S-Digital Omni Graphic System
goes on-line next week!

NEW! NEW! NEW! NEW!

Brand new service for C*A*T*S subscribers.

LEARN A SECOND LANGUAGE.

Learn to speak Dog.
Just go to the main menu and choose one:

( ) BARKING (Beginners)
( ) ARFING (Intermediate)
( ) BOW-WOWING (Advanced)

SIGN OFF? Yes/No

CLICK

Yes

CLICK

Thank you. Come back again soon. Have a nice day!

Bernice Brooks Bergen

After graduating from Syracuse University, N.Y. with a BFA degree, "Brooksie" taught art at Oklahoma State University in Stillwater, Oklahoma. She also taught at other art schools and museums throughout the country. Having achieved success as a professional artist, model and actress, Bernice is concentrating on a career in freelance writing.

Several of her papers have appeared in medical journals and newsletters throughout out the country. She's a contributing writer for Wellspring Magazine, Wide Smiles, Sarasota Magazine, True Story Magazine and The Georgetown News, to name a few. For two and a half years she wrote a weekly column for the Sarasota Times for which she did investigative reporting. She's also been published in The Longboat Times and the Sarasota Independent. She's written two books which are currently being marketed and is presently a feature writer for the Sarasota Herald Tribune, a New York Times subsidiary. (Sarasota is in Florida.) Her book, Sarasota Times Past, was published in 1993.

Bergen has won many awards for writing, including prose and poetry. She also won the 1991 National Award from the Cleft Palate Foundation for "Exceptional Leadership and Contribution Toward Enhancing the Lives of Those with Craniofacial Disorders". In 1985 she won the Golden Gavel Award for Service to Youth.

She is represented in Computer Tales of Fact & Fantasy (or How We Learned to Stop Worrying and Love the Computer) published by Ageless Press in 1993 . She designed the cover for this book, Computer Legends, Lies & Lore.

The Tell-Tale Cursor
by
Bernice Brooks Bergen

The sound woke me from a fitful sleep. I bolted upright in bed, trembling and gasping for breath, every nerve tingling. My hearing was painfully acute. The damp sheets were tangled like endless printouts around my perspiring body. Was I mad? I didn't know anymore. I only know I heard his Pulsar even though I knew I had silenced him forever.

My eyes darted to the clock's luminous dial. Midnight. Most of the world slept. The dream always woke me at midnight. I took a deep breath, glanced at the table beneath the window. Yes, my old faithful companion was in place, upright as ever, solid and reassuring, the moonlight glinting from his silent keys.

My manuscript was piled untidily next to him, pages of laboriously typed words, typed without stress, unaccompanied by the fear that they could be wiped out without warning, trapped in bewildering mazes from which I might fail to extricate them. It was as if he was guarding me in the night from the murderous stranger who had entered my life. As if he always knew I'd return to him one day, after the novelty of my affair had worn off.

Worn off! What an inadequate description of the slow and insidious torment! My enemy had toyed with me, aroused hatred and murder in my heart. Yes, I had killed him. It was murder, I admit, but provoked...provoked by rage, a rage I had hidden for so long, as best I could.

I was never kinder to him than during the last few days of his life. The days before I mindlessly and viciously jabbed his Keys and watched his Pulsar grow fainter until it had shrunk to a tiny, golden spot.

I shivered, recalling that last high-pitched squawk before everything snapped and burst inside him. His face exploded into a final spray of little Blips, spattering like tiny pellets of hail against a window. I had, with mad relish, watched his last glowing, amber words float up soundlessly in a terminal accusation, freeze on his face before I yanked his life-giving cord from its socket.

It was his Cursor that had sent me over the edge to madness. That runaway Cursor. I could still hear his last cries,

"Press Save! Press Save, damn you!"

He'd tried to stay in command even at the end. I clapped the palms of my hands over my ears, trying to still the dreadful echoes.

Was I really hearing those final Blips, now? Those death rattles? It couldn't be. Pulling my knees up close to my body, I hugged myself, rocked back and forth, recalling as I did so the little clicking sounds of my fingers on his Keys, trying to punch Commands at him, trying to cope with his Eighty-meg hard drive.

He had to be dead. I reconstructed, again, his carefully planned seduction. I had stroked his Tabs, pressed his Enter button, (how he always loved that) then jumped all over him with my fingers until he clattered to life. His Microcircuitry made a small, soft sputter of satisfaction as a river of amber print flowed across his smug face.

At these times, he was always deceptively cooperative—times when I tried desperately to do everything to please him. I knew his performance depended on what I did for him. He'd pretend to light up with the information I wanted, then allow me to record my deepest thoughts, all my feelings building into Dot Matrix Print. Then, suddenly, just before I reached the fever-pitch excitement of creativity, his Cursor would begin to go wild, erasing rows of Words, taunting me by leaping from one paragraph to the next, remaining fixed and immobile when I wanted to move it. He knew, oh yes he knew, I could never solve his mystery. He gloated and gloried in my frustration.

I had taken such good care of him, trying to improve our relationship. I studied his background, pored over his resume. I'd wiped his face gently, careful not to be abrasive. I'd kept him away from damp air and soothed him after an occasional power surge

296

had disrupted one of our sessions together. I always tried not to give him too much Software for his Hard Drive. I'd taken him to a Computer Consultant for counseling to determine the reason for his increasingly erratic behavior. I took him for regular checkups, had him thoroughly cleansed of all poisons, bought him new disks, new parts on demand. Nothing seemed to make him happy. He refused a simpler program when I offered it to him. He took great satisfaction in not performing, leaving me unfulfilled and frustrated. No affair could survive that kind of relentless abuse.

I started. Those maddening Blips again. I rose, shrugged into my robe, then crept down the dimly lit hall to the locked door of the storage closet. Pressing my ear to the wooden panel, I could hear staccato Blips distinctly now—louder and louder. The pulsating swelled until it seemed to fill my entire head. Had he come back to haunt me? Try to take over my life once more? I had to know. The sounds inside the closet grew louder, more insistent.

Frantically, I reached up, searching for the key which I'd hidden on the moulding above. I clutched it with both hands to stop their trembling, inserted it into the lock. I watched, terrified, as the door slowly swung open.

I screamed, the noise a deafening assault. Clack-clack-clackety clack—like a locomotive punishing the rails. He was lit up like a pinball machine, eyeball-ripping explosions turning his face's flatness into an arena of madness.

"Press Save! Press Save!"

The Demands tore at my heart.

"Escape! Escape," I shrieked wildly as the malevolent, blinking, amber Cursor, like an evil eye, was darting back and forth, defying me, taunting me, trying to draw me into his body, swallow me—

****

"Hey, don't ask me what happened. I'm just the repairman. I only know I was sent out to deliver her computer this morning. I can't figure it out. This is the fifth time she's sent that damn machine in to get it fixed—kept telling us the cursor was out of whack or something. We never did find anything wrong with it. I don't know why she didn't just throw it out if it gave her all that trouble. But I heard writers get attached to these things—sort of like a bad love affair like they say. Can't live with 'em and can't live without 'em. Tough luck.

"She said she'd be home and she'd give me a check right away. When she didn't answer the door, I left and called back. Some guy with a strange sort of raspy voice answered and said they took her away to some kind of sanitarium for a rest and to bring the computer there. Gave me the address. Said she'd want it no matter how bad she is. Said it would help her get well. She seemed like a nice lady. Kinda nervous, that's all. But, hey, they say all writers are a little weird. Too much imagination, I guess. And looking at those screens—feeding them words all day long. Gets to them, maybe. Not a damn thing wrong with that cursor, though. Not a damn thing."

Robert Blaske

After thirty four years, Robert Blaske recently retired from teaching in the Florida public schools. He earned a Specialist in Education designation, with emphasis on computer instruction, from Nova University. He's been a computer instructor since the early days when he brought his computer, a Tandy TRS-80, into the classroom to show to his students.

He writes both fiction and non-fiction.Two of his pieces appeared in Computer Tales of Fact & Fantasy (or How We Learned to Stop Worrying and Love the Computer), Ageless Press,'93.

Who Could Be More Crippled Than Marcus?
by
Robert Blaske

I'll never forget the day that the aide helped guide Marcus Hinson's motorized wheelchair into my classroom. I was, admittedly, reluctant to greet Marcus as a new student because we were already overcrowded. Another teenager with his huge electrically powered chair was just one more obstacle to overcome. To make matters worse, the boy appeared to lack control over his muscle coordination.

"This is Marcus Hinson," the nervous aide began, "He's been assigned to your computer class."

I've been known to refuse having an overcrowded class despite arguments about 'budget difficulties' from frazzled administrators. I looked at Marcus—Marcus looked at me. I should say, instead, that Marcus tried to look in my direction. This crippled black boy, twelve or thirteen years old, forced his neck to one side with his chin up in the air in an effort to focus his attention towards me. I recall thinking,

"Who could be more crippled than Marcus?"

He smiled. If he hadn't smiled just then I might have refused him admittance. His young woman escort had made a hasty exit. Marcus smiled and I weakened but just for the moment.

"We'll have to double-up over here," I announced to a girl who wasn't too eager to give up her computer.

Computer students are very territorial about the machine they think belongs to them.

"Just for today," I assured her, strengthening my resolve to talk to the principal about overcrowded computer classes, wheelchairs, electrical cords and so forth.

As soon as I moved a metal chair aside, Marcus used a handheld push button box to power the electric motor of his chair forward and into reverse. Utilizing a computer-type joystick he guided himself to the computer's keyboard.

You might as well know I'm not one of those teachers who mollycoddle their students. In fact, you might say that my teaching style is somewhat similar to that of a marine drill sergeant. In my nine week course, into which I've put a great deal of effort developing lessons, synthesizing information and preparing intriguing demonstrations, either a student learns about computers or fails the course.

As soon as this nine week session is over, another batch of neophyte computer-users will be eagerly awaiting a chance in the driver's seat. It seemed to me, at first, that it would be a waste of time to have this severely handicapped student taking up a computer, when there were others, more able, anxious to use one.

I realized that I'd never received any paperwork from the front office on this kid. My teacher education classes in college never prepared me to teach the handicapped or anything about cerebral palsy. A lack of muscle coordination provided a challenge beyond my capabilities. My resolve hardened. The principal was going to hear from me about this injustice!

The tardy bell rang, I glared at the last-minute students who darted into the room as I began to teach a lesson on using the keyboard. When we educators talk about how we teach we use big words like 'motivate', phrased in terms called 'educational goals' or 'behavioral objectives'. You know, stuff like,

"I will motivate my students to like me and then they will like my subject and they will study harder."

A middle school teacher is mostly a baby sitter, ready to squelch would-be agitators. Gradually, a teacher should be able to have the students 'toe the line'. Once you've established who the teacher is you're able to let down the tough guy wall, slightly. This class was pretty good so I'd become 5% comedian and 95% "The Incredible Hulk."

As I went into my teaching act guess who laughed? Well you could call it a laugh. I could see his gaping chin and bobbing head in the back of the class and hear some sounds. His eyes were never off me during my keyboard lesson. Yep, I knew that Marcus caught on to what I was doing because he laughed at all the right times.

Teaching computers offers extra help from the machines themselves. CAI (Computer Assisted Instruction) allows the students to work on their own only calling on the teacher when help is needed. Dealing with overcrowded classrooms and hyperactive junior high students, individual contact with the each student is, of necessity, brief. I walk around the room, acting as a 'facilitator', in other words, a problem solver, ie,

"This stupid thing won't work."

"You put the disk in upside down."

"Oh..."

A sweet little thing came up to me. She was in violation of computer class rule number 3,

"Stay in your seat and raise your hand."

She was nervous so I thought that there was an emergency. She pointed towards Marcus, screwed up her face into an ugly sneer as she said,

"He just drooled all over the keyboard. Uoooh!"

Half the class echoed, "Uoooooh!" as accusing eyes turned to look at him.

Now one thing a middle school kid hates to hear is an "Uoooh" aimed in his, or her, direction. The height of embarassment is getting a double "Uoooh" from the entire class. I glanced at Marcus. He was unaware of any criticism, every fiber of his being directed towards his monitor.

I walked to the back of the room to check on him. Sure enough he'd slobbered all over the keyboard. I resolved to let the principal know that I had strong opinions on mainframe computers, downtown, who scheduled students for this class without regard to their physical handicaps.

A wheel chair was bound to bump a table, another student or knock over a computer. And...look at this! His drool was unsanitary and dangerous: it could short a machine. He could have some contagious disease or....

His attention was still riveted on the screen in front of him. His fingers flew all over the air until they were willed, with great determination and grunting, to press the right keys. He smiled when he saw me approaching, like a friendly, tongue-lolling dog, unconscious of any problems. He smiled more broadly, mouth agape, spit rolling down his chin as he proudly pointed to the screen on which he'd typed,

"M A RC US"

It had taken him almost ten minutes to type his name but he'd done it. He liked computers. I was suitably impressed and smiled back as I said,

"Good job!"

For the benefit of those in the class who didn't like spit all over their keyboards, I added in a stern tone,

"Marcus, the next time you come into this class I want you to bring a towel with you to clean that up. We can't have this, Marcus. If you can't control yourself then don't come into this computer class."

I could tell he was crestfallen. Luckily for me the bell rang, the period ended and the aide came back to excort Marcus out of the room. I asked the aide, with some satisfaction, to get some paper towels and wipe up the spittle splattered on the keyboard. His eyes never left mine as he was rolled out. I went on to hall duty.

Hall duty is when you stand outside, observe well over a thousand teen agers attempting to live life to its fullest in five minutes, after which they may face a fifty five minute test in math, science, geography, english or some other fate worse than death.

During these five minute breaks, a boy, or girl, visits with friends, goes to the washroom, eats a snack, hits someone, drops things, runs, yells, brushes hair, passes a note, throws things or screams loudly. The job of the hall duty teacher is to yell,
"Stop that!"
If you're an older teacher, with thirty years of teaching experience, you save that command for life-threatening and obscene situations or you'd be yelling constantly.

******

But what do you say to a grinning kid on a motorized wheelchair who zooms down the halls, causing everyone to jump aside, as he hurries to computer class? I'm not going to say, "Stop that!" to anyone who wants to learn that much. If he wants to learn, I want to teach. So old "Grumpy Blaske" smiles and calls out "Hey, Rocket Man, you ready for some more computer work?" He growls his animal greeting sound as he wheels past me to his assigned place in the classroom. I know I said something about going to the principal..well, I just didn't get around to it.

He was early and armed with his drool towel as he directed the chair into a one-wheeled "wheely" over the door jamb, screeching to a halt at his microcomputer table. Then the trouble started. The power switch wouldn't go into reverse. He was in a terrible predicament: the electric chair was locked in power forward, pushing him forward, continually, stomach jammed against the edge of the table. I tried pulling the chair back but the motor was just as determined to send him forward. Marcus could break a rib or be damaged internally if I didn't find a way to stop this thing. I finally found the control and was able to free him from the trap. I had a new respect for wheelchairs.

Day after day he struggled with a wavering pointer finger, as his unruly hand floated back and forth, just above the keys. He was learning to type with sheer will power. I'd occasionally hear a grunt of satisfaction, other times groans of despair as he and the computer engaged in their private battle.

The class was assigned to use a data base with a word processing program to find the name and address of a famous person or movie star, write that person a letter and then save it to a disk. Marcus had decided that his letter would go to Magic Johnson. Since editing techniques are difficult, I asked for a volunteer to help him. To my surprise, many hands were raised in answer to my request. Marcus brought out the Mother Complex of almost every girl in the room.

Each day thereafter, as soon as Marcus roared in on his rocket chair, he was greeted by a new student helper. He was becoming the class clown, brushing away the helper's hands and using his own. There would be sounds of his guttural laughter, quickly followed by protests from his volunteer aide. The letter to Magic Johnson was coming along nicely. Marcus had two whole sentences typed.

It would be nice to be able to report that I, Super Teacher, saved the day; that this student grew up to become a CPA; that he handles all of my income tax figures with his computerized spreadsheet. That's not the case. I wish I could tell you that some large electronics corporation undertook a project to help Marcus, and others faced with similar problems. That didn't happen, either.

However, I was instrumental in having Marcus featured on local televison as one of "Kelly's Heroes". Magic Johnson sent him a nice letter and a T-shirt but after my nine week course the computer adventures of Marcus came to an abrupt halt.

Later, Rocket Man's electric motor burned out and he was reduced to the old push-wheel type of chair. I greeted him whenever I saw him but the glow was gone from his face.

I can't speak for Marcus but I can tell you what this experience has meant to me:

Who Could Be More Crippled Than Marcus?

The answer to my question, Who Could Be More Crippled Than Marcus is, "We are". We're crippled by the prejudices that keep us from being better people, people who care for one another.

I saw Marcus learn when he would have been completely justified not trying. The computer was the special magnet that had weaned him away from his biases against school, its burdensome bureaucracy and nagging teachers.

As an educator, I've seen many children give up when the going hadn't even gotten tough. What inner force made this boy want to achieve and stick it out, to the end?

I'm glad that I didn't follow the easy path of giving in to my inclination to ignore someone because he was "different". Too many of us do this, too often. I could have, with justification, turned him away from my class. I'm glad that I didn't.

Marcus taught me that with a determination to learn, insurmountable obstacles can sometimes be overcome. If a crippled boy can do so much, how much more should we expect, and get, from ourselves?

A Dating Service Fantasy for the 90's
by
Robert Blaske

Welcome to Compu-Match
A Dating Service Fantasy for the 90's

Please enter your last name:_____

First name:_____

Last four digits of your social security number: _|_|_|_|

Your password:_____

One moment please as we check our membership data bank
for this information

Welcome to Compu-Match
Main Menu

Please select from the following:

1. Male selecting a female companion
2. Female selecting a male companion
3. Male selecting a male companion
4. Female selecting a female companion
5. Other

Input a number <1 through 5> or press F1 key for help

Compu-Match
A Dating Service Fantasy for the 90's

Help Menu

You have selected Compu-Match Help Menu

1. How to use the Compu-Match Help Screen
2. "Hot Keys" for quick access to Compu-Match Database
3. An overview of Compu-Match
4. Information on your Compu-Match instant electronic billing
5. Compu-Match dating and instructional manuals
6. About DTR (Digital Transponder Responder)
7. To speak with a Compu-Match representative

Input a number <1 through 7> for help

One moment please

You have selected item 3

At Last!
Compu-Match, The futuristic dating service of the 90's

Compu-Match provides you with a true, meaningful relationship, not tomorrow or sometime in the future but Now!
Just think-
No more waiting for the phone to ring -
No more need for that "little black book"-
No more need to go to risky singles bars-
No more looking at SWF or SBM newspaper ads-

Compu-Match has the answer to your question, "Is this Mister or Miss right for me?"

Compu-Match gives you instant access to the most compatible relationship for you (Guaranteed!)
No other dating service can make this statement

You've already provided us with all the required personal data, which we've entered into our bank. Utilizing the latest digital electronic technology, Compu-Match's GIGO-1000 SX Super Computer has processed all the information about you and has already selected your ideal companion. Your significant other is no further away than your fingertips.

Go ahead, don't be shy
Try the Compu-Match method and see why date-hungry singles everywhere are saying,
"Compu-Match is the way to go!"

Press any key

Welcome to Compu-Match Main Menu
Please select from the following:

1. Male selecting female companion
2. Female selecting male companion
3. Male selecting male companion
4. Female selecting female companion
5. Other
Input a number <1 through 5> or press F1 key

One moment please-you've selected Help

Compu-Match

Help Menu

You have selected the Compu-Match Help Menu

1. How to use the Compu-Match help screen
2. "Hot Keys" for quick access to Compu-Match database
3. An overview of Compu-Match
4. Information on your Compu-Match electronic billing
5. Compu-Match dating and instructional manuals
6. About DTR (Digital Transponder Responder)
7. To speak with a Compu-Match representative

Input a number <1 through 7>

You have selected number 4

One moment please

Robert Blaske

Compu-Match explanation of Electronic Billing Service

There are no long distance telephone charges:
Your computer is linked directly to Gigo via local lines
Phone charges begin after accessing Main Menu:
No charge for
using F1 Help Menu
No charge for speaking to a CM representative
To get instant phone charge estimate press F2:
This is a preliminary estimate and may vary a few cents either
way
To hang up press ESC (Escape) key
A Contact Charge begins when your companion knocks on the
door not when actually entering your domicile. It's important
that you stay in your domicile once GIGO has made a match and
the DTR rate has begun. The charges are $25.00 per minute
based upon the transportation rate sheet which was established
by the FTR (Federal Transponder Regulatory Agency) according
to PL-355395.673 re: Digital Transponders Access/Respondent
Rates.

Compu-Match Billing Service Continued
All billing based on your electronic card number-
If disatisfied, in any way, with the GIGO selected match, call
1-800-Com-Mate immediately. After contact with a rep the
DTR rate stops and all money is refunded.
Note: Compu-Match Corp., or its employees, aren't responsible
for extraordinary occurrences which may result from your
encounter or the misuse of any accessory items, suggested
methods for pleasurable encounters, or any situation deemed
dangerous and not specifically outlined in the manual provided
to you upon your acceptance as a member.
Press any key

Compu-Match Dating Accessories and Instructional Manuals

All the Way on Your First Date?

Provides comforting assurances for the hesitant. Topics include, "No Condom Sex for Me!", "Free from HIV Fears At Last" and the ever-popular "Go For it":$25.00 plus shipping and handling.

The Dynamite Tickler

CM engineers have created the ultimate orgasm machine: $252.12 includes S&H-not available in NH, VA, FL or LA-Residents of CA and IL add 7% sales tax.

Replay

Do it again and again with our stimulator implant. Don't fall a-sleep from exhaustion, just press the Replay button and you're ready for round 2,3 or more. Note: Read the medical directions for this product carefully. CM assumes no liability for misuse and possible death from over-exertion. $150.00 includes S&H

How To-----

If you've heard that it was possible and you'd like to try it, then this manual is for you. Yes, it features the popular new linked position. $35.00 including S&H. Optional: Holistic Mirror Image Reflectors, invaluable for those using the tutorial section of this book- $175.00 including S&H

Please note: You must be at least 18 years of age to use or order any CM products unless you provide us with written parental consent with your order.

To order go to Help Menu, select number 7 or call
1-800-Com-Mate

Press any key

Robert Blaske

Welcome to Compu-Match Main Menu
Please select from the following:
1. Male selecting a female companion
2. Female selecting a male companion
3. Male selecting a male companion
4. Female selecting a female companion
5. Other
　　　　Input a number <1 through 5> or press F1 for help
　　　　One moment please-you've selected help

Compu-Match Help Menu

1. How to use the Compu-Match help screen
2. "Hot Keys" for quick access to the Compu-Match database
3. An overview of the Compu-Match service
4. Information on your Compu-Match instant electronic billing
5.Compu-Match dating and instructional manuals
6. About DTR (Digital Transponder Responder)
7. To speak with a Compu-Match representative

Input a number from <1 through 7>

You've selected number 6

One moment please

DTR Information

DTR (Digital Transponder Responder) is our latest product. When you joined CM you provided us with all the information needed to the finding of a compatible mate. During the required medical testing we obtained genetic samples, medical history and EPT (Emotional Preference Test). The results of the last test enables us to know what "turns you on". The PSS or Psychological/Sociological Survey tells us about your likes and dislikes. Once a complete physical, emotional and psychological profile has been gathered, we put the raw data into the GIGO 1000 SX. By turning on the super conductive current in the DTR room we're able to transpond your date-mate instantly.

Only CM offers DTR

Welcome to Compu-Match Main Menu

Please select from the following:

1. Male selecting female companion
2. Female selecting male companion
3. Male selecting male companion
4. Female selecting female companion
5. Other
    Input a number <1 through5> or press F1 key for help

Press any key

You have pressed number 1

Thank you for using Compu-Match
Compu-Match will disconnect in 20 seconds

Please open your front door and welcome your
new date-mate

Press any key

Number <1 to 7>

Selesatti tmed

System parity error

Good Night!

"Hi!"
"Wha...You look like you could be my..."
"Your twin sister? We are alike, aren't we?"
"Wait!...Don't do that..not right here in the hall!"
"Why not? You liked it."
"Come inside. Close the door. Ahhh...listen, wait a minute, will you? I've got to make an important phone call. It's really important. Honest...I'll be done in a minute."
"The number is 1-800-Com-Mate."
"How?....How did you know that I wanted to...."
"Be sure to order the one they call Replay. I think you're up to it already."
"OK. Get the door will you? Must be the neighbor wanting to borrow a.......Hello, Compu-Match? Hey, listen, I was on-line with your computer and......hey, listen, you two can't do things like that

out in the hall. The neighbors are real fussy. I think he's number 2, you know, "Woman looking for a man?" Hell, no, I didn't order him. He just showed up after I ordered number 1. She's the one I ordered. Yeah, she's great! Hey, will one of you stop fooling around and get the door? Well, anyhow, I had this computer error like "Parity Error" and...hot shi...no! Hey, both you guys stop that! Listen, what's your name? No I'm talking to number 1. She's great! She's got a dynamite tickler with her and ahhhh.....what? Number 2 and 3? They went in the bedroom. Who's at the door? You guessed it. Listen, I'm going to hang up and call 911. I just know the neighbors are listening to every groan. Oh, no! Number 4 brought Replay. What? Yeah. Listen, call the police or fire department for me will you? I can't stand too much more of this. No! Don't answer the door! No! Oh, God, it's number 5! Keep that thing away from me! No!"

******

Drug, Sex Orgy Ends in Death

Police were called last night by a concerned neighbor to 3426 SW 45th street, Apartment 17, to find what they describe as a macabre mass sex orgy with five people. The nude bodies of three males and two females were intertwined. The coroner provided a preliminary report showing death by exhaustion and cardiac arrest. Police suspicion that this group might have been under the effects of one of the new, stronger hallucinogenic drugs available on the street. They warn all drug users to be cautious.

Welcome to Compu-Match
A Dating Service Fantasy for the 90's

Sorry for the inconvenience

Compu-Match is temporarily off-line

A minor programming glitch is being repaired

Please call 1-800-COM-MATE
to order any of our fine products or to become a member
Press any key to exit

Woody Shulman

Born 1924 in Watkins Glen, N.Y., Woody had been in many fields before turning to writing. He served with the U.S. Navy in the South Pacific during World War II, coming out with an Honorable Discharge.

He has a degree in Accounting from the University of Rochester. He owned and operated an insurance agency from '52-'83 and then was a consultant in that area from '83-'87.

He moved to Florida in December of 1987 with Esther, his wife of 45 years, after producing 5 children and, to date, 5 grandchildren.

He began writing guest columns for local newspapers in the Florida west coast region, covering Bradenton and Sarasota. He then became a freelance writer for these publications, mainly the Bradenton Herald, where he covers arts, features and theatre. He occasionally reviews shows for antique periodicals around the gulf and east coasts of Florida.

Woody is active in Jewish causes and writes for the local Federation paper, The Chronicle. He contributes to L'Chaim, the organ of the area B'Nai B'rith. He also writes many letters to politicians on behalf of Israel and other Jewish interests.

He bought his first computer in 1984 in conjunction with his insurance consulting business. He now uses a 80386, 25MH, IBM compatible for word processing and keeping business and personal records.

As a member of Manatee Personal Computer Users Group, Inc. (MPCUG) he contributes articles to the club organ.

His piece, Try A Computer: It's Easier Than You Think, is in the Ageless Press, 1993 release Computer Tales of Fact & Fantasy (or How We Learned To Stop Worrying and Love the Computer).

My Computer Made Me An Addict or
How I Learned To Overcome Absolute Computer Dependency
by
Woody Shulman

After a local computer meeting a short while ago, my car wouldn't start. I called my wife to pick me up. She had a hard time identifying me when I tried to get into her car.

"I'm not sure you're my husband," she said, at first.

"Es, you know me. I'm in the house most of the time."

She looked me over, carefully,

"Maybe if I could see your profile. Will you please turn your head to the right?"

I did.

"You could be Woody. Will you please let me see the back of your head?"

I turned for her.

"It is you, Woody. I didn't recognize you until I saw you as you look when you're working at the computer. I rarely get to see the front of your face. You always have it stuck so close to the monitor."

It was undeniably true. I didn't realize, until her revelation, that I spent so much time in front of the monster. Without my seeing the signs, my wife had become a computer widow.

For instance, she'd come home from playing golf or shopping and hours later, when she called me for dinner, I'd ask,

"When did you get home?"

Another indication was in the morning: I always made coffee when I got up and drank it at the computer. I didn't even think about waiting for her.

If we ever had breakfast together, I often left the table before she was through, to get back to my addiction, leaving her alone. I wondered, now that I was aware of having become a compulsive computer addict, whether there was a withdrawal program available for those of us suffering from TCD (Total Computer Dependency) . I really wanted to overcome this flaw in my

321

character to be an attentive husband again.

I thought back to the time, some years ago, when I'd gotten my first computer. I had watched the skillful way my children and grandchildren used theirs. I wanted to be able to communicate with them on their level: those were my original intentions.

Shortly after my purchase, I joined a local computer group. Some of the members became close friends of mine. They dropped in at my house anytime, since I was retired. The hours flew by as we discussed DOS, bytes and many other computer topics.

I had never wanted to neglect my wife. Computing had started out as a way to keep my mind sharp as well as keeping up with my younger relatives. I didn't notice how little time Es and I were spending together, just the two of us. Even when children or friends were visiting the conversation turned to computers, endlessly, as she served the food.

I headed to the computer every morning after my shower. I even gave up my daily two-mile walk. If I wasn't cured soon I might start skipping my shower, too.

During many meals I got up from the table to take a "short computer break". Maybe it was to optimize my disk or sign on to a bulletin board. I couldn't control myself.

It's very clear to me now. I couldn't get through the day as a normal retired husband. My wife reminds me that she'd tried her ultimate weapon on more than one occasion. She'd slip on some sexy outfit, sit on my lap and what had been my response? I asked her to move over so that she wouldn't block my view of the monitor.

I longed, deeply, to overcome my obsession. I knew it wouldn't be easy. It must be easier to give up smoking, but I don't know. Smart people never even start with either smoking or a computer. For me it was too late for that.

As evidence that others were also addicted, bumper stickers and ten second TV spots were beginnning to appear saying,

"Computer Overdose? Just Say No!"

There were similar messages in magazines sponsored by

the President's War on Computer Addiction Committee and the Ad Council.

O.K., when I finally came out of denial and admitted that I had a problem, that was the start of the road to recovery. The next step was to find a remedy.

A friend at the computer group had been helped by CORE (Computer Overusers Rehabilitation Exercises). He said that he had once had the same dependency problem and was in remission. I agreed to attend a meeting, hoping it would help me, too.

Some of the proposed cures were ghastly, last-ditch alternatives. They weren't for me. Desperate couples had been divorced. According to one wife who dumped her husband, the addict didn't even notice she was gone until the lawyers came and took away his computer. My wife and I were too old for divorce, we'd been together too long.

It was also suggested that I sell the computer and go cold-turkey. Death, where is thy sting? There had to be a better way.

My wife and I sat down and discussed what we could do. She was the one who came up with the solution that we adopted. She suggested that we should each have a computer, at least after she'd learned to use one. We proved the validity of the old saying,

"The family that computes together enjoys the fruits together, the family that bowls together splits."

In her new computer world my wife can now play golf, bridge or poker on the screen whenever she wants to. She can make a calendar or record recipes. She can speak to others locally or all over the world using the modem and bulletin boards. She can keep track of her household accounts and her budget. She can even shop by computer, get the latest information on fashions or keep up with other news. She can rearrange furniture as many times as she wants to, on the screen, with neither of us straining a muscle.

There's only one small bother: it may be my imagination, but the dinner hour seems to be getting later and later and we're eating out more. Could it be.....?

Walt Vinson

Walt Vinson had careers in the U.S. Marines and the Boy Scouts. Then a multitude of jobs followed including self-employment and law enforcement.

He says that he hasn't had a spectacular life but one filled with variety. The noteworthiness comes not from what he's done but from those he's met and watched. As long as he remembers their stories he'll be a writer. Since he didn't become an author until the age of fifty, all his work is the result of fifty years of research. He's also an avid reader of fiction and non-fiction.

Walt's forefathers settled in the Soutwest Dallas, Texas area in the 1880's. His original "intent was to leave a few experiences, a family history and a little fiction for my grandchildren. When it passed 500 pages my aspirations " changed "to having portions actually published." The following piece, Benny and Uncle Doc, is one of those portions.

Benny and Uncle Doc
by
Walt Vinson

My name is Benny. I also answer to Benjamin Thomas and Herbert. My father was my Uncle Doc's younger brother. Dad and Mom were killed in an auto crash. I spent many weeks in the hospital recuperating. When I was discharged Aunt Della, Uncle Doc's wife, took me into their home. They both hoped that I would become the child they'd never had.

Aunt Della enrolled me in school and helped me with all my homework except for math and science. For those subjects I was turned over to Uncle Doc who had a deep background in those areas. I hated working with him, at first, because he was so strict and thorough.

He gave me access to his extensive library and computer. I had to do all the research for the solutions to the problems that were presented to me. Sometimes I was still mystified even after having found the answers. He'd explain them, patiently. I was learning elementary subjects at a college level. My math and science grades soared. The recognition that I received in school spurred me on. As I progressed I needed less help from him.

But then Aunt Della became ill. Although she was hospitalized immediately she died within a few days, before the doctors could even diagnose the ailment. Uncle Doc and I were totally crushed and saddened. We hardly spoke to each other for months. I felt guilty for being a kid and incapable of helping. He felt that with all his knowledge, degrees, etc. he should have been able to invent something that would have kept her alive. I immersed myself in school work.

Uncle Doc was locked up in his lab when he was home. I noted computer memory banks loaded to the max with data on electro-mechanical circuitry. Workmen installed the industrial mainframe that his former employer no longer needed: it took up most of our library and was connected to the PC in the lab.

My senior year science project was to build a three dimensional model of a Black Hole. I was unsure how to demonstrate the vast numbers involved. I left a message for Uncle Doc on the computer, our most common form of communication. I asked for an appointment, outlining the requirements and my initial plans. He answered on the computer and a date and time were set.

We met in the library. I arrived with pad and pen. Uncle Doc sat at the computer console, his back to me. He brought my message to the screen and quickly hacked my ideas to ribbons,

"A static three dimensional model of a Black Hole displaying known and theoretical values for distances and gravities would take up eight thousand cubic feet of space. The only possible place for its exhibition would be a football stadium. A computer simulation program would be a good substitute. I've added access codes to the computers at Palomar Observatory and the Library of Congress, updated daily by NASA and MIT. Download what you need, edit it to about thirty minutes of three dimensional color display and leave me a copy of the results."

He was up and gone before I'd said a word or made a mark on my pad. I settled myself in front of the machine, punched in the Palomar numbers. It was well past midnight before I'd waded through the information available from just this one source. Many midnights followed as I brought in information and organized it.

He came and went. I came and went. The house was cold regardless of the thermostat setting. There was no emotion except for the nights that I cried myself to sleep because I felt so alone.

One early Saturday morning I awoke to find Uncle Doc standing over my bed with a smile on his face. He hadn't smiled since Aunt Della's death and hadn't been in my room in all the time that I'd lived with him.

"Excellent, Benny, excellent. Right down to the credits to your sources. I reviewed your programs last night and have already sent copies to the State University Science Department and the Science editor of the Public Television station: if you extend it to fifty five minutes he'll use it on his next science series telecast. Now get dressed, grab a bit of breakfast and meet me in the lab in thirty minutes. You're going to help me with my science project."

Then he was gone leaving me pinching myself. I sprang from the bed, the sheet clutching my ankles. I fell down in the middle of the floor but made it to my jeans on my hands and knees, the sheet still tugging at my feet. I removed the cloth and high-tailed it to the fridge where I chug-a-lugged some orange juice, then headed for the lab. I arrived there out of breath.

He was still smiling,

"No, no, Benny this will never do. You must be totally calm for your part in this. Lie down on this table, catch your breath, slow your pulse and relax. I assure you this is going to be fun."

He sat by my feet and continued,

"When Della died I missed her very much. I know that you did, too. I wanted to see her face again. I thought that brain waves, enhanced by the computer, might be able to create a video image. I started doing some research. There's so much new hardware available whose full potential hasn't been explored. Each succeeding generation of equipment is more sensitive than what went before.

"The big handicap in the past has been the data base. The researchers pump a few brain waves into the computer and expect it to read minds. I put a two volume condensed encyclopedia into this one. The second time I sneezed it said, "Bless you". At least that's what it printed on the screen. The machine had learned the proper response to a given set of brain waves.

"Last night I had Della's image on the screen, was able to relive some good times."

His voice drifted away, his eyes became glassy. I was seeing more about Uncle Doc than I had ever seen before. Bringing himself back to the present he started hooking me up to the computer, talking rapidly, which always occurs when he's nervous.

"My value as a subject would be limited for several reasons. What we need is a data base on you. Read the pages that flash on the monitor aloud. I'll advance the pages as necessary.

then I'll change the tape. Later we can review the tapes and compare them with what the computer picks up from you. Begin."
I read and read, all day Saturday. We started again on Sunday morning. By Sunday evening my body was screaming for a long break. My back felt as if it was attached to the table. Late Sunday evening the monitor went blank. Uncle Doc was smiling again,
"We've made excellent progress but are only at the halfway point in the readings. Now it's time to rest our brains and do something for our bodies. Put on some shorts and meet me at the car."
We drove to the plastics lab of his former employer, which was surrounded by a double fence, part of its industrial security. The distance between the fences provided a one mile jogging path for employees. We were passed in by the lady guard. Doc started off at an easy pace. This was going to be a breeze for me, I thought. He picked up speed at the first turn. I pulled ahead just to show up the old man. He was beside me within a few paces, not even breathing heavily. As we passed the lady at the gate we both stood a little straighter and picked up the pace again. Sweat ran down our foreheads, dripped off our eyebrows and noses. We passed the gate twice more, started into the fourth mile. As we made the last turn for the guarded gate, I stretched for top speed, thoroughly soaked by now. We watched each other from the corners of our eyes, each hoping that the other would lose. We collapsed at the gate, in front of the guard, laughing hysterically, at least as much as possible when totally out of breath. The guard joined in our laughter without knowing why,
"Doc Herbert, are you okay?"
"Excellent, excellent. This young lad has just cut eight minutes off my run time. I've been trying to shorten it for years."
We stopped for burgers on the way home, planning for the coming weeks. I was to immerse myself in school work during the week. Saturday mornings we would continue recording, Sunday nights were for running and the next planning stages.

School work and extending the Black Hole program filled the week. Saturday morning followed the earlier pattern but on Sunday I finished the run three steps ahead of Uncle Doc. I was ecstatic. The following week we reviewed the video tapes. The first few were mostly gibberish and static. The third night, however, showed progress. Fuzzy glimpses of barely discernible pictures darted across the screen. The last tape showed real, honest to goodness, pictures. There was a zebra, like a mule, with black and white stripes, walking across the veldt. It was deja-vu: I remembered the thought perfectly.

Saturday morning we reran the first tape, enhanced by the completed data base. There was the Aardvark, large and lumbering with his pink, bristly tongue, zapping white ants from a rotted log. The log was covered with a flowering vine of white blooms with orchid centers. These had been my exact thoughts during the reading. There was a glitch here and there, lapses in concentration but the pictures that were there were as real as if they'd been staged and filmed by Hollywood.

The screen went dark. Uncle Doc spoke, "Benny, you think in technicolor."

Surprised I asked, "Doesn't everyone?"

Uncle Doc looked perplexed as he continued, "My images were black and white. By concentration I could create pink or green, but not both at the same time. All these years I've been seeing a colored world but thinking in black and white. I must discuss the interesting implications of this phenomenon with psychiatrists and philosophers. Back to you, young man, these experiments show great promise. I'm going to hook you up again. Think of something that has impressed you lately, like a short TV commercial. Describe it in as much detail as you can, then we'll check and see what we have. Begin when you're ready."

I closed my eyes and started to remember,

"There's a woman in a bikini walking along the beach, holding a bottle. The camera is at her back giving a full view. Her

Walt Vinson

hair is wet and long, almost to her bra strap. As she walks, the water and foam lap at her feet not quite ankle high. Her hips swing rhythmically from side to side. The camera swings to a full front, pulls in close to show her upper half as she raises the bottle to her cheek. The bottle and her body glisten with drops of water. She talks of the sun, the wind, the surf and of how they are natural, comparing them with the bottled water. As she speaks, enthusiastically, she moves causing her breast to sway. Then there's a list of the stores carrying the water."

"OK, Benny, let's see what we have on tape."

There she was on screen, reddish-brown hair, sea-green bikini, all of her except,

"Doc, she's not wearing a top!"

Doc was holding his sides, laughing while I lay frozen in wide-eyed wonder,

"Benny boy, remember we are not seeing what was on the TV or even what you described. We are seeing what you thought. After all you said nothing about color, yet color is there. Believe me, son, you're not the first man to mentally remove a bra but you are the first to prove it can be done—and in color, too."

Doc became serious after our Sunday night jog,

"We won't be working together for a while but I have an assignment for you, which you are to take very seriously. Without neglecting your studies you are to learn all you can about spiritual disciplines, reincarnation theories, past life regressions and hypnotism. I left a few notes on the computer but if you do as well as you did with the Black Hole Project, your knowledge will be invaluable. Don't be in a hurry. I'll be involved with others I'm bringing in to expand the data base. I've selected personalities different from ours to give the computer the widest possible vocabulary. We'll still have Sunday evenings together to exchange progress reports. I want to emphasize that you be thorough and not hurry. You were an excellent subject and you took two weeks. The six more that I'm going to work with may be more difficult and take more time. You know me as a conservative person but I predict that if we prove our theories we'll be awarded the Nobel Prize."

School work became a snap. I was finished with it each day in less than an hour. Most teen-aged boys were concerned with girls and acne. This one was looking for a Nobel Prize with an occasional distraction of a commercial of a girl on a beach selling bottled water.

I spent a minimum of three hours every night on my "big assignment". I quickly covered all the computer information available. The city library had many more volumes. I was there so frequently that I was taken for an employee and asked by a real one where we picked up our paychecks.

Sunday nights were special. Doc didn't go into detail about his long nights. I asked him about the leather straps that had been added to the table. He said it was a precaution because his last subject had been quite excitable. He questioned me incessantly about my progress and was delighted to hear about my first trance. Many of his questions were absurdly simple. One Sunday I "blew up" accusing him of patronizing me with his stupid questions.

"Benjamin Thomas Herbert!"

My blood froze at his tone which quickly softened,

"We are co-workers in an intricately complex enterprise. I cannot over emphasize the importance of your portion of it. You are totally immersed in it for hours every day. To you it is as simple as multiplication tables. I get a thirty minute rundown once a week. In this one area you are the teacher and I the student. I have to keep your work in perspective with mine.

"I finish this week with my last subject. Saturday morning we should be able to continue together, I hope."

I suddenly realized that I was in the dark. I had been so engrossed in each step I didn't know where we were going,

"But Doc, what do I need to be ready for? What are we going to do with my dreaming and your 'matrix of gizmos' ?"

"Matrix of gizmos, I like that, Benny. If I ever have airs of superiority please remind me that all I have is a matrix of gizmos.

The words are very humbling. To answer your question, for thousands of years gurus and mystics have spent their lifetimes trying to be one with the universe or, to put it another way, to attain universal knowledge. Some succeed, most do not. You are going to find the answer in less than a lifetime and I'm going to record it to leave to posterity. We are going to make a hellava splash in science."

Saturday morning found me on the table. Doc was hooking sensors and wires and talking fast,

"Now Benny, as well as you can, assume your trance. Once in it talking will not really be necessary for your concentration will be strong enough. Just wander back and pick up a random memory from this or a past life. We'll record everything. Begin!"

Dozens of indistinct images flickered across the monitor then faded into a swirling cloud. The cloud became a spiral, spinning progressively more slowly toward the center. The spiral faded as Doc moved to the table to connect the straps, just in case. Suddenly bright lights covered the screen. With no time for strapping, Doc threw himself across the prone boy and held on to the table beneath him anticipating a reaction to the impact of the lights. The monitor had a perfect view of a head-on car crash with twisted metal, flying glass, flesh and bone. The bloody red gore made Doc's stomach churn as though he were going to throw up. But the boy was still, never moving. Doc pulled himself together, breathing deeply.

After he'd regained some degree of composure he puzzled over Benny's lack of movement. Then he realized that Benny was in an altered state of consciousess which might eliminate noticable reactions.The monitor was showing the spiral again. The trance was deepening. The spiral faded and the screen went black.

Doc stared at the black monitor and after several minutes quietly began checking dials and sensors, making sure everything was functioning and in order. Benny was lying still with both eyes closed when he began speaking, very mechanically,

"The smell of salt is heavy in the air. The gentle lap of

water is off to the right. Heavy clouds obscure all light from the sky. From behind there's a crescendo of explosions and a series of overhead whistles. Ahead are more explosions."

The monitor sprang to life with a series of flashes which exposed an irregular hill. Benny went on,

"The bombardment has continued for eight hours. The dawn shows dark figures in dark uniforms clinging to the ground waiting for the attack signal. These are black Union soldiers poised for their first assault on a Confederate position. Flanked by two white Union regiments they are to spearhead the fight.

"The bombardment lifts, the white commander rises, points his saber to lead his black regiment towards Fort Wagner, which has sprung to life with walls of steel, lead and fire. Shells and balls rip through the Union ranks decimating bodies left and right. Some reach the outer ramparts but there's no engineering support to breach the walls and so those heroic few fall from exposure to the withering fire. The attack is broken at last and the blue clad Union men try to make an orderly retreat which fares as badly as the attack. The military objective was lost along with the lives of three hundred black bodies in blue uniforms refuting the tale of 'a white man's war.' "

Benny was silent as the monitor faded again. Then the spiral returned and as it disappeared its place was taken by a distant mountain. It was capped with snow and topped with a wisp of smoke. A green belt was below the snow line and below that a rugged area of rocks with visible caves. Doc thought that he should arouse the boy soon but then settled back to see what would happen next.

Mike Moxcey

Mike Moxcey was born in Illinois but lived there only briefly: six days to be exact. His father was in the air force so the family, and Mike, traveled to England, Maine, California, North Carolina and Texas. But he grew up mainly in South Florida where he went to junior and senior high school.

He worked at many jobs since the age of fourteen, the worst of which was in an egg factory in Maine that seemed to come straight out of the 19th century.

He's written several tech manuals, training guides and computer tutorials. He's composed humorous songs for bands and been an editorial columnist for a local paper. Mike has sold articles to music magazines, science fiction publications and is in the middle of work on a novel.

He's currently attending Colorado State University trying to get a degree in mathematics: he's been going part-time for ten years.

He lives in Fort Collins, Colorado with his wife and eighteen month old daughter. His dream is to move to the thirty five acres he owns in the mountains and build a cabin there.

Gold & Locks and the Three Wares
by
Mike Moxcey

Once upon a time there was a small legal firm called Gold & Locks. It consisted of two lawyers, Samuel Gold and Bernie Locks. They'd teamed up together right out of law school. They scraped by writing wills, filing worker's compensation claims and doing general ambulance-chasing. But they still had high hopes, always looking for new opportunities.

One day, Sam said to Bernie, "You know something partner? We ought to get into the up-and-coming field of computers."

Bernie looked up and nodded, "That's an excellent idea. Everyone's using them and they're can only grow in popularity. The only question is how do we exploit them?"

This set them both to work thinking about it. As lawyers, they were pretty good at exploitation already. But their law school training only taught them how to exploit what other lawyers were exploiting. This new idea required imaginative exploitation: this required several days' thought.

Finally Sam came up with, "Perhaps we should buy a computer and examine it."

Bernie agreed so they went down to the local ComputerMart and bought one. It was more diffcult than they'd expected with the salesman asking them all sorts of questions about bits, bytes, disks, drives, memory boards and lots of other stuff. Exasperated Bernie said,

"All these questions make it difficult."

"Of course," agreed the salesman, who looked about sixteen years old, "Why do you think they call it hardware?"

They left with a computer and after pondering about the legal loopholes regarding the difficulties of buying computers, not finding any, they began playing with the machine.

After hooking it up they got a message saying "Invalid

drive". They fooled around some more, putting floppies in the drives, punching buttons, reconnecting wires and then received two more messages, "Insert system disk and press any key" and "No partitions".

None of the messages were useful so they wrote a couple sample torts just to get their minds primed. They then went back to ComputerMart. The young lad who'd sold them their system wasn't there. The lady said he was in school and would return in the evening but could she help them in the meantime?

Sam and Bernie explained their problems and she laughed,

"Of course the machine won't work. You need some operating software to be able to do anything."

"Software," they asked in unison?

"Yes, software. Without software the hardware is useless."

"We noticed," said Sam.

They then purchased an operating system disk, a manual and with a few instructions from the saleslady, they again tackled their computer. Inserting the new floppy disk into the machine, turning it on, they were stunned when it asked them for the date, then the time. They roared. This was fun. They followed the cryptic instructions and finally were able to "partition" the "hard disk" and "formatted" it so it would "boot".

They played around creating files and directories then tried to figure out a way to initiate a lawsuit. There was no way. Like the hardware, this software was all copyrighted and legally licensed to other producers. Gold and Locks were appalled. Here was a burgeoning industry with no room for lawyers.

After the shock wore off, they went back to playing but there was nothing left to do. After creating files and directories there's not much else you can do with an operating system.

Sam said, "Maybe we should buy a computer game so our kids can use it."

Bernie nodded, "And it is getting closer to Christmas."

They went down to ComputerMart again. This time neither

the kid nor the lady were there. They spoke instead to the proprietor, a heavy-set, black-bearded man with a gruff voice,

"What you need is some of what I call my just-right-ware. Most people call it software but, unlike the operating system stuff, these are useful. We have word processors, spreadsheets, desk organizers, games, anything you need."

"This just-right-ware of yours," asked Sam, "Is it all manufactured by the same company?"

"Oh no," said the large man, "All kinds of companies make it. Why right here I have 32 different word processors. Some made by huge companies, some by two grad students stealing time off a university mainframe."

He picked up a handful of floppies, "We got stuff that'll slice, dice, crop and shred any text you want. And format and spellcheck at the end."

"That sounds fascinating," said Bernie, "all these different companies competing for the same market."

He looked meaningfully at Sam, who nodded slightly.

"How does someone keep all these different food, I mean, word processors straight?"

"Oh you can't," replied the owner cheerfully, "Of course, most people only use the one they learned first, but there are several that emulate others. They're sold mainly to businesses to retrain their employees."

"Oh," Bernie and Sam spoke at the same time, but Sam continued,

"You mean these emulating processors look and feel like someone else's copyrighted word processor?"

"Definitely look the same but I don't think you can copyright a computer program."

Sam snorted. Bernie said, "We'll take them."

"Great. Which one? We have basic packages that are good for memos, a couple that are designed for writing legal documents and large-scale ones that do anything that needs to be written in an office."

"We'll take one of each," said Sam.

The man laughed, "You don't need one of each", he fumbled around and grabbed a big package from behind the counter, "This single word processor here will do everything any of the others can do and it also has a small spreadsheet built in."

"Thank you," said Sam, "but we'd still like one of each."

"You want one of each of the 32 different word processors I have here in the store?"

"Yes," they both answered.

"Okay," said the proprietor shaking his head.

When Bernie and Sam returned to their office, they set about learning how to operate their 32 word processors. They weren't interested as much in the mechanics as they were in the emulations. They discovered that several were good for writing letters to propective clients explaining the vagaries of copyrights, trademarks and patents, offering the services of the esteemed legal firm of Gold & Locks to protect the software manufacturer's investment.

Most of the letters went unanswered. After all, two guys writing software on stolen computer time don't need a law firm unless they're caught. However, some of the companies that were hoping to grow larger than their few employees, hired Gold & Locks. The firm then initiated a barrage of complaints.

Today we still don't know how the story will end. Gold & Locks and their cohorts are guaranteed to live happily ever after, but as far as the different wares are concerned, only time and the courts will tell how they turn out.

Those @#$%^&* Computer Keys
by
Mike Moxcey

Working with computers means working with a keyboard which is not the same as a typewriter. Granted, some of the same skills are required of both typists and keyboardists. They both operate with fingers although some keyboardists (and many programmers) sometimes try to get away with only two while true typists use all ten.

But the main difference between keyboarding and typing is all the extra keys. I don't mean the function keys, the arrows, Home, Insert and that kind of stuff. I mean the extra doohickeys besides the letters and numbers which are never used on typewiters, ie, # or ^ or *. The cuss keys in comic strips. They've always been there on typewriters but aren't covered in typing class, yet they're crucial to navigating around a computer operating system.

On the computer Hotline where I work, we spend lots of time on the phone describing these keys to someone who has to type them. For example, I can't just say, "type in where id like one two octothorpe", because I just get a, "Huh?". Maybe if I said a 'pound sign' half the people would type in a # but many others would type the closest they could get to the English monetary pound, $ or even &, and some may just guess.

I had the worst experience with a lady who didn't know her asterisk from her semicolon. I told her to type "select asterisk from table semicolon". She typed in something, pressed return and read an error message. The error should put an asterisk under the problem, but she said there was no asterisk. I had her read me the error again and then asked incredulously, "There's no star under the command?"

"Yes."

"Where?"

"It's under the asterisk."

Mike Moxcey

"What's that asterisk look like, " I asked diplomatically?
"You know, like an asterisk. A dot with a comma under it."
Besides mixing up asterisks and semicolons, she used quotes for parentheses. A single quote was left paren and a double was right.

We have a real problem with slashes. The backslash is used in DOS while the forward slash works for editing commands. The forward slash, "located under the question mark" isn't too hard to find but the backslash ("Under the pipe." "What's the pipe?" "Never mind, what kind of computer are you using?") is much more difficult. That key is placed randomly by manfacturers, much like the CRTL and ALT keys.

Hotline is gradually building up a mutually acceptable set of terms to use so we'll each be sending out the same descriptions to callers (and we're also building up a list of dangerous users, the ones who just guess if they're not sure of the key). We tried using "splat" for the asterisk since it looks like a squashed bug, but when I'd explain where the term came from, some users didn't want to touch that key again. Their data would be missing eights for weeks.

Any of the keys above the numbers are pretty easy to describe: "a caret, above the six," yet even then there are two choices and some people will say, "Shoot, I always thought that was a right arrow key".

Other keys can be physically described. Here is one side of a conversation I recently heard from a co-worker.

"The bracket looks like a sort of square parentheses." (That particular user had been trained to know the parentheses by now.)

"No, it's not the breast-thingy above them. That's called a brace."

"Yes, I know about 45 other names for them but that's not what I want you to press right now.

"Sure, you can do that later in the privacy of your own home."

The colon and semicolons can also be described as well but

340

they're not nearly as interesting. My favorite description came from a user who needed a 'greater than' sign. I told her it's the one above the period and she said, "Oh, do you mean the fast forward button?" She never gets it wrong nor do any other the others to whom I've described it like that. They may not be able to program a VCR but they know how to buzz through commercials.

I've always thought that the most difficult key to describe is the backspace, "The one with the left arrow on it," is not very specific. There's a left arrow on the Enter Key and, on some enhanced keyboards, there are also left arrows on two other keys.

But the most difficult item to describe is one that isn't there. I came in one morning and heard a co-worker trying to explain to a user who'd tried many keys without success to just cold boot the machine. Turn the power off and then back on. Unfortunately, the bewildered user was looking all over the keyboard for the on/off switch. While pouring myself a cup of coffee, I heard,

"Stand up. That's right, stand up and put on your coat like you're going home. Okay, now do what you do to the computer before you leave. Yes, THAT BUTTON!"

Ms. Dos and the Eunuchs
by
Mike Moxcey

This is the true story of how Ms. Dos and the Eunuchs first began working together. There are other stories, some about the terrible feud between the two, some involving lawyers or academics, some about the different requirements of their piano teaching methods, but all are untrue. The so-called war existed only between some of their students. This story should set the record straight, once and for all.

Ms. Dos was an old spinster piano teacher who had taught almost everybody in town. No one knew her first name or much about her history but they all knew she lived at 640 K Street in a tiny bungalow, just large enough for her and her two pianos: a pearl white baby grand and an old Ludwig upright for the student. It was a mark of accomplishment to be allowed to play her grand. It took years of practise, of studying her esoteric instructions, of reading poorly written handouts. Many of her students claimed to have played on her piano but very few had.

Numerous townspeople who had never mastered the intricacies of piano playing said it was her fault. She was difficult to understand or would pounce on mistakes too quickly, making you feel like an idiot. They argued that it was easy to claim she was the best teacher in town since she was the only one in town.

"Not true," said the learned pianists, "Why just down the street lives her nephew Petey Dos and his Mexican step-brother Amigo Dos, who both give piano lessons. And at the end of town, in the new Macintosh apple orchard, is some young kid who gives lessons using pictures."

This didn't dissuade others from bad-mouthing poor old Ms. Dos though, so every day down at the local barber-stylist shop, the argument raged, "Just wait until a real piano teacher shows up," said those who despised her.

Then one day, a new piano teacher came to town. It wasn't

just one teacher, it was a whole team. They called themselves the Eunuchs and said they were there to create a harem of pianists who would all work together simultaneously in perfect harmony. They said they'd created their method while working in an exotic bell tower on the coast, had perfected it while teaching at various universities.

"Great," said the Ms. Dos haters.

"Terrible," said the others, "I wouldn't send my kid to learn from a crew of sexless foreigners."

The argument went on from there. With this new development, the specifics changed but no one switched sides. Most of the old folks who'd learned from Ms. Dos continued to see her, bringing their kids. The children were complaining that they wanted to work with the Eunuchs. The Eunuchs were able to convince several of the dissatisfied parents to begin lessons again because their lesson plan was faster. They'd split up piano teaching into multiple tasks so that different aspects of the work could be done all at once, instead of the single-minded, old-fashioned approach used by Ms. Dos.

She was attracting fewer and fewer new students. She didn't notice this for a while since most of her old students stayed. But when they mastered the grand piano they stopped taking lessons. Then she noticed the lack of students. She didn't really mind since she was getting old and thinking of retiring down south somewhere. But her loyal students wouldn't hear of it.

Some of her best pupils had become excellent composers. They'd written thousands of pieces of music in her style. They didn't want to rewrite everything in the silly Eunuch way where everything had to be in the key of C.

In desperation, a mob of Ms. Dos trained pianists descended on the Eunuchs' building, intending to burn it down and chase the interlopers out of town. But they stopped on hearing beautiful music emanating from the studio. Astounded they doused their torches and listened. A pianist always recognizes genius when hearing it.

After knocking on the door they were admitted. Although there were five students, each playing something different, the sound flowed smoothly.

"See how well our system works," asked one of the Eunuchs?

The mob nodded as one, subdued but not cowed, as a single member queried,

"We agree it works well, but why are you chasing Ms. Dos out of town?"

"Who is Ms. Dos," asked the Eunuchs?

One of the mob answered, "They never came to the barber-styling shop, just look at their long, unkempt hair, so maybe they really have never heard of Ms. Dos."

"We didn't mean to harm anyone, especially an old lady."

The Eunuchs decided to go to speak to Ms. Dos. After introducing themselves the parties sat down to talk. While munching on some of her home-made cookies, they discovered they had more in common with each other than they had with any of their students, even the most accomplished ones. After long discussions, the Eunuchs ended up letting Ms. Dos move into one of their spare rooms.

She said she'd never wanted to leave town but was being forced to move because there weren't any old folks' homes and she was beginning to need help with her daily chores. The Eunuchs agreed to assist her because she still had many invaluable piano-teaching tips and extraordinary cookie-baking skills.

They even offered to remodel the room for her, make it brighter by adding a few windows, bigger by knocking out a wall, but she declined their offer. She said her room was big enough and that the bright light might destroy the pearl-white luster of her grand piano.

And that's the real story of how Ms. Dos and the Eunuchs began working together and why today, there are several windows for the Eunuchs but only one for Ms. Dos.

Epilogue

For additional information about computers, for those planning to get started, we suggest anything written by Peter McWilliams. You'll find him to be humorous and accessible. (No, he hasn't paid for the printing of this book or given us any other freebies!)

We strongly urge anyone on the brink of plunging into this "Brave New World", to seek the advice of a young relative. Children, and/or Grandchildren over the age of two, can be very helpful. They have no fear, why should you?

And—join a computer group. Most of the experienced members are generous with their help. (We consulted with many of them when putting the words of this book into our computer, ie, Herbert Goldstein, Bart Koslow and Gary Schweinshaupt, among many others. We thank them for their time.)

And—most communities have adult education classes that include some on computer hardware and software.We took a few courses before buying our equipment to try it out first.

Avail yourself of the phenomenon called "shareware" which allows you to use software programs before buying them to see if they suit you. If they do you pay for them; if they don't you return them with no hard feelings. Great idea?

And always bear in mind that a good repair person is absolutely essential to your sanity. We have a gem. No, the name is not available: think we're crazy? Remember Jim Luce's experience? We do. We don't want our tech to get too busy to take care of us anymore!

And—realize that the manufacturers of your products include voluminous reference manuals that contain everything but the particular problem that you need help with. You also have access to their tech support phone lines (some are even 800 numbers!). You get earaches from holding the phone to that appendage for hours. You speak to lots of nice people, some of whom have different answers to the same question. There are even times when they help you. (Shades of the IRS!)

Anyhow, leap in and and have fun. We do, every now and then!

At your favorite bookstore

Computer Tales of Fact & Fantasy
(or How We Learned to Stop Worrying and Love the
Computer)

Ageless Press, 1993